ALAN M. BLANKSTEIN

Foreword by Michael Fullan

Failure Is NOT an Option®

6 Principles for Making Student Success the *ONLY* Option

Second Edition

A JOINT PUBLICATION

CORWIN
A SAGE Company

NATIONAL EDUCATION ASSOCIATION

nea.org

Great Public Schools for Every Student

For information:

Corwin
A SAGE Company
2455 Teller Road
Thousand Oaks, California 91320
(800) 233-9936
Fax: (800) 417-2466
www.corwinpress.com

SAGE Ltd.
1 Oliver's Yard
55 City Road
London EC1Y 1SP
United Kingdom

SAGE India Pvt. Ltd.
B 1/I 1 Mohan Cooperative
Industrial Area
Mathura Road,
New Delhi 110 044
India

SAGE Asia-Pacific Pte. Ltd.
33 Pekin Street #02-01
Far East Square
Singapore 048763

Printed in the United States of America

Library of Congress Cataloging-in-Publication Data

Blankstein, Alan M.
Failure is not an option®: 6 principles for making student success the *ONLY* option/Alan M. Blankstein; foreword by Michael Fullan, A Joint Publication with the HOPE Foundation and the National Education Association. —2nd ed.
      p. cm.
Includes bibliographical references and index.
ISBN 978-1-4129-7923-8 (pbk.)
   1. School improvement programs—United States. 2. Academic achievement—United States. 3. Educational leadership—United States. I. Title.

LB2822.82.B53 2010
371.2′07—dc22   2009032762

This book is printed on acid-free paper.

09   10   11   12   13   10   9   8   7   6   5   4   3   2   1

Acquisitions Editor:	Debra Stollenwerk
Associate Editor:	Julie McNall
Editorial Assistant:	Allison Scott
Developmental Editor:	Faye Zucker
Production Editor:	Melanie Birdsall
Copy Editor:	Adam Dunham
Typesetter:	C&M Digitals (P) Ltd.
Proofreader:	Gail Fay
Indexer:	Sheila Bodell
Cover Designer:	Anthony Paular
Graphic Designer:	Rose Storey

PRAISE FOR ALAN M. BLANKSTEIN'S
FAILURE IS NOT AN OPTION®, SECOND EDITION

Failure Is Not an Option is more than an audacious slogan; it is a carefully drawn road map to creating successful schools, even in the most challenging contexts. Alan Blankstein describes ten familiar paths to failure that raise critical cautions for education reformers and then systematically outlines six key elements to support excellent and equitable schools. He offers vivid examples, cases, and strategies, buttressed by research and the wisdom of practice, to enable committed educators to work effectively to reinvent schools. Everyone who cares about the future of public education should read this book.

Linda Darling-Hammond
Charles E. Ducommun Professor of Education
Stanford University

Alan Blankstein has written the new handbook for school transformation. *Failure Is Not an Option* lays out a road map for educators aspiring to create a great public school. In this richly researched book, Blankstein writes in clear, accessible prose about ideas that work. Blankstein's six principles form the scaffold for improvement plans, and the book is chock-full of how-to tips based on the experiences of real educators in real schools. Blankstein is an unabashed cheerleader of the talents of the men and women who lead and teach in America's schools. He reminds educators that, while change takes sustained, hard work, it can start right now, with something as simple as a warm welcome to each student every day. This book will be easy for educators to pick up again and again to review, reread, and renew their own commitments to make sure that failure is not an option for any student.

John Wilson
Executive Director
National Education Association

A book that should be read by every teacher; it establishes in the clearest way possible that teachers must be responsible for learning, not just teaching. Using six powerful principles, Alan Blankstein provides the information teachers need to be able to do this. The book is a wonderful blend of philosophy, theory, and, through numerous vignettes, practical examples of the principles in action. Eliminating failure as an option cannot be achieved on a large scale by teachers acting as individuals; to make "failure is not an option" a reality, teachers must see this as a shared responsibility, and this book shows how it happens now in some places and how it can become the way we operate in all schools.

Ken O'Connor
Educational Consultant
Author, *How to Grade for Learning*

If you liked the first edition, you should rush to buy the second; if you didn't read the first, get ready for a moving experience. This book is for administrators and teacher leaders who embrace their work as a calling rather than as a job. Blankstein's six principles for making schools work for all students should be printed on the back of every educator's business card, and the cases and details bring them to life. This edition deepens the message that the real work of school reform is messy and hard but within our reach if we welcome ambiguity and aim high.

Karen Seashore Louis
Rodney S. Wallace Professor
University of Minnesota

This passionate and wise book builds on years of collaborative learning, teaching, and leadership. It is filled with understandings as well as many practical suggestions, guidelines, tools, and stories from the field that support the whole child and the whole school community working effectively for children's healthy development and capacity to learn and to soar.

Jonathan Cohen
President, Center for Social and Emotional Education
Adjunct Professor, Teachers College, Columbia University

Alan Blankstein provides a compelling framework for improving schools—a framework that will excite, motivate, and sustain itself over time. This is a book to be read again and again.

Thomas J. Sergiovanni
Lillian Radford Distinguished Professor of Education and Leadership
Trinity University

There is something special about witnessing a school that has changed the way it does business. Those places are remarkable examples of what is possible for every child when "failure is not an option." This book illuminates the pathway to high performance so that others can muster the courage to do what is right for every student. As a strong proponent of teacher leadership, networks, and the power of teams, I applaud this book for its passionate ideas and forceful strategies. We can no longer wait for someone else to make the change happen; we must join forces to make success the norm for all, and this book is a valuable asset in that endeavor.

Deborah Kasak
Executive Director
National Forum to Accelerate Middle-Grades Reform

Rich in new examples, more relevant research, and great stories of success, this second look at comprehensive school improvement adds even more practical wisdom and concrete ideas for making schools better. It is readable, accessible, and useful to every level and every leader in schools.

Kent D. Peterson
Professor
University of Wisconsin-Madison

In our work facilitating inside organizations, we have found over and over again that great leaders bring two vital characteristics to their work: passion and clarity. In *Failure Is Not an Option,* Alan Blankstein brings the passion that inspires others to share in a powerful vision, and the clarity that points to what to do, and what not to do, to make the vision a reality. The six principles of the FNO framework and the impressive resources provide educational leaders at all levels with the vision and the tools for successfully facilitating transformation in their world.

Michael Wilkinson
CEO, Leadership Strategies
Author, *The Secrets of Facilitation*

The new edition improves on a book that many educators have found to be useful by including more examples as well as chapters on family engagement and sustainability. The book provides a helpful and accessible synthesis of what is known about school change. It addresses many barriers that principals and teachers face, provides useful strategies for overcoming the barriers, and provides explicit guidance on how to implement these strategies in a manner that engages the entire school community.

David Osher
Vice President, Education, Human Development, Workforce
American Institutes for Research

You don't often come across a book that links theory and practice in a compelling way. *Failure Is Not an Option* is a passionate and inspiring read. Backed by evidence and offering useful resources, the book provides a picture of how to make a difference to persistent challenges in school quality and equity. The stories about schools and districts are filled with moral purpose, determination, and humanity. If any book about education will make you feel "Yes, we must!" and "Yes, we can!" this is it!

Louise Stoll
Former President, International Congress for School Effectiveness and Improvement
Visiting Professor, Institute of Education, London, England

Failure Is Not an Option, Second Edition is a book that administrators should read, share with their learning communities, and keep in their professional libraries. Blankstein is an amazing visionary whose work is impacting the lives of administrators across the country. The two editions of *Failure Is Not an Option* are the most influential books in education in the past decade. Blankstein writes in a way to empower all stakeholders to be a part of the plan while emphasizing everyone's responsibility for student learning and success. In his latest book, he shares compelling cases from actual principals, providing concrete examples and resources for educators to use. We are a real-life example; these principles really do work. I will continue to lead my extraordinary school with tenacity, courage, and hope, because at Jackie Robinson School we truly believe that, "Excellence in education is really our *only* option!"

Marion Wilson
Jackie Robinson Public School 37
Brooklyn, New York

Failure Is Not an Option is overflowing with enthusiasm, optimism, and a motivational spirit. This book is a convincingly well-developed blueprint for sustainable school improvement, as well as a call to action for all dedicated educators committed to meaningful school reform and student progress. The wonderful second edition leads the reader on a journey to discover the realities of student success and a comprehensive look at what to do to prevent failure.

Sean J. Walsh
Principal, Roland Hayes Intermediate School 29
Brooklyn, New York

Contents

List of Case Stories and Case Examples

This icon indicates a Beacon of Hope school district. See Chapter 1 for a list of such districts highlighted in this edition.

Chapter 8. Principle 4: Data-Based Decision Making for Continuous Improvement

Chapter 9. Principle 5: Gaining Active Engagement From Family and Community

Chapter 10. Principle 6: Building Sustainable Leadership Capacity

List of Resources

These Resources for *Failure Is Not an Option,* Second Edition can be found

1. At the HOPE Foundation Web site at www.hopefoundation.org.

2. In the *Facilitator's Guide* to *Failure Is Not an Option,* Second Edition (ISBN 978-1-4129-8174-3) available for order at www.corwinpress.com.

Resource 1. FNO Snapshot Rubric for Educational Leaders

Resource 2. FNO Student-Success Model and Critical-Success Factors

Resource 3. Williamston Zoomerang Survey: Tying Professional Development to Results

Resource 4. FNO Tuning Protocol

Resource 5. Williamston Graphic Organizer and Rubric for Writing

Resource 6. Williamston Professional Development Agenda

Resource 7. Strategies for Making Time

Resource 8. Self-Assessment

Resource 9. Strategies for Dealing With Resistance

Resource 10. Running River Elementary School Mission Statement

Resource 11. Development Process for Mission, Vision, Values, and Goals

Resource 12. Worksheet for Developing a School Improvement Plan

Resource 13. Pyramid of Support at Coyote Ridge Elementary School

Foreword

The six principles which form the foundation of the second edition of Alan M. Blankstein's *Failure Is Not an Option* are as solid and comprehensive as when they were formulated in the first edition. It is no accident that these premises have proven correct as change stories and successes have unfolded since the first edition six years ago. This powerful book addresses all of the elements that are absolutely necessary for effective and enduring educational reform. Blankstein takes the key pieces of strategic reform ideas and weaves them into a coherent whole. In the first four chapters, he clearly and convincingly establishes the foundation for courageous action—why failure is not option, why courageous leadership is crucial and what it looks like, 10 common routes to failure and what to do about them, and why and how professional learning communities are central to successful reform.

Having established the philosophical and values base for reform, Blankstein proceeds to tackle the very difficult how-to questions. He does this through the six principles, with a chapter focusing on each. The six principles again cover the waterfront of effective reform: mission, achievement for all, collaborative teaching, using data, active engagement of the community, and sustained leadership for continuous improvement.

In addition to getting the content right and doing it in a comprehensive way, *Failure Is Not an Option* is chock-full of interesting vignettes, case studies, and tested techniques for addressing difficult issues. The techniques in the Resources are invaluable in their own right. Particularly powerful is how Blankstein provides both sides of all key points. He describes what is wrong, and then *what right looks like.* He systematically poses challenging questions, and then proceeds to outline solutions to each challenge. All throughout the book there are ideas and strategies for pursuing practical applications to perplexing problems.

In this second edition, with the experience of others using the six principles, several other contributions are now apparent. In new cases we see the *synergy* of the principles in action within schools, within districts, and across districts. There is more precision in peer-to-peer observation in coaching and assessment for learning that shows how the principles get operationalized up close. We see how the ideas play out in diverse settings. And the critical question of how to sustain the focus on success is tackled. On top of this, the second edition has many more practical, rich resources to assist the readers in applying the ideas in their own context.

Failure Is Not an Option is a deeply passionate call to arms, combined with an entire arsenal of information—from the worlds of both research and classroom practice—to enable the reader to take systematic, continuous, and effective action. As we grapple with the new opportunities in the Obama/Duncan "race-to-the-top" era, this book is essential reading because it is simultaneously inspiring and practical.

—Michael Fullan
University of Toronto

Acknowledgments

O buntu is a concept and word that has great value in South Africa. Obuntu means that we are inextricably bound to one another and is roughly translated as "I am because you are." Similarly, it is has become apparent to me that those who have supported me personally in fundamental ways have also supported this work. They are named below, along with the professionals who have contributed directly to this book.

BEFORE FAILURE WAS NOT AN OPTION . . .

My grandmother Sarah was there for me as an infant when no one else was. She later taught me what courage, compassion, and commitment look like. She, the Jewish Child Care Agency, and God were no doubt responsible for my surviving infancy and early childhood.

When I was 13, Harry Haun befriended my mother. While their relationship did not endure, he has been a friend, supporter, and father figure to me since.

At age 17, I met Dr. Myland Brown, who made it possible for me to attend college through the Educational Opportunity Program grant that he administered. He has been mentor to hundreds of young people, and I was able to find him again and show my gratitude by joining others who were honoring *his* academic success as the Black Distinguished Alumni of Ball State in 2001. We have been in close touch since then.

When I was 18, I met my college sweetheart, Reneé Fleming. She has since galvanized the world as the most renowned opera diva of our time. Yet she still remembers her "early fans" and has been a constant supporter. She is now Honorary Board member of the HOPE Foundation.

In 1981, I met Africans for the first time while studying French in Canada. Adama Sy, Oumar Dicko, and Kadi Ly (whom I met years later) changed my life by introducing me to the love, grace, warmth, and dignity of Malians—even in the face of extraordinary poverty. While students together, we shared meals from the same bowl from the warmth of their homes. All of them have since advanced to the top tiers of leadership in Mali to help their countrymen and women, and they remain among my closest friends.

In 1988, I met the now Executive Director of the HOPE Foundation and my best friend of more than 20 years. Nancy Shin has contributed directly and in many more important ways to this work. She, along with her husband and my teacher, Jeff Pascal, has given me much direction and guidance. In addition, Nancy's support, friendship, and unwavering commitment have made the past 20 years of the HOPE Foundation's success possible—and joyous!

Melanie and Phillipe Radley have been like surrogate parents since we met in 1989, when Melanie was working for Chancellor Richard Green in New York City. As good parents would, they have always been available and have shown up during the tough times in particular! In the same year, 1989, I met and began mentoring with quality guru, W. Edwards Deming, whose brilliance altered the course of events in Japan and, later, the world.

Shortly after apartheid ended in South Africa, in 1994, I had the honor of meeting one of our world's great spiritual and moral leaders, Arch Bishop Desmond Tutu. Although his calendar, life, and heart would seem to have been too full for *one more thing*, he has graciously become Honorary Chair to the HOPE Foundation, and continues to provide inspiration for me on a personal level.

Our Board of Directors comprises some of the most talented, brilliant, and committed people I have ever met, and this isn't a superficial analysis: I have known some of them since I was in graduate school! They include Larry Barber, Felicia Blasingame, Maurice Elias, Marilyn Hartman, Barbara Huff, Fred Mathews, Larry Rowedder, Bill Scott, David Spencer, and Paul Stafford.

Failure Is Not an Option, First Edition

The first book was born out of a conversation I had over breakfast with Tom Koerner, a wonderful person and committed educational leader, who is the Executive Director Emeritus of the National Association of Secondary School Principals. He encouraged me to write the work, and I did so over the next three months. Maurice Elias (mentioned above, but never mentioned enough for all he has done for this field!) put me in touch with Faye Zucker who became my editor and brilliantly navigated a rapid publication process of the work through Corwin. Along with others named above and below, these people played a critical role in bringing this work to fruition.

I learned from my heroes—Dalai Lama, Arch Bishop Tutu, and Nelson Mandela, among them—that those who take leadership roles will experience mountaintops and profound valleys. Mostly, it is just tough climbing, with the winds of commitment, faith, and passion at one's back. After the first edition of this book, I delighted in meeting tens of thousands of readers whose dedication and enthusiasm for enhancing the lives of children was very moving. Receiving the Book of the Year Award from National Staff Development Council (NSDC) was surprising and humbling, and the birth of my child Sarah was miraculous and the greatest joy of my life.

I quickly descended to the lowest point imaginable after Sarah's mother indicated that her commitment had always been "day-by-day," and she unveiled plans to go across the country with our daughter who had just celebrated her first birthday.

Thus began the trial of my lifetime in which the goal was emotional and in some ways physical survival for me and my daughter. Fortunately, and I think divinely, some 32 people came to my aid in very powerful and meaningful ways. Some are already named, and a few showed up briefly and then just disappeared like angels in the night, offering me a place to stay or the words I needed to go on during a moment of exhaustion or near collapse. All said in effect, "You are right; this was not just, I stand by you, and I will help." All of these people made this second edition of *Failure Is Not an Option* possible: Patrick and Patricia Efiom, Valerie Grim, Bruce Ecker, Chen Dong (Joey), Cam Danielson, Ben Sanders, Kiki Diarra, Kathleen Curry, Judi Williams, Lynne Morrow, Kayton, Al Assad, Pat Cortese and Terry Wisniewski, Laurie, Jake and Hilary Mindlin, Edna Lenchner, Esther and Kwame Dakwa, Brian McKibben, Jeffrey Willsey, Jan Nobuto, Mary Deitz, Sam and Patty Ardery, Marlena Johnson, and my loyal, rock-solid friend, Zenobia Washington, who meant it when she said, "You know me—I'm ride or die!" and spoke with me to assure that I would make it through *every* single day!

Contributors to *Failure Is Not an Option*, Second Edition

As with the first edition, this book has been graced by some of the great researchers and practitioners in our field. Michael Fullan, Andy Hargreaves, Dean Fink, Linda Darling-Hammond, and Pedro Noguera all made significant contributions to this for which I am grateful. In addition, we drew heavily from a project underway with Jay McTighe, and informed by Ken O'Connor, to update Chapter 8.

Case stories were contributed by practitioners whose insights, commitment, and years of experience in creating learning communities through the Failure Is Not an Option process were inspiring. They include, from Shambaugh Elementary School: Principal Shawn Smiley, Chris Rasor, Diane Pelkington, Colleen Kobi-Berger, Lydia Beer, Nancy Noel, Susan Lothamer; from Brooks Wester Middle School: Principal Scott Shafer, Anh Pham, Beverly Green, Charlene McKinzey, Dave Hodgson, Debbie McDonald, Debbie Minardi, Doug Arnold, J. J. Stroud, Janna Allen, Jill Wylie, Judy Collier, Karen Swanson, Kasey Holder, Malana Rudnicki, Marshella Stone, Mike Pringle, Penny Martin, Sue Gerlach; from Icenhower Intermediate School: Principal Duane Thurston, Reggie Rhines, Tamara Liddell, Robyn Rinearson, Hayley Rambo, Stefanie Kahl, Kim Wood, Melissa Jackson, Channon Mata, Juliana Gregory; from Williamston Middle School: Principal Christine Sermak, Rhonda Jaskowski, Tania Dupuis, Katy Maiolatesi, Sherri Petersmark, Tim Kelly, Tammy Hosford, Laura Hill, Anne McKinney; from the Sunnyside School District: Dr. Manuel Isquierdo, Jan Vesely, Lorena Escarga, Peggy Weber, Dr. Jeannie Favela, Dr. Alex Duran, Dr. Sharon Hooker, Dr. Julia Lindberg, Sue Tillis, Cheryl Siquieros, Jim Ridge, Keith Maynard, Roxana Rico, Bob Sterner, Brenda Harford, Jacque Croteau, Hans Schot, Juanita Diggins, Noah Tonk, Joe Peters; from the Mattoon School District: Larry D. Lilly, David Skocy, Tom Sherman, Susan Smith, Bill Harshbarger, Mary Eddy; and from Wichita: Assistant Superintendent Greg Rasmussen, and principal Donna Welty. Thank you for taking the time to not only implement but also to share your successes and challenges with others.

Reviews of early iterations of this work from Mary Deitz, Ken O'Connor, Carol Tomlinson, Dennis Sparks, Paul Houston, Sharon Kagan, David Osher, Father Val Peter, and Louise Stoll were extremely incisive, encouraging, challenging, and greatly appreciated! Thank you for bearing with me under the time constraints we worked within.

Numerous practitioners weighed in on this work as well, and their advice challenged me to think more deeply and consider many changes to the work. They include Jennifer Walts, Calanthia Tucker, Carol Anne Russler-Boyer, Carol Godsave, Dr. Jo Ann Pierce, Ronald Gorney, Phyllis Wilson, Marilyn Rogers, Peggy Saunders, Rosemary Manges, Diane Williams, Trudy Grafton, Barbara Gillian, Mary Dietz, Wendy McVicar-Lew, David McAdam, Kari Cocozzella, Deborah Wortham, Carolyn Powers, Ed Dawson, Gail Cooper, John McKenna, Linda Jonaitis, and Mike DiDonato.

The impetus for creating this second edition came directly from Corwin's new and dynamic president, Leigh Peake. I surely would have spent this summer another way without you! Thanks for fanning the flames.

It was kind and wise of Leigh and my Senior Acquisitions Editor, Debra Stollenwerk, to allow my original editor, Faye Zucker, to work on this with me. Faye, your array of talents is worthy of yet another chapter in this book! Yet, in brief, you know we would never have accomplished this within our timelines without you. Thank you, Debra, for so deftly clearing the path for us along the way to this work's completion. With Debra, Faye, and Leigh at Corwin, thanks go to the extraordinary leader and CEO of SAGE Publications, Blaise Simqu; Julie McNall, associate editor; and Melanie Birdsall, production editor.

Joining the team to create this second edition was a bright Cornell PhD student, Barrett Keene, and one of the sharpest assistants I have ever had, Christina Eads. Thank you both for showing that failure is not an option mentality, and welcome to the team!

PUBLISHER'S ACKNOWLEDGMENTS

Corwin gratefully acknowledges the contributions of the following reviewers:

Margarete Couture
Elementary Principal
South Seneca Central School District
Interlaken, NY

Laurie Emery
Principal, Old Vail Middle School
Vail Unified School District
Vail, AZ

Tara L. Fair
Principal
Central Middle School
Edmond, OK

Sheila Fisher
Principal
Maria Weston Chapman
    Middle School
Weymouth, MA

Barb Gillian
Principal
Alton High School
Alton, IL

Dr. Roberta E. Glaser
Assistant Superintendent, Retired
St. Johns Public Schools
St. Johns, MI

Carol Godsave
Assistant Professor,
    Educational Administration
The College at Brockport,
    State University of New York
Brockport, NY

Ronald Gorney
Principal, Genesee
    Elementary School
Adjunct Professor, LeMoyne College
Auburn, NY

Trudy Grafton
Principal, Study Elementary School
Fort Wayne Community Schools
Fort Wayne, IN

Kathy Grover
Assistant Superintendent
Clever R-V School District
Clever, MO

Jane B. Huffman
Associate Professor,
   Educational Administration
University of North Texas
Denton, TX

Suzette Lovely
Deputy Superintendent,
   Personnel Services
Capistrano Unified School District
San Juan Capistrano, CA

Rosemary Manges
Educational Consultant
Education Service Center, Region 10
Richardson, TX

Jacie Maslyk
Principal
Crafton Elementary School
Pittsburgh, PA

Gregory A. O'Connell
Principal
Cedar Rapids Community Schools
Cedar Rapids, IA

Jo Ann Pierce
HOPE Foundation Consultant
Principal, Duncan Public Schools
Duncan, OK

Bethany Rayl
Assistant Superintendent for
   Curriculum and Instruction
Clio Area Schools
Clio, MI

Carole Anne Russler-Boyer
Sixth-Grade Math Teacher
   and Team Leader
Jefferson County Board of
   Education
Charles Town, WV

Peggy J. Saunders
Assistant Professor
Weber State University
Ogden, UT

Dr. Louise Stoll
Visiting Professor, London Centre
   for Leadership in Learning,
   Institute of Education,
   University of London
Former President of the
   International Congress for
   School Effectiveness and
   Improvement

Dr. Calanthia Tucker
Cluster Superintendent, Retired
Fairfax County
   Public Schools
Falls Church, VA

Dr. Jennifer C. Walts
Curriculum Coordinator
Taylors Creek Elementary School/
   Liberty County School System
Hinesville, GA

Diana Williams
Leadership Coach
Coaching for Results, Inc.
Millersport, OH

About the Author

 **Alan M. Blankstein** is Founder and President of the HOPE (Harnessing Optimism and Potential through Education) Foundation, a not-for-profit organization, the Honorary Chair of which is Nobel Prize winner Archbishop Desmond Tutu. The HOPE Foundation is dedicated to supporting educational leaders over time in creating school cultures where failure is not an option for *any* student. Founded in 1989, the HOPE Foundation has focused for the past decade on helping districts build leadership capacity to close gaps and sustain student success.

The HOPE Foundation launched the professional learning communities movement in educational circles, first by bringing W. Edwards Deming and later Peter Senge to light in a series of Shaping America's Future forums and PBS video conferences from 1989 to 1992. The HOPE Foundation now provides some 20 conferences annually, highlighting their long-term successes in sustaining student achievement in districts and regions in 17 states and parts of Canada and South Africa.

A former "high risk" youth, Alan began his career in education as a music teacher and has worked in youth-serving organizations since 1983, including the March of Dimes, Phi Delta Kappa, and the National Educational Service (now Solution Tree), which he founded in 1987 and directed for 12 years.

In addition to authorship of this award-winning book, Alan is publisher of three *Failure Is Not an Option* video series and, with Paul Houston, is senior editor of the 13-volume *The Soul of Educational Leadership* series. Alan also coauthored the *Reaching Today's Youth* curriculum and has published articles in *Educational Leadership, The School Administrator, Executive Educator, High School Magazine, Reaching Today's*

Youth, and *Inside the Workshop.* Alan has also provided keynote presentations and workshops for virtually every major educational organization.

Alan served on the Harvard International Principals Centers advisory board, as board member for Federation of Families for Children's Mental Health, as Co-Chair of Indiana University's Neal Marshall Black Culture Center's Community Network, and as advisor to the Faculty and Staff for Student Excellence (FASE) mentoring program. He also served as advisory board member for the Forum on Race, Equity, and Human Understanding with the Monroe County Schools in Indiana and on the Board of Trustees for the Jewish Child Care Agency (JCCA), in which he was once a youth in residence.

To my darling Sarah,

The first edition of this book was dedicated to your great grandmother, whose name you have. Her grace, artistry, and big heart were also passed on to you.

Grandma Sarah believed in me at times when no one else would or could, and so she passed on to me the spirit of never giving up on a person. This enabled me to find you again when your future and our relationship were cast into perilous waters. I hope that one day, you too will be able to fully love, embrace, and dedicate yourself to those who need this from you.

In the meantime, you are already a little light of joy and hope for all who know you, and especially for me. My love for you is unending, and nothing will come between us again. For us, success is the only option!

CHAPTER 1

Why Failure
Is Not an Option

Never give up
No matter what is going on
Never give up
Develop the heart
Too much energy in your
country is spent
Developing the mind instead
of the heart
Be compassionate not just to
your friends but to everyone

Be compassionate
Work for peace in your heart
and in the world
Work for peace and I say again
Never give up
No matter what is happening
No matter what is going on
around you
Never give up

—His Holiness the Dalai Lama (given to poet
Ron Whitehead with permission to share with everyone)

In times of drastic change, it is the learners who inherit the future. The
learned usually find themselves beautifully equipped to live in a world
that no longer exists.

—Eric Hoffer, *Reflections on the Human Condition*

In the spring of 1970, the *Apollo 13* spaceship faced repeated crises as it circled the moon. Most Americans, including many of those working at

NASA's ground control center, gave up hope for the survival of the *Apollo 13* crew. Newscaster Walter Cronkite described the challenge: "Perhaps never in human history has the entire world been so united by such a global drama."

At one point, when the ground control team became aware of the ship's inability to reach Earth with its current power supply, the director of flight operations, Gene Kranz, assembled the NASA team. He had been told that they had only 45 hours to get the astronauts home before the power ran out. Marking a point on the chalkboard halfway between their current position and Earth, he stated, "That's not acceptable!"

The group exploded into a cacophony of reasons for their assessments and explanations of the limitations they faced. Then the voice of one team member rose above the rest to point out that everything depended on power. Without power the astronauts would not be able to communicate with the ground crews, they couldn't correct their trajectory or turn their heat shields around. Everything would have to be turned off. Otherwise the craft would never make it to reentry.

When asked what he meant by "everything," he replied, "At the current rate, in sixteen hours the battery is dead; so is the crew. We have to get them down to 12 amps."

The crowd erupted at this idea. "You can't even run a vacuum cleaner on 12 amps," said one. Another objected to the idea of shutting down everything, as he felt that the guidance system at least must be kept running. Another NASA scientist was concerned that this course of action had "never been tried before," and still another added that it had "never even been simulated."

Scientific data eventually prevailed over the fear of the unknown and the untried nature of the proposal to turn off the power. Kranz was adamant in response to his crew's fear of the many unknowns, telling them they had to figure it out, that the teams in the simulators would have to work out scenarios for re-entry to Earth. He ordered them to find all the engineers and assembly workers who had designed and put together all the switches, circuits, light bulbs, everything connected to the power supply, and to work out a way to reduce the use of every amp possible in the spacecraft. Pointing at the mark he had made on the chalkboard, he said, "I want this mark to go all the way back to Earth with time to spare. We never lost a man in space, and we're sure as hell not going to do so on my watch!"

Gene Kranz's motto was "failure is not an option." And he led his crew to success by bringing the astronauts safely back to Earth.

FAILURE IS *NOT* AN EDUCATIONAL OPTION

Many educators would intuitively agree: Failure is not an option for today's students—at least not one we would conceivably choose. Although clearly, students *may* fail, and indeed many do, the consequences are generally too dire to *allow* for such an option (Springfield, 1995). Students who don't make it through high school earn substantially less in wages (Springfield, 1995) and may have far greater rates of incarceration and drug abuse than do their peers.

Rosa Smith, former superintendent of the Columbus, Ohio, schools, had an epiphany one morning when she read some statistics about the U.S. prison population. Some 75% of the prison population, she found, is Latino or African American, and 80% are functionally illiterate. She felt a new sense of purpose: Her work was no longer about teaching math or science but about saving lives!

The ability to articulate such a clear and compelling message to all educational stakeholders—inside and outside of the school building—is the beginning of defining what Michael Fullan (2001a) refers to as "moral purpose." Leaders who tap this clear sense of purpose in themselves and others are addressing the beginning of what we refer to in this book as the *courageous leadership imperative.*

Many leaders have yet to discover their moral purpose or develop their courageous leadership abilities. A popular keynote presenter, Rick DuFour, recounts his reaction to a superintendent who challenged the importance of educating *all* children to *high* standards. The superintendent told DuFour, "This isn't brain surgery. No one is going to die here! Some kids advance a little, some a lot. Isn't that the way it goes?" DuFour retorted that this cavalier attitude reminds him of a little office building he once saw in a small town. On the office door were posted two signs: "Veterinarian" and "Taxidermist." Underneath was printed these words: "Either way you get your dog back!"

Failure is not an option for public schooling, either.

Leaders in Western society have long articulated the close tie between a strong public education system and democracy itself (Dewey, 1927; Glickman, 2003; S. J. Goodlad, 2001; Putnam, 2000; Putnam, Leonardi, & Nanetti, 1993). Schools are clearly for the common good, and they serve as the gateway to, and potential equalizer for, economic and life success for millions of underserved children.

As Michael Fullan (2003a) states, "A high-quality public school system is essential, not only for parents who send their children to these schools but also for the public good as a whole" (p. 4). Failure is no more an option for the *institution* of public education than it is for the children within that institution (Glickman, 2003; S. J. Goodlad, 2001).

Yet, we have seen countless threats to public schools in recent years. They include the rise of vouchers—even for religious schools (Walsh, 2002)—as well as the concerted entry of large, for-profit corporations into the public education arena. Even more troubling is the rise of the for-profit prison industry whose executives gauge the number of prison cells to build based on literacy rates in *second* grade (M. P. Williams, 2002)! David Lawrence points out that

> a child who can read by the third grade is unlikely ever to be involved with the criminal justice system [while] four of five incarcerated juvenile offenders read two years or more below grade level. Indeed a majority of them are functionally illiterate. (Lawrence, 2009)

As the global recession forces educators to compete for scarce resources with health care, the military, and other sectors of the economy, it often appears that *public* policy itself is harmful to *public* education. A greater level of courage and commitment are needed now—more than ever before—to meet these and other grave challenges.

Luckily, a growing number of policy makers are providing hopeful signs. The Obama administration's spending priorities; the whole-system change efforts underway in Toronto, Canada; and massive public investment in educational R&D through the National College of School Leadership in the United Kingdom are examples. Even opinion leaders from business (e.g., Bill Gates; Warren Buffett) are again seeing education as *the* vital renewable resource in which to invest:

> The country that uses this [financial] crisis to make its population smarter and more innovative . . . is the one that will not just survive but thrive down the road. We might be able to stimulate our way back to stability, but we can only invent our way back to prosperity. And for this there is no script—only a heart of courage and a hungry mind. (Friedman, 2009, p. WK8)

Indeed, that is what this book is about. We are all in uncharted waters together. Developing courage, collective commitment to our children, and faith in our actions—even in the absence of full information—is essential to brave the storm.

THE AIM OF *FAILURE IS NOT AN OPTION:* HOW HIGH-ACHIEVING SCHOOLS SUCCEED WITH ALL STUDENTS

How did Gene Kranz persevere under such dire circumstances and unrelenting odds during the *Apollo* crisis? What are the elements of this kind of courageous thinking and action, and how does one develop them? How could he harness the urgency of the situation, yet maintain his composure with three lives at stake and the whole world watching? What kind of organizational culture allows both for the open commentary from "naysayers" and for the ability to quickly move beyond those initial reactions to concerted teamwork?

This book addresses these questions with a unifying framework for action. Parker Palmer (1998) indicates that most professional development (and books like this) answer the "what" or "how" questions: *What* should I do, and *how* should I do it? This book answers these questions in detail. In addition, we address the two questions often ignored yet crucial to success: *Why* am I doing this, and *who* do I need to be to succeed?

Perhaps more than in any other profession, educators have pursued their calling for a noble reason. Indeed, what could be more compelling than undertaking a profession that *literally* places the future of *children* in your hands?

Educators don't have the distractions of fame and fortune to cloud their thinking about *why* they are here! So there must be another reason—a more profound *why* that leads to all the hours of toil, the deep concerns for the success of young people, the countless evenings and weekends attending plays and ball games.

Reconnecting with this *why* is imperative to sustaining one's passion and focus in light of the barrage of attacks that *public* education and all those involved with it regularly endure. Standing up for why we are in this field is essential to our personal and professional well-being. Equally important, it is imperative for our very future—and that of our children. In this, failure is indeed not an option.

Ironically, the single most important element for success in any endeavor is often omitted from books such as this. While it is easy to focus on what *others* need to do, or on how to *structure* an organization, or on what *policies* need to be handed down to staff members, the *real* determinant of success will no doubt be *you!* You, the person reading this book. This book grapples—most notably in Chapter 2—with the thorny issue of *intro*spection to assure *external* results. Make no mistake about it: Failure Is Not an Option begins with *you!*

THE STRUCTURE OF THIS BOOK

Failure Is Not an Option begins in this chapter with an overarching moral purpose (Fullan, 2001a) for schools: *sustaining success for all students because failure is not an option.* This provides coherent direction for our work and answers the question "*Why* are we in this profession?"

The following chapter addresses the *who* question by formalizing what we have discovered to be the mental framework of thousands of highly successful leaders. We call it the courageous leadership imperative. The components of this imperative are described in Chapter 2, and specific examples and processes for developing this kind of courageous leadership are provided. Leaders of every variety can produce short-term gains in student achievement. A courageous leadership imperative, however, is necessary to *sustain* significant gains. This is especially true under challenging circumstances. Leaders who adopt the five axioms that compose this imperative are more likely than others to successfully adapt to shifts in educational spending, priorities, personnel, and policies. Ultimately, it is the internal strength of the leader and the school community that will act as ballast, rudder, and engine for the ship during stormy weather.

Chapter 3 gives a realistic depiction of the common factors that have derailed many change efforts. More important, it provides specific processes and strategies for keeping initiatives on track.

Chapter 4 provides an extensive research base to answer the *what* question. It offers six principles for creating and sustaining a learning community with relational trust as the foundation. These principles are drawn from more than a decade of research on the topic and 20 years of practical experience in the field. The research is clear: Building such a community is our best hope for sustained school success (Darling-Hammond, 1997; Drucker, 1992; Fullan, 1993; Joyce & Showers, 1995; Louis, Kruse, & Raywid, 1996; Newmann & Wehlage, 1995; Senge, 1990). How this community is defined, constructed, and sustained will be addressed beginning in Chapter 4.

Finally, we address the *how to* question in Chapters 5 through 10. In these chapters, we provide detailed, field-tested processes for creating professional learning communities in which failure is not an option (Figure 1.1).

In sum, this book builds on more than two decades of intensive work with educational leaders to reshape school cultures for *sustained* student success. Our work began with W. Edwards Deming in 1988 and continued with the work of Peter Senge, Michael Fullan, Andy Hargreaves, Maurice Elias, Shirley Hord, Dennis Sparks, Pedro Noguera, James Comer, Tom Sergiovanni, and thousands of school leader-practitioners who have been at the forefront of creating true learning communities.

A NEW IMPERATIVE FOR A NEW CHALLENGE

In times of great challenge or dynamic change, such as schools are now experiencing, organizations must develop cultures that are significantly

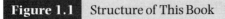

Figure 1.1   Structure of This Book

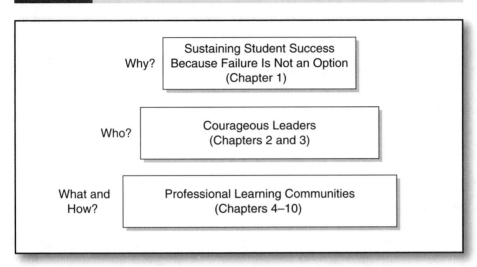

different from those needed in stable times. Like most organizations, schools tend to seek consistency and equilibrium. But as Pascale, Millemann, and Gioja remind us, "Prolonged equilibrium is a precursor to disaster" (2000). Avoiding equilibrium enables living organisms to avoid extinction in periods of great change.

Michael Fullan (2003a) advises educators to "move toward the danger" instead of hunkering down in difficult times. It is better to face the danger with a proactive approach than to wait for the danger to surprise you.

This is not at all easy. Most people are not easily swayed to move toward the danger. More commonly, people face threats by avoiding the challenges at hand or, at the other extreme, embracing every possible solution to the point of losing focus. Other reactions to challenge include

- Looking outside their own sphere of influence for reasons why students are not succeeding;
- Seeking a quick and easy solution;
- Avoiding or ignoring the data;
- Shooting the messenger; and
- Total burnout and utter collapse.

The courageous leadership imperative (described in Chapter 2) provides an alternative to these options, cutting through the many reasons to forestall *meaningful* action while minimizing less substantive, or even counterproductive, *hyper*action. There will always be obstacles to changing (see Chapter 3), but the courageous leadership imperative deeply roots a school's purpose and passions in ways that are enduring and stabilizing in the context of rapid change. At the same time, relational trust within the learning community (Chapter 4) and processes for implementation of the FNO system and framework (Chapters 5–10) will help create a culture adaptable to extensive change. Knowing *who* we are as educators and leaders and *why* we are here provides an enduring source of strength. *How* we fulfill our individual and collective purpose, however, must be flexible and adaptable.

PEOPLE ARE THE TOUGH PART OF CHANGE

In *The Answer to How Is Yes*, Peter Block (2002) reflects on how so many of his major corporate clients refrain from committing to action, replacing action with an ingenious barrage of "How?" and "Yeah, but . . ." questions and comments. Even when professionals know what to do and how to do it, they are often reluctant to take courageous action. Mark Twain once quipped, "Quitting smoking is easy—I've done it a thousand times!" Like the smoker who knows better or the gambler who occasionally wins, we can become wedded to what worked at one time or what works once in a while.

The human aspect of school change is the most difficult, yet essential, element for success. Perhaps because of this, it is often overlooked, minimized, or dismissed.

Without clearly addressing the human dimension of change—the *who* and the *why* of school reform—the outcomes of efforts to change will be disappointing. Tom Gregory (2001) encourages us to identify the "educational bogeymen whom we're afraid to confront" and who "tend to evaporate when we muster the courage to push them aside" (p. 580), while Dennis Sparks (2002) reminds us that the challenge to change our schools is a human and emotional one as opposed to being mainly technical or cognitive.

This is true outside of education as well. Corporations spend billions annually in fees for "change consultants" (Pascale, 1997–1999), but reports from the "changed" corporations indicate that a whopping 70% of those efforts fail (Pascale, 1998). Pascale et al. (2000) attribute this to "social engineering":

> "Social" is coupled with "engineering" to denote that most managers today, in contrast to their nineteenth-century counterparts, recognize that people need to be brought on board. But they still go about it

in a preordained fashion. Trouble arises because the "soft stuff" is really the hard stuff, and no one can really "engineer" it. (p. 12)

This book provides direction and support for the difficult but essential "soft stuff." Readers will find many new examples of school leaders, teacher leaders, and school improvement teams working together to define who they are as individuals and as organizations and why they collectively are engaged in the endeavor of building and sustaining success for *all* students.

LIMITATIONS OF THIS WORK

We approach the task of this book with both caveats and conviction. The first major caveat is that there is no *formula* for success.

The initial "formula" for success in the *Apollo 13* example given earlier had to be entirely tossed aside. It was replaced with processes for creating *new* approaches to success using data, past experience, a willingness to reconsider all assumptions, and the climate for challenging one another's assumptions toward reaching a widely understood and commonly desired outcome. Most important, the NASA story exemplifies the courageous leadership necessary—in the face of nearly certain failure—to maintain a sense of hope and optimism, composure, and urgency. And to *act* on the best information possible toward what was ultimately a successful rescue of the three men in *Apollo 13*.

Formulas for success are suspect. As Peter Drucker (1992) stated, the reason we have so many *gurus* is because we can't spell *charlatan*. That being said, we *do* share some convictions and experience regarding "best practices" for reculturing schools and districts toward sustainable student achievement, guiding principles for success, and using time-tested truths about leadership and implementation of initiatives, while taking into account the complexity of change. The trick is sorting all this out, being accurate and precise without oversimplifying, and providing specific steps for action in the face of intricate challenges. That's the balancing act this book aims to perform.

TAPPING GREAT WISDOM

Finally, we draw from an array of literature and practice from all areas, including organizational development technologies, educational change, PLCs, practice and research, enlightened corporate approaches to leadership development, youth psychology, and enduring wisdom of the past.

To that end, we fashion this book in terms described by last century's leading champion for young people's potential. Janusz Korczak (1967) directed a school for Jewish street children from 1912 to 1942, until Warsaw came under Nazi occupation, and Korczak voluntarily tied his fate with that of his street orphans:

> This book is designed to be as short as possible because it is addressed primarily to a young colleague, who, suddenly thrown into the whirlpool of the most difficult educational problems, the most involved conditions of life, and now stunned and resentful, has sent out a cry for help.
>
> A fatigued person cannot study thick volumes on education at night. One who is unable to get enough sleep will be incapable of implementing the precious principles he has learned. This shall be brief so that your night's rest may not be disturbed.

Chapter 1 Resources

Resource 1. FNO Snapshot Rubric for Educational Leaders

Resource 2. FNO Student-Success Model and Critical-Success Factors

Resource 3. Williamston Zoomerang Survey: Tying Professional Development to Results

Resource 4. FNO Tuning Protocol

Resource 5. Williamston Graphic Organizer and Rubric for Writing

Resource 6. Williamston Professional Development Agenda

These Resources for *Failure Is Not an Option*, Second Edition can be found

1. At the HOPE Foundation Web site at www.hopefoundation.org.

2. In the *Facilitator's Guide* to *Failure Is Not an Option*, Second Edition (ISBN 978-1-4129-8174-3) available for order at www.corwinpress.com.

WHAT IS NEW: LESSONS LEARNED FROM LEADERS USING *FAILURE IS NOT AN OPTION*

What I am saying is that even relatively advanced work such as creating professional learning communities does not push the adaptive envelope. It is necessary but not sufficient for sustainability. It's critical to do, but we need more.

—Michael Fullan, *Leadership & Sustainability: System Thinkers in Action*

The prior edition of this book was designed to explicitly outline the *who, what,* and *how* of becoming a high-performing school and learning community. It was meant both for getting started and for advancing one's school or district. As the quote above indicates, that goal no longer sufficiently "pushes the envelope."

While there are many more places that use the term *professional learning community* (PLC) to describe themselves now, it is often a misnomer. To gain the greater clarity necessary to move forward, this edition provides more examples and nuanced descriptions of high-performing communities that engage all learners and close gaps within and between schools.

Thankfully, some of the foremost researchers and writers in our field have shared their expertise with us to provide some of this clarity, as you will see in Chapters 9 and 10, which feature compelling contributions from Pedro Noguera and the team of Dean Fink and Andy Hargreaves, respectively. In Chapter 8, we draw heavily from our work with Jay McTighe as well.

In addition, many extraordinary practitioners have advanced the field since the first edition came out (Blankstein, 2004), and we have been honored to work with some of them in a sustained manner. It is humbling and exciting to see what many of the 200,000 readers of the first edition of *Failure Is Not an Option* have done to give that text additional life and energy through the creative and effective ways in which they have actualized it. Some have taken pieces of the book to make adjustments in their work. Others have moved their entire schools, districts, provinces, and regions forward in a sustained manner, often with the support of the HOPE Foundation.

The latter group has certainly pushed the envelope with their concerted and courageous implementation of the six principles embodied in this book. Many of these leaders have taken on the kind of "second order change" (Heifetz, 1999; Stoll & Temperley, 2009) that Fullan refers to in the opening quote of this section; taking on challenges for which there is no known script or easy answers.

While the original tenets of the book hold true and in fact are retained in this edition to bring new and intermediate readers forward, those aforementioned districts and award-winning schools' practices provide a rich and energizing new depth to the work. In addition to what we have learned from the five districts and one region highlighted in this book, this new edition of *Failure Is Not an Option* incorporates lessons learned from our work and the work of our colleagues in Canada, the United Kingdom, Australia, Finland, and South Africa.

Lesson 1: Ideas Have Consequences

The Failure Is Not an Option (FNO) mentality has in and of itself shifted the conversation significantly in thousands of schools and districts. Much like the concept held in "Highly Reliable Organizations" (Stringfield, Reynolds, & Schaffer, 2008), in which failure would mean disaster and therefore is almost completely mitigated, the concept of FNO has led school leaders and their teams to create places where, as the children in one district put it: "Success is the only option!"

Ideas and single statements alone certainly do not change school systems. As noted previously, however, they have been an essential starting point for many, many leaders. Marion Wilson, principal of PS 375, Jackie Robinson School in a tough part of Brooklyn, New York, decided with her staff that Failure Is Not an Option and "Excellence is the only option," thus beginning a journey in which they went from being a "D" school to an "A" school in her three-year tenure.

The power of clarifying and articulating intentions cannot be underestimated. As Dennis Sparks (2007) writes, "Knowing what we want and being proud of it increases the likelihood we will achieve the results we seek" (p. 8).

CASE EXAMPLE

The Power of an Idea: A New Start

When Shawn Smiley first became principal, he told his new staff that failure was not an option. They could no longer say they were failing and "so what?" Teacher and leadership team member Diane Pelkington recalls how she reacted: "We had to find a way to succeed, and he's not going to accept failure in our building any more. Just hearing that and having a leader who believes, truly believes that, helps everybody else get on board. It gives us that same desire to make our building a strong building once again. I was so impressed. I had not heard that before—'failure is not an option'—so I *clearly* remember that moment."

This determination on the part of the principal and school staff to assure success across the board had significant consequences as can be seen by the scores for current reading levels below.

Grade	Quarter 1	Quarter 4
Kindergarten	51%	97%
First	80%	84%
Second	46%	67%
Third	61%	75%
Fourth	48%	63%
Fifth	48%	70%

Source: Personal communication, Shawn Smiley, Nancy Noel, Susan Lothamer, Chris Rasor, Diane Pelkington, Colleen Kobi-Berger, Lydia Beer, Marcy Bestard, & Deb Hyatt, 2009.

Note: These were percentages of students per grade level reading at grade level; K–3 were measured from DIBELS and 4 and 5 were taken from Scholastic Reading Inventory (measured in LEXILE).

The idea that no child will fail is still relatively new:

The old mission was about providing access for all to basic education and access for a relatively elite to university education. . . . The new mission for schools is to achieve 90–95 percent success. (Fullan, Hill, & Crévola, 2006, pp. 1–2)

Yet once this becomes the clear picture of a core group of leaders, it begins to spread and develop in a manner that reflects the character of the new owners. For example, the teachers participating in the Courageous Leadership Academy at Shambaugh Elementary School in Fort Wayne, Indiana, developed their own institute for the district based on similar information and titled it "Failure Is Not an Option . . . One Student at a Time."

Most important, when a learning community agrees that success is the only option for their students, they have to come to terms with a whole new set of actions to support the new agreement for a no-fail school (Blankstein, 2007; Corbett, Wilson, & Williams, 2002). Indeed, ideas have consequences, and while not sufficient in and of themselves, the clear articulation and commitment to them is the precursor to any substantive change.

Lesson 2: The Marathon Starts Before the Race Begins

We still see teachers engage in really short one- and two-day workshops rather than ongoing, sustained support that we now have evidence changes practices and increases student achievement.

—Linda Darling-Hammond, Ruth Chung Wei,
Alethea Andree, Nikole Richardson, and Stellos Orphanos,
Professional Learning in the Learning Profession

We would never expect a marathon runner to begin her training at the starting line of a race. Yet many schools launch a new initiative in such a manner. Lacking the necessary strength, endurance-building of the staff, and preparation in laying the groundwork for change, the initiative and those leading it run out of breath long before the race is over. School change can occur in a minute, but sustainable change is a marathon.

Consider the following scenario reported by Karen Seashore Louis (2008): "The busy and well-respected principal, eager to find new resources for her school, attended a workshop in which the work of DuFour and Eaker was discussed. Arriving back at school, she announced that they would be implementing PLCs and assigned teachers to cross-grade-level work groups to analyze the school's literacy data" (p. 44). Not surprisingly, the staff was not prepared to run this new marathon. As Louis reminds us, "Culture cannot be permanently altered in a short time frame of one school year" (p. 48).

The reasons that school leaders often do not create the conditions for success are many and include the following:

- Lack of awareness around change theory.
- Lack of understanding of necessary *precursors* to change.
- "Program" mind-set in which one thinks, "There has *got* to be an easy *solution* I can just buy!" There is, but it works only short-term, if at all.
- Belief in the marketing of *solutions* by the corporations that sell them.
- Comfort in continuing ways of the past, and no desire to push the envelop.
- Minimal time or focus to redress all the above; only time to repeatedly endeavor short-term solutions.

Our research indicates that school district readiness is critical to long-term success (HOPE Foundation, 2009a). The methodology we use to prepare for the marathon of sustaining student success is instructive for any change effort and includes these steps:

Step 1: Clarifying Intentions and Desired Methodology

As indicated above, this is a critical and often time-consuming step. Numerous calls have come into our offices from district leaders indicating they would like us to "do a Courageous Leadership Academy" for their district without clarity as to what that actually is, what they would gain, why exactly they want it, or who in their district really supports it. For some organizations, the request alone might be sufficient to move forward! Yet a successful outcome warrants adequate time and dialogue, and there are children's futures at stake. Put another way, being in sync on operational definitions alone takes time:

There is considerable variation regarding the delineation of the PLC components, as well as how they operate to contribute to the increase in staff learning and competency that, in turn, results in desired student learning outcomes. (Hord & Hirsh, 2008, p. 25)

It is essential and worth the effort to clarify what is needed, by whom, and why prior to beginning a new initiative.

Step 2: Self-Assessment

Teams often engage in dialogue using book studies as a catalyst to better understanding of the six principles of FNO, how to apply them, and what they are doing with them. Many use the FNO snapshot rubric (Resource 1), and critical-success factors (Resource 2) to get an overview of their current status.

Step 3: Assuring Readiness

To determine school and district needs, team-based readiness surveys are taken with the help of a professional development specialist at the HOPE Foundation. At a later point, it is often the case that the steps to assuring readiness and ultimate sustainability of the effort will include creating breadth of motivation (large-scale buy-in), depth of understanding, and commitment (Hargreaves, 2005).

Step 4: Building Successful School Teams

Once there is sufficient clarity around the nature of the marathon to begin, and leaders at both district and school levels have helped define the focus of the work, then school-based leadership teams can be formed to facilitate the change. These teams would have a common core commitment to student success, yet have varied titles, talents, and experience bases. There would likely even be some who have not yet fully bought into the effort, who might later become liaisons to bring naysayers and other resisters in the school on board.

Invariably, as efforts proceed through the Academy that follows, the leadership teams come to see themselves as facilitators of change, and the teachers on and off the team go from "doing their job," to "running their school." In the words of Reggie Rhines (personal communication, 2009), sixth-grade counselor and lead team member at the Icenhower school in Mansfield, Texas, "We've become facilitators, and you'll even have people come up and ask some specific questions about how this ties with Failure Is Not an Option in their classrooms."

The ability of team leaders to translate into schoolwide practice what they are learning at Courageous Leadership Academy meetings is critical so as not to create an inside-outside division of the staff. There are various "reentry strategies" for engaging the entire staff in the learning. At Icenhower, for example, the leadership team does more than present to those who are not in the Academy:

> As individuals on other teams as well, we are responsible and accountable to team members, so we infuse what we have learned in the academy into our work within our department, on academic teams, and in faculty meetings. So what we learn becomes standard practice throughout the school. (Rhines, personal communication, 2009)

Lesson 3: Relational Trust Trumps Technique

> *The first couple of times the teachers went in [to observe other classrooms], they did so empty handed. It was just to build trust. The protocol was to follow up with an e-mail just saying something positive that was noted during the visit. We didn't call it "instructional walks;" we called it "peer-to-peer." This was all to build trust before we got into specific strategies for instructional improvement.*

> —Duane Thurston, Principal,
> Icenhower Intermediate School, Mansfield, TX

Everyone we spoke with in our fieldwork concurred with the research—without relational trust, there will be no student achievement gains (Bryk & Schneider, 2002). Of the 21 correlates between a principal's responsibilities and student academic achievement identified by Marzano, Waters, and McNulty (2005), fully 12 of them are directly related to relationships the principal has with his entire learning community; Richard Elmore (2000) recommends that principals "rely more heavily on the face-to-face relationships than on bureaucratic routines . . . the most powerful incentives reside in the . . . relationships among people in the organization."

Yet despite all the evidence, many are still dismissive about making relational trust an agenda item, equating it with "singing Kumbaya" or going to the forest for trust walks. And while there certainly *is* a place for these two activities as well, it would not go to the core of what practitioners need to succeed, nor are they what we are advocating. In the words of Christine Sermak, principal of the Williamston Middle School at Ingham Intermediate School District, "We can do all these mini-feel-good sessions and share personal stories, but it doesn't get to the root and heart of what would take us to the next level as a building" (see Case Story 1, Six Lessons Exemplified Across a Region).

Knowing one another is certainly critical to advancing the work. Tom Sherman of Mattoon Community School District in Mattoon, Illinois, recalls,

> At our initial meeting we had 20 people in the room representing the 5 building leaders, some teacher leaders, and the district. It became evident within the first 30 minutes that even among the 20 of us, we didn't know each other, let alone the 600 staff members in our districtwide project. The relationship piece was huge! (Personal communication, 2009)

Developing an affinity for one another also helps. Creating entire "Firms of Endearment," where employers "love their employees," is even better (Fullan, 2008). Yet, trust is also built on taking tough actions in a fair and data-based manner. Allowing everyone their dignity through times of change will make success more likely.

CASE EXAMPLE

 Trust Built on Truth

Principal Shawn Smiley recalls,

I had been looking at grade-level data at the end of quarter two. I have three sections of kindergarten, and one classroom was not moving as I knew they could. I got the three grade levels' data sheets and marked out the teachers' names and asked for a meeting with the grade-level team.

Previously, we discussed sharing lessons, data, asking for help from our in-house resources in staff meetings. We had talked of shared models, peer mentoring, and precision planning of lessons through the use of data in collaboration. Still, this teacher was not moving forward as I had expected her to. As she and I sat in my office and discussed the grade-level data sheets, she noticed that one classroom was not performing as the others had. She noticed the trends, identifying factors, and lack of growth in areas where growth is expected, relative to the amount of growth she had seen in the other two classes. She looked at me, smiled, and asked, "What is this teacher doing?"

I replied, "You tell me." Then she knew it was her class. She felt as though she had cheated her students. She felt terrible about what she had done. . . . She never intended to let her students slide under the radar.

From that day forward, she was no longer closed off from outside help. She was a regular contributor to collaboration. We saw a fire that I, in my short time here, had not seen to date. She had fired herself and hired a new self. I had a brand new kindergarten teacher from that day forward.

Source: Used with permission of Shawn Smiley.

This principal combined pressure and support very effectively. Being caring, compassionate, and patient—especially in the midst of crisis, high-demand, and the pressures of time—is not wimpy. It is courageous, and it is hard. Consider the following about relationships from a tough corporate CEO, speaking to Ivy League business school students:

> How many of you have taken courses on how you talk with an employee you are firing? How do you talk with a person who comes to your office late at night to tell you that her daughter is sick, and she won't be in the following day? . . . As managers and leaders of people, those are the kinds of questions that one deals with probably 80% of the time. (Bryant, 2009, p. 2)

These are the words of the vice chairman of Wal-Mart Stores, Eduardo Castro-Wright, who is likely not advocating Kumbaya. This dichotomous thinking of either soft or hard, either relationships or results, is one of the challenges we face in creating a common language of leadership and a common language of success. Once we get past that, we will still need to meet the challenge of building capacity. Where does one learn the soft skills that lead to the hard outcomes? Without a systematic approach to this, we will continue to believe that "leaders are born" and suffer a continually diminishing pool of qualified applicants.

We have learned a great deal from excellent practitioners in the field about the specifics of building relational trust as a foundation for the sustainable learning community, and we will examine specifics in more detail in Chapter 4.

Lesson 4: School Culture Is Queen (and King!)

Probably the most important and most difficult job of the school-based reformer is to change the prevailing culture . . . ultimately a school's culture has far more influence on life and learning in the schoolhouse than the state department of education, the superintendent, the school board, or even the principal can ever have.

—Roland S. Barth, *Learning by Heart*

While there are many quick solutions that focus on techniques of collecting and analyzing data or changing teaching strategies, the enduring payoff comes in shifting school culture (Blankstein, 2007). Schools and districts implementing the principles in this book have found creative ways to express their collective values and core culture so that they are personalized and permeate the organization.

In working intensively in Mansfield Independent School District, the fastest growing district in Texas, we came across the use of symbolism and story tied closely to the mission and academics of Icenhower Intermediate School. In the words of Icenhower counselor Reggie Rhines,

> When we just started our campus, kids selected the Alaskan Husky as our mascot, which naturally led to our academic teams being named after Alaskan cities. We follow the Iditarod Dog Sled race every March and the teams do integrated units that connect all disciplines to the race. Our principal, Duane Thurston, went to the race once and the kids connected with him online which was exciting.
>
> The Red Lantern is now a symbol of our school. In the Iditarod Race, it goes to the last place team to finish, and the light stays on until that team crosses the line. This has become a symbol of our tenacity. We keep the light on during the race as a reminder that no one is forgotten or left behind. This is the spirit of our school when it comes to our students. (Personal communication, 2009)

New stories of struggle and success permeate this second edition. We use them as well to help other schools create high-performing cultures.

Lesson 5: The Answer Is in the Room—Networks Work

The book study galvanized a lot of action around here as people started realizing that it wasn't so much getting outside expertise as it was having a methodology to tap the expertise we already have.

—Gail Cooper, Principal,
Pottstown Middle School

If the answer is in the room, imagine what would happen if we expanded the size of that room, from the school house to the district, to the region, and then to the province or state. Constructive networks purposely facilitate knowledge sharing among practitioners within a given geography. The most systematic use of networking schools is in England, and it began in 2002 (Fullan, 2005). Two years prior, the

HOPE Foundation began this process in one district (see Chapter 3) in the United States (Hargreaves & Fink, 2004, 2005).

More recently, networking has been extolled as one of the most promising strategies for sustainable improvement in education (Fullan, 2005; Hargreaves & Shirley, 2009; Southworth, 2009). The successful districtwide change process will incorporate many of the lessons described, including solid preparation for the change and transference of the knowledge beyond the leadership team to the entire network. This approach involves lateral learning as well as accountability and support across the entire district or region. And while it is conceivable that a district would undertake a major change process alone, "All improving districts that we know about have active partners . . . that help build districts' professional capacity" (Fullan, 2005).

When done well, the effectiveness of this kind of work results from multiple factors:

• *Leaders can enhance their impact.* The influence of the school leader on student achievement is only through indirect means via three aspects of staff performance: (1) building staff capacity, (2) motivation and commitment, and (3) changing working conditions (Leithwood, Day, Sammons, Harris, & Hopkins, 2006). In general, the leader's influence is strong on *working conditions,* moderate on *motivation and commitment,* and weak in relation to *staff capacity.* That's because there is only one principal to every 25 to 100 teachers. A district leader alone has even less chance of developing the capacity of his entire staff. Development of capacity is time-consuming and more likely to happen when it occurs laterally, rather than hierarchically. Further, when leadership is widely distributed across the entire learning community, the influence of this collective leadership is up to three times higher than reported for an individual leader (Leithwood et al., 2006, p. 12).

• *Professional learning works when it is sustained, school-based, and embedded in teachers' daily work* (Darling-Hammond, Wei, Andree, Richardson, & Orphanos, 2009). Good networks enhance on-site learning. Yet, a disconnect remains between most professional development and the actual work of teachers and leaders back in their schools and districts. Only 10% to 20% of U.S. teachers experience *meaningful* professional development (PD) (Fullan, 2009); yet, more than 90% of them have participated in PD consisting primarily of short-term conferences or workshops. In contrast, "other nations that outperform the United States on international assessments invest heavily in professional learning and build time for ongoing, sustained teacher development" (Darling-Hammond et al., 2009).

- *Networking increases the speed of knowledge transference.* By structuring productive conversations, those involved get many more ideas, which are based on real practice in a similar and relevant context.

- *Networking increases the likelihood of implementation.* The ideal networking construct includes necessary support from, and accountability to, one's leadership team, school, district, and external partners.

Lesson 6: FNO Is a System and Framework for Action

If a student doesn't graduate, it is not just the twelfth-grade teacher's issue. It is also the second-grade teacher's issue; and an issue for the preschool and middle school teachers, and the administrator at the elementary level. How do you put all those pieces together?

—Tom Sherman, Mattoon
Community School District, Illinois

Many readers of *Failure Is Not an Option* have confirmed for us that the six guiding principles were not to be implemented in a discrete manner but were, in fact, interrelated and acted together as a comprehensive system. Creating common mission, vision, values, and goals (Principle 1), for example, is a leadership capacity builder (Principle 6). Implementation of any of the principles requires a collaborative team (Principle 3) and data-based decision making (Principle 4). Making the connections across the six principles allows schools and districts to name, organize, and then strengthen their current best practices within one cohesive system.

Similarly, a common framework and theory of action is essential for school or district change. It makes sustainable improvement possible (Fullan, 2009). Without it, efforts are random at best, and cacophonous at worst. The quality guru W. Edwards Deming used to explain that temporal spread—a theory of action—is necessary for any improvement to be understood and recreated, and for the theory itself to be revised if necessary (personal communication, 1989).

Having a common framework for action helps schools do the following:

- *Scale up and bring new people on board.*

Using a Common Framework to Build Cohesion

Principal Scott Shafer of Brooks Wester Middle School in Mansfield, Texas, reports,

The Mansfield Independent School District has been one of the fastest growing school districts in the state of Texas. Growth came so fast to this small town that within 5 years the district went from one high school to three.

When you had one high school everyone knew the procedures and expectations within the school. The problem is that as the district began to grow, each school began to have different ways of doing things, which can be good in many ways but not in other ways.

The district did not have a uniform grading system, performance standard, or policy regarding separation of behavior and achievement in grading. The state of Texas had outlined what was considered passing, or an A, B, or C, but there was no policy on how often grades should be taken. What was the minimum or maximum number of grades a teacher could take in a grading period? How were tests weighted? Did they count more than once? What about homework? A closer examination of the district showed that not every department within many schools had common performance standards or grading scale.

Source: Used with permission of Scott Shafer.

• *Focus the effort and avoid initiative overload.* In the words of Scott Shafer (personal communication, 2009), "When we started the process, we thought we were a pretty good school. This has allowed us to direct our purpose, narrow our focus, and drill down on specific areas. Since then, our scores have gone up in all areas."

• *Create synergies and cohesion across the district.* When everyone is speaking the same language, learning is greatly enhanced!

CASE STORY 1: SIX LESSONS EXEMPLIFIED ACROSS A REGION

The first Case Story of this book comes from Williamston Middle School, part of the Williamston Community School District within the Ingham County, Michigan, regional service center area, about an hour outside of Detroit. Under the leadership of Cindy Anderson, seven districts in the region became a part of the same Courageous Leadership Academy (CLA), facilitating a regionwide sharing of knowledge and resources. The systems approach as well as all the other lessons of this chapter are exemplified in this Case Story.

CASE STORY 1

 Six Lessons Exemplified Across a Region

"Our building is working on relational trust; however, we still need an outside group or someone to help get us to the next level," said principal Christine Sermak to the regional educational center coordinator Nancy Fahner. Thus began a multiyear project in which "we began through attending conferences and building our school improvement team. That helped us move in the same direction."

Teacher team members Tania Dupuis, Anne McKinney, Laura Hill, and others had already begun the trust building with students in various ways, including getting them to draw numbers or animals when entering the cafeteria indicating where they would sit and then learning about one another through questions placed at their tables. The adult trust building began in the CLA (Courageous Leadership Academy) with a self-assessment:

> Just giving the leadership team the chance to really review what great things we're already doing in our school was a refreshing change! We then looked at the many activities we have going on: which we want to stop or continue, and others we want to start.

Relational trust was intentionally *deepened*.

> We did mix-it-ups by seating people with others not from their content area (like a PE teacher, ELA eighth grade, and sixth-grade science teacher) and tackling issues like building

crosscurricular activities or how to tear down the walls of cliques. When all the ideas were collected and presented for us to choose from, it was powerful.

This was the foundation for more intensive, professional relations to come, focused on teaching and learning.

The Answer Is Down the Road

Relations were also *expanded* districtwide:

During the CLA, we had time to build relations with other schools in and outside of our district. So we sent a team to Okemos, which is in another district, since they were also creating their values. We placed theirs, the CLA values, and our own values on a table, and discussed them all. We gave everyone two stickers to vote on up to five values and ultimately reached consensus around what ours would be.

Learning across districts became the norm as well. We sent a team to Haslett Middle school, just 15 minutes away, to see how they were handling academic labs for their students struggling with literacy and numeracy; and we did the same thing with a high school in the Holt district that developed a skills-based report card.

Year One Actions

"We began building sustainable leadership from the start by bringing everyone into the process," said Christine Sermak. The leadership team was diverse and open to anyone who would commit to making every academy session. It included one parent and one board member as well. Two SMART (Specific and Strategic, Measurable, Attainable, Results-oriented, and Time-bound—see Chapter 5) goals were developed by the school staff and they aligned with those from the district:

1. By the end of the year, all teachers will incorporate writing using a common graphic organizer, editing tool, and rubric.

2. We will develop the whole child (physical, emotional, and behavioral aspects included).

Professional development was created to address these goals, and assessed accordingly. After the professional development (PD)

(Continued)

(Continued)

for Goal 1, for example, a Zoomerang survey was taken of all, asking questions ranging from their understanding of the session to their intended use of what they had learned. (See Resource 3 for survey questions.) The data-based determination of instructional planning followed, as did alignment of our PD (as described in the student-success model; see Resource 2). The model helps to embed training and assure changed practice.

Getting everyone to do meaningful walkthroughs necessary for writing and achieving the SMART goal was made easier due to the trust that was built prior.

> I know Laura's favorite ice cream, and that is a wonderful thing to begin with. What the academy allowed us to do, however, was share our work with one another using tuning protocols (see Resource 4) and that allowed us to get to know one another on a professional basis while building trust.

Initially, the walkthroughs were presented by lead team members, not the principal. They were done on a voluntary basis, in a nonjudgmental and nonevaluative manner, and the successful outcomes were trumpeted. Here is an example of an e-mail sent out following a class observation in Year One:

> I "walked through" Shelley Kranz's room on Thursday, 11 December. She taught a lesson on push/pull factors that influenced Irish and German immigration to the United States in the mid 1800s. My first observation was that Shelley has set up her room and technology in a way that made much better use of the space available than how it was in my room. Shelley seemed to have a very informal relationship at times with her students, lots of smiles, but also was able to rein them back in when needed. She set aside a significant amount of time at the beginning of the period to discuss relevant school events and questions the kids had about them. For example, the food drive was discussed and encouraged.

To further refine the common tools outlined in the first SMART goal, principal Christine Sermak and a small group of teachers decided to pilot the writing across the curriculum with two science teachers, an art teacher, a PE teacher, and a Spanish teacher.

We partnered them with a language arts teacher who helped walk them through a writing assignment using the common graphic organizer and rubric that we had developed prior (see Resource 5).

The first year success was manifest in part by our taking ownership and finding our own answers. Everything wasn't coming from Christine anymore . . . we were the ones kind of leading the school and it had a different feel than having an administrator always giving direction from the top. Everyone was investing in the whole system.

Year Two Outcomes

An e-mail goes out now if a teacher is going to teach using the graphic organizer, for example. Others will sign up to watch that, and someone from central office will cover their classroom. It is now the expectation that everyone will see someone's classroom, and have his or her class opened for viewing as well. We were able to do this due to the relational trust built in year one.

Staff meetings are now often focused on a particular student's work. Teachers use the common rubric to collectively view and analyze the work and then strategize around how to improve teaching accordingly. This leads to more embedded PD and more walkthroughs around what the team had determined they would do in the grade level or crosscurricular meeting.

"Collaboration has increased and intensified," said math teacher Laura Hill, "I've been working with a teacher who teaches an academic lab but is really strong in writing and literacy. We'll get together over lunch and I'll pick her brain about using the editing tool in my math class. She'll give me a good idea, and I'll say 'how about if we do that as partners!' Then we'll send out an e-mail for others to watch and give us feedback."

Teachers and other staff are also taking the formal lead in continuous learning and improvement. "They talked about their experience in front of the whole staff. It worked extremely well which led to everyone signing up to see another teacher teach writing."

Resource 6 shows the agenda for a full PD day they conducted. The district mission is on top, followed by the FNO six principles, and the focus is on achieving the SMART goal in this case study.

(Continued)

(Continued)

Growing the leadership capacity to collaborate focused on teaching for learning and based on a foundation of trust has been the key to this schools' success. The numbers below more of the story:

	2004–2005	2008–2009
Referrals (administrative)	1152	368
Detentions (number of detentions)	265	207
Excessive absence/tardies (number of students with 15 + incidents)	119	11

Source: Used with permission of Christine Sermak.

Think It Through . . .

How did the school in Case Story 1 use the larger network to expand their learning opportunities? What was the basis for their tapping into this network? How can your school or district access information internally and externally? How were new initiatives introduced to minimize resistance? How did this initiative minimize overload and maximize cohesion? Which of the six principles do you see in action above, and how do they act together as a system? What is your district doing to provide a common system and framework for action?

Throughout this second edition of *FNO*, readers will find other examples from Williamston Middle School and the Ingham Intermediate School District in Michigan, as well as examples from Wichita, Kansas; Fort Wayne Community Schools in Indiana (Shambaugh Elementary School); Mansfield Independent School District in Texas (Brooks Wester Middle School and Della Icenhower Intermediate School); Pottstown School District in Pennsylvania (Pottstown Middle School); and the Mattoon Community School District in Mattoon, Illinois. We've marked these "Beacons of Hope" with a special icon ⊗. Unlike the other school examples highlighted in this book, not all of these districts are award winners—yet. They range from small to moderately large, are progressing at a fairly impressive rate, and have been using FNO as their systemwide umbrella for anywhere from one to five years. The courageous work of these districts, as they advance and "push the envelope," lends valuable insight for intensive, strategic, and advanced FNO users.

CHAPTER 2

Courageous Leadership for School Success

The ultimate measure of a man is not where he stands in moments of comfort, but where he stands at times of challenge and controversy. Courage faces fear and thereby masters it; cowardice represses fear and is thereby mastered by it. We must constantly build dikes of courage to hold back the flood of fear.

—Martin Luther King, Jr.

L eaders across disciplines and throughout time have seen *courage* as the essential human virtue. Consider this small sampling:

Courage is the mother of all virtues because without it, you cannot consistently perform the others.

—Aristotle

Without courage, all other virtues lose their meaning. Courage is, rightly esteemed, the first of human qualities, because . . . it is the quality that guarantees all others.

—Sir Winston Churchill

Courage may be the most important of all virtues, because without it one cannot practice any other virtue with consistency.

—Maya Angelou

Courage, the footstool of the virtues, upon which they stand.

—Robert Louis Stevenson

Leadership has for centuries been closely associated with courage. Richard I, King of England from 1189 to 1199, was renowned for his courage and dubbed by troubadours "Richard the Lionhearted." More recent Western interpretations of courage have associated it with war, battle, and fallen or surviving heroes, yet the word itself comes from the French root *coeur*, or "heart."

Having heart was among the greatest virtues in many early Native American societies, and courage was systematically developed in young men (who were, not coincidentally, called "braves"). "The greatest brave was he who could part with his cherished belongings and at the same time sing songs of joy and praise" (Standing Bear, 1933). Eastman (1902) recounts that his grandmother encouraged him to give away what he cherished most, his puppy, so that he would one day become "courageous and strong." These young braves were taught to face their inner fears of loss. Many would later extend this courage to the ultimate sacrifice of their life for those members of the tribe, especially children and their elders, who were unable to defend themselves. Such a sacrifice for children was natural and consistent with many Native American cultures.

Eddie Belleroe, a Cree elder from Alberta, Canada, recalled a conversation with his aging grandfather. He asked, "Grandfather, what is the purpose of life?" After a long time in thought, the old man looked up and said, "Grandson, children are the purpose of life. We were once children and someone cared for us; now it is our turn to care" (Brendtro, Brokenleg, & Bockern, 1990, p. 45).

Many educators constantly make sacrifices and face fears on behalf of children. We at the HOPE Foundation work with them nationwide. We know, as just one example, a principal who fought with the bus driver's union to create an ever-changing, flexible bus schedule that serves itinerant and homeless children. We work with thousands of teachers who daily put their practice on the line in an unwavering commitment to children who are years behind grade level. Every day, these teachers, and their students, face the very real possibility of failure.

These professionals have a courageous leadership imperative (CLI). The CLI is defined as acting in accordance with one's own values, beliefs, and mission—even in the face of fear, potential losses, or failure.

Rudy, another courageous colleague, recently ran a big-city school district. One day he met with one of his principals to ask why the children in his school were consistently underperforming. The principal took Rudy to the window of his office, pointed to the children entering the school, and said, "You see those poor kids? Most of them have one parent, if that; they can't read; and they probably don't even speak the language. They just aren't going to make it!" Rudy fired the principal that day, although the political consequences were serious. In another large school district working with us, the leadership analyzed the strengths and needs of 34 elementary schools. Acknowledging that they could no longer settle for the dim improvement results they'd experienced, they decided to "get the right person on the right bus," which resulted in eight principal changes and seven assistant reassignments within one year. That was followed by one resignation and one retirement but a net gain as the needs of each building now matched the strengths of the principals and assistant principals for the buildings. Transition meetings followed to clarify expectations and smooth the change process, and the entire school community then realized how serious the district was about improvement.

The courageous actions described above are not calculated in terms of personal risk. They are not designed for personal gain. These educators acted in accordance with their hearts. They do what they have to do because of who they are and what they value. They do it because of the young people whom they are charged to protect, nurture, and help develop into successful young men and women. Developing such courageous leadership individually and organizationally, and leveraging it to assure sustained student success, is the subject of this chapter.

WHEN FAILURE IS NOT AN OPTION

Following a conversation with Archbishop Desmond Tutu, Nobel Peace Prize laureate, we asked his personal assistant if fear of failure ever influenced them in their struggle against apartheid. Oupa Scene responded,

> We never considered failure. Even though we were under apartheid, we had some African neighbors who were doing even worse than us! We drew strength from one another; we would reminisce and conceive of a brighter future for our country . . . a day when everyone

could eat, lodge, and have other basics of life; a day when we could create a space program that would rival NASA in the U.S. While so many of our brothers died, we never considered defeat. (Personal correspondence, 2003)

What makes it possible for people facing such horrific odds against success to persevere until ultimate victory? If they can do this under such circumstances, are there lessons for teachers who face daily struggles in the classroom? For school administrators looking down the barrel of steep budget cuts? For superintendents and district personnel dealing with massive turnover?

A TEST OF COURAGE

Courage is a natural virtue—but it's also a virtue that can be developed. Although we tend to mystify this "mother of all virtues" (Aristotle) and idealize it in the realm of conflict and war, acts of courage can be found regularly in daily life, as noted previously. But it's important to take note that courage can be *developed.*

One's capacity for courageous action can be quickly gauged by this informal test that has been given to more than 3,000 educational leaders since 2002. Imagine that you are in a new town or city and are on your way to shop at a nearby mall. As you approach the mall, you discover that it is on fire. You do not know the nature of the fire, only that it began shortly before you arrived. There are no fire trucks in sight.

Would you enter the mall? Most of us would say "No!" Our instincts tell us that it would be foolish to do so. There is a difference, after all, between foolish behavior and courage. But under what circumstances, if any, *would* you enter the mall? Would you enter if

1. A big sale is going on?

2. People are in the mall (who might be trapped)?

3. Children are in the mall (who might be trapped)?

4. Your children are in the mall?

None of those we surveyed said "Yes" to question 1, though some laughed. About 5% of those surveyed said "Yes" to question 2. An additional 25% responded positively to question 3. Every person who was asked question 4 emphatically answered that they would enter that mall to save their own children.

Although we do not claim that this is a scientifically administered survey of educational leaders, it does provide an interesting glimpse into the nature of courage and what evokes that virtue. For example, no one surveyed responded to question 4 with another question. Questions about particulars *did* arise when those surveyed were asked to respond to question 3 ("How many children are there?" "Has the fire department already been notified?" "Do I know where the entrance is?" and so on). This implies that the need for specific "skills," "strategies," and "how to?" information may diminish as the relevance of the task at hand grows for the individual.

The lesson is, in part: "People are willing to make sacrifices if they see the reason why. . . . People need to know the stakes are worth it" (Heifetz & Linsky, 2002, p. 94). In short, where there's a will, there's a way. Conversely, where there's no will, there may also be no way!

The need to *act* can be more compelling than the *fear* of action, its consequences, or possible failure. Countless examples—from *Apollo 13*, from the struggle against apartheid, from the educators cited previously, and from our own research—indicate that this is the case. Courageous leaders can develop their own internal fortitude as well as tap and develop a courageous leadership imperative throughout their organization. In fact, it is imperative to engage the heart or courage of people throughout an organization:

> As the strategy unfolds, leaders must pay close attention to whether they are generating passion, purpose, and energy . . . on the part of principals and teachers. Failure to gain on this problem is a surefire indicator that the strategy will fail sooner than later. (Fullan, 2003a, pp. 62–63)

THE COURAGEOUS LEADERSHIP IMPERATIVE

The CLI not only begins with the "end in mind" (Covey, 1989) but also requires a resounding commitment to that end. The link between success in a given endeavor and our belief in our *ability* to succeed is well established (Bandura, 1986; Goddard, Hoy, & Hoy, 2000; Goleman, 1995; Love & Kruger, 2005; Sternberg, 1996). In education, a vast body of research indicates that the belief system of teachers heavily influences their students' possibilities for success (Clark, 1988; Cole, 1989; Fenstermacher, 1986; Nespor, 1987; Pintrich, 1990; Weinstein, 1989). In short, "positive expectations yield positive results" (Kouzes & Posner, 1999, p. 68).

Research on highly reliable organizations (HROs) takes this concept of positive expectations and belief systems a step further. These HROs embrace the core concept that *failure is not even an option.* In fact, for these organizations, failure would mean disaster, as they are responsible for such things as clean water, electrical power supplies, and air traffic control. One study of two types of HROs—air traffic control towers and regional electrical power grids—considered applying "HRO response" to meeting the demand for high-quality instructional services for *all* students. This study indicated the strong likelihood that what was learned from HROs can be applied to work in schools (Stringfield, Reynolds, & Schaffer, 2008).

Rossi and Stringfield (1997) wrote, "We found much support for the HRO construct [for potential use in schools] and for its dependence on an established network of high-quality relationships among all stakeholders" (p. 6). Among the cited principles of HROs were

1. The central goals are clear and widely shared.

2. All staff in HROs share a belief that success is critical and that failure to achieve core tasks would be absolutely disastrous.

3. HROs build interdependence among all staff. (Rossi & Stringfield, 1997, pp. 6–7)

Our interviews with thousands of school leaders over the past two decades have yielded findings similar to those immediately above. We found that those administrators who hold an unshakable belief in the ultimate success of their staff and students have far better results than those who do not hold such a belief. Moreover, leaders with a CLI take that belief a step further. They are unwilling to conceive of failure in the long term. Setbacks along the way are rapidly turned into learning experiences that fuel advances toward future successes. As a result, these leaders are more likely to see projects through to completion, inspire others to high levels of performance, and commit to sustaining achievement for *all* students.

What are the elements of such a CLI, and how can they be developed? The next section addresses these questions.

FOUNDATIONS FOR SUCCESS

The CLI was distilled from an extensive literature review on educational leadership and conversations with thousands of leaders over the past

Developing a "Failure Is Not an Option" Philosophy

In a three-year study documenting schools that embraced a philosophy of "all children can learn and it's my job that they do," Corbett, Wilson, and Williams (2002) discovered Granite Junior High School, located in a poor urban community. Granite students' success rate on standardized tests compares favorably with wealthier schools in the district. This is due in great part to the staff's consensus position that every assignment by each student must be completed at a level sufficient to earn a B. In essence, all assignments receive one of the following:

A—Above and beyond.

B—The basics. You know your stuff.

I—Incomplete. You need time and support.

To earn an A, students had to complete extra-credit work. To attain a B, students needed to meet the quality standards clearly defined in advance by each teacher. Teachers had to address many structural challenges to make this philosophy work, including how to handle the open-endedness of the incompletes. According to the study,

> The ninth-grade teachers established the end of each marking period as the deadline for assignments . . . while the other two grades continued with the more open-ended approach . . . ninth grade also resorted to using C's and D's [still avoiding F's]. (Corbett et al., 2002, p. 86)

Granite Junior High School embraced a common philosophy, behaved in accordance with it (culture), and created structures and teaching strategies to accommodate it. In the traditional school's equation of Time + Efforts = Learning, the time spent on students and the teaching efforts (including alternative pedagogies) are shifted only marginally in response to students who don't learn. At Granite Junior High,

(Continued)

(Continued)

however, learning became the constant; time and instructional approaches became the variables that could be manipulated in order to assure student success.

Source: Adapted with permission from *Engaging Every Learner* (Blankstein, 2007, p. 13) and *Effort and Excellence in Urban Classrooms* (Corbett et al., 2002).

20 years. Preliminary findings in the most recent study still underway shows that the most successful leaders demonstrated characteristics that mirror those of highly reliable organizations listed earlier. These leaders do not consider failure to be an option. Specifically, leaders who turn failing schools around and keep successful schools moving forward over time exhibit characteristics that can be summarized in the following five axioms:

1. Begin With Your Core

This axiom refers to first clarifying the driving *internal* core of the leadership and the school community. "Authentic leaders build their practice inward from their core commitments rather than outward from a management text" (Evans, 1996). The core is defined here as the intersection of one's purpose, values, and intention. Determining one's core is a profound and intensive process that provides the enduring roots necessary to sustain efforts in the face of opposing forces. Elaine Wilmore (2007) defines our core values as

the central part of our lives. They are what we stand for and what we are willing to put on the line for the sake of honor and integrity. They are established within us and are guiding principles of how we live our lives.

School leadership often requires balancing the interests of varying groups. For example, parents on the "right" may want to reduce access to certain reading texts for their children, whereas parents on the "left" may highly value those same texts as well as the concept of free access to information. How can leaders attend to the many disparate interests that tug at them without losing their own center? As one high school principal puts it,

> The non-negotiable that I come back to most often is being true to myself—heeding the call of my heart, *my core,* for better or worse. Sooner or later a great leader is going to stir the pot and, if great things happen as a result, is going to get splattered and slopped on. (Hallowell, 1997, p. 55; italics added)

Although mission statements address why schools exist (e.g., to assure that all students learn), the axiom of "beginning with your core" goes a level deeper. It answers the questions "Why do I care?" and "What am I willing to do about it?"

Clarifying one's core as a person and a leader is perhaps the most difficult and most fundamental of all acts (Bennis, 1989). We should not be surprised that it is also rarely undertaken. In fact, one could find many understandable reasons for passing over this critical axiom, and there are many reasons why such practices are seen as unnecessary or impractical among modern-day educational leaders:

1. There is too little time to do *anything,* much less "getting to one's core"! Donaldson (2001) refers to the "leadership-resistant architecture" of schools in which there is a "conspiracy of busyness" (p. 11) that leaves little time to convene people to plan, organize, and follow through. Although most leaders find this leaves them with little time for reflection, the most effective among them make allocating their time properly a priority nonetheless.

2. There is an impression that "self-discovery" is "soft" or an otherwise unnecessary aspect of leadership. Our work with leaders indicates otherwise and more closely concurs with Warren Bennis's (1989) pioneering work in the field.

> "Know thyself" is the inscription over the oracle at Delphi. And it's still the most difficult task any of us faces. But until you truly know yourself, your strengths and weaknesses, know what you want to do and why you want to do it, you cannot succeed in any but the most superficial sense of the word. (p. 40)

3. Acting on aspirations and ideals can be painful. Such actions expose leaders to what Ackerman and Maslin-Ostrowski (2002) refer to as

the inevitable "wounding" that true leaders experience. It becomes easier and less risky, therefore, to just do what is mandated by the district, state department, or province.

4. Leadership is a lonely role to begin with. This isolation is compounded by the sense many leaders have that it is not safe to be themselves, even with their staff. They can become a "prisoner to their roles" and suffer from what Kets de Vries (1993) refers to as the "impostor syndrome."

5. In almost every society we researched there have been or still are mentors, spiritual guides, elders, and others who systematically assist people in self-development and self-discovery. Many African societies we visited still use rites of passage with their young boys and girls. Several Native American societies use "vision quests" to help prospective leaders uncover their purpose in life. Such practices have been seen as essential to leading a meaningful life, and especially to leading others to do the same. This is no longer the case in most Western societies, and many people simply don't know where to begin such a search for self.

CASE EXAMPLE

 Finding Purpose

Carolyn Powers is director of elementary administration for the Fort Wayne Community School District in Indiana. She reflects,

What do you want people to say about you once you leave? Are you here to make the adults in the building happy or to ensure that the children learn? It is difficult to stay focused on student learning when the pressure of status quo tugs at you from the existing culture. You have to look yourself in the mirror each day and say I will do what is right for the students under my watch.

There are many ways that educational leaders can reach their core. Livsey and Palmer (1999) suggest answering the following questions in pairs to get to "the heart of our life as a teacher":

1. Why did I become a teacher?

2. What do I stand for as an educator?

3. What are the gifts that I bring to my work?

4. What do I want my legacy as a teacher to be?

5. What can I do to keep track of myself—to remember my own heart? (Livsey & Palmer, 1999; Covey, 1989).

Another way to get individuals to discover what lies at their core is through an activity that can be undertaken in groups of about 8 to 15. One group or several can do this activity at the same time within a room.

Ask everyone to begin by sitting in a circle while the activity is explained, and then break into groups of three. Each member of the triad recounts a story from his or her own life that captures the essence of the person in some way. For example: "When I was a young teenager, I saw a couple of other teenagers robbing an elderly woman, and I intervened."

The person telling the story then draws out the elements that describe some of his or her essential personal characteristics. In the above example, the storyteller might say: "This shows the essence of who I am and what I value because I protect those who need help, and I am not afraid of the consequences." Others in the triad may add to the list of characteristics and see if the storyteller agrees with them.

Someone else in the triad can write down each personal characteristic to share with the larger group. It is also possible to build an affinity diagram from everyone's notes in order to discover the "common core" of the group. This, in turn, can be used as part of the development of the school's mission or values (to be described in Chapter 5). The full group is reformed at the end of this sharing session, and everyone has the opportunity to briefly share their story and corresponding "essential" or "core" characteristics.

Educators can also get to their core by reflecting alone on these critical questions:

1. What do I *value* most? Another way to ask this might be, What behaviors can I *not* tolerate and why?

2. What do my past life patterns, strong interests, and passions tell me about my *purpose* in life?

3. How do my values and purpose in life overlap with what I am doing *here* in my current role? What are my *intentions* relative to the work I am now doing?

Defining the answers to questions 1 and 2, and ensuring alignment between this and the intentions of one's current work as a leader, will help to maximize the effectiveness of such an exercise. This process takes time, yet it builds a feeling of personal authenticity and therefore enhances trust within the organization.

"Leaders who are followed are authentic. Integrity is a fundamental consistency between personal beliefs, organizational aims, and working behavior" (Evans, 1996, p. 184). Defined in slightly different terms, leaders with the greatest credibility and moral sway know who they are. Their *purpose, values,* and *intentions* relative to their work are aligned. The next four axioms deal with leaders' *actions*.

2. Create Organizational Meaning

What's really important to being our best is concentration and focus on something that is meaningful to us.

—James M. Kouzes and Barry Z. Posner, *Encouraging the Heart*

Victor Frankl (1959/2000) wrote persuasively about people's fundamental need for meaning in their lives. Despite the current focus on testing and standards, educators need more than incremental gains on their students' test scores to establish a motivating connection to their work. Similarly, students need to see the relevance of schoolwork in their lives. This is essential to gaining sustainable achievement or anything more than short-term results on tests. As one 14-year-old student shared with us, "What do I care about Romeo and Juliet? I ain't goin' to college . . . an' most of my friends ain't even made it to be 20 years old!"

The drive to create meaning guides the creation and communication of deeper meaning in the lives of all stakeholders, which in turn unleashes energy toward substantive school improvement. It also provides a sense of hope to those in despair. Such hope is a vitally important ingredient for success (Cooper, 2007; Evans, 1996; Fullan, 2001a; Hargreaves & Fullan, 1998).

One way to create organizational meaning is through reframing. Although a budget cut may demoralize a school community, for example, it could also be an impetus for change and an opportunity to rally the troops. It could be seen, therefore, as an opportunity to gather people together to discuss how the community can collectively make their current work more effective, drop things that are not working, and learn about how other schools are dealing with similar challenges. It could even be the impetus for a school community that was otherwise isolated to undertake action research on "best practices" for dealing with budgetary constraints.

 Reframing in Action

From "Throwaway" Child to Ray of Hope

A principal faced a challenge with a minority parent who had little or no trust in the authority figures at the school. The children in the family were sent to the office on a daily basis, and the parents were furious and felt their children were being singled out.

Instead of avoiding the conflict and allowing the staff to label the family as unreachable, the principal chose the students as examples of how to offer quality interventions that lead to academic success. Intensive interventions were set in place for the children. Each time a new milestone was reached within the classroom, the parent received a positive call. The children began learning. The successes were shared each month at the staff meeting. The staff started believing that they really could make a difference.

At an open house the parent told the superintendent, "At first I didn't understand what this school was all about, but now I know that they are trying hard to teach my children."

Creating Positive Meaning Across the District

When state-testing results continued to label most of the 54 schools within this urban district as failures, the Board of Education and Superintendent got to work. Realizing that there were many success stories as well as schools that missed the mark by only a few points, a Balanced Scorecard was created.

This document allowed schools to show gains in targeted areas for improvement. Success stories began to be shared with the community as well as with the students. Setting clear and measurable goals for the purpose of student improvement provided reasons to celebrate in Fort Wayne.

All leaders are faced with crises at some point. Leaders are also regularly faced with challenges. A leader's most productive reaction to such situations is to create positive meaning from them for themselves and for the people in their organizations.

3. Maintain Constancy and Clarity of Purpose

Sometime in the 1970s, advertisers must have quietly signed a pact: *All products should now and henceforth be deemed "new and improved"!* Educators, like most of us, gleefully bought the "latest" and most "improved" lawnmower, car, and soap. As a profession, we have also adopted this same regrettable concept—creating, consuming, and abandoning the latest educational fad every few years.

But the educator who purchases a quick and convenient "initiative du jour" is buying a mirage. Most of these new initiatives are later deemed ineffective and evaporate—or worse, they are kept indefinitely without further evaluation. In the latter case, the educational "bookshelf" is filled with a confusing array of possible ways to proceed. This approach is disjointed at best, and it is demoralizing for an already overburdened staff.

This axiom—to maintain consistency and clarity of purpose—moves us toward a disciplined approach to both clarifying and holding fast to organizational purpose. It saves time that would otherwise be spent changing directions and filling vacancies for departing, dispirited staff.

The "constancy of purpose" portion of this axiom (Deming, 1986) is made possible by first clarifying that purpose. In the *Apollo 13* example, the purpose was clear: Bring the astronauts back alive. Had the purpose been vague (e.g., at one point there was still question as to whether they should attempt a moon walk) or the constancy of that pursuit wavering (e.g., had ground control given in to the pessimism surrounding their superhuman mission), the astronauts would never have made it home.

Maintaining clarity and constancy of purpose accomplishes two major goals. First, it helps reduce stress among staff—stress that arises from multiple priorities coupled with insufficient time to accomplish them. Tom Williams (2001) surveyed current elementary and secondary principals in Ontario and found that more than 80% will retire by 2009. Three of five of their top "dissatisfiers" had to do with lack of time to perform their jobs properly. Most have since retired.

Gail Connelly and Gerald Tirozzi (2008) note that,

traditionally, assistant principals and teachers have stepped up to the plate, ready and willing to fill the shoes of a former principal. Now, *in the face of an ever-increasing amount of responsibility* placed on the shoulders of school leaders, many assistant principals and teachers are foregoing the opportunity to take over the top spot.

Reports from Australia indicate that they share similar challenges as applications for the principalship continue to decline (Barty, Thomson, Blackmore, & Sachs, 2005).

As one principal told us, "I feel like I need to be all things to all people. And district priorities shift like the desert sands. It can be overwhelming at times." Adhering to the axiom of clarity and constancy of purpose helps provide continuity and coherence in an otherwise ever-changing landscape.

Second, maintaining clarity and constancy of purpose leads to greater success within those areas of focus. Evans (1996) explains, "Studies of high-performing systems show that their leaders provide direction that is clear, strong, and unambivalent. . . . Clarity brings many advantages. The first is to foster trust" (p. 213). Evans goes on to advocate that any given team or individual considering a multifaceted project undertake "one thing at a time" (p. 218).

There are several ways to keep focus clear and constant:

1. Be fanatical about the positives of a project. Continually point out the milestones that are being reached along the way. Celebrate success. Encourage experimentation and refinements where necessary. Empower people to continue the efforts on their own in order to build momentum.

2. Systematically drop what should *not* be pursued. Involve stakeholders in creating a list of such activities or projects to determine "what needs to be done that is not being done now, and what can we quit doing so we can do what we need to do?" (Schlechty, 1992, p. 106).

3. Provide a sense of urgency to the area of desired focus. In Chapter 1, we described a superintendent who determined that she and her staff were not teaching math and science, but saving lives! Such "reframing" in compelling and urgent terms helps to focus people on desired outcomes.

4. Provide continuous feedback using data. Ensuring that pertinent data flow directly to those involved with a project (as opposed to being filtered through the leader) is even more powerful and focusing.

5. When necessary, stretch out timelines to meet the goal. It is better to provide the time needed for success than it is to have several half-completed projects.

Effective leaders help their school community succeed by first personally defining their core, making meaning for their organization around core values and core purpose, and continually clarifying and focusing on priorities that are aligned with that purpose.

4. Confront the Data and Your Fears

In *Good to Great*, Jim Collins (2001) observes that successful companies consistently and accurately assess current performance with an eye toward improvement. "Facing the brutal facts" is often difficult; they can be unflattering! In addition, educators tend to correlate certain types of assessment with personal and critical evaluation by administration (Hargreaves & Fullan, 1998; also see Chapter 8).

Naming and facing fears constructively can be the first step to overcoming them, thereby expanding the range of possible actions. Take these classic world events, for example:

1. The May 13, 2003, issue of the *New York Times* reported: "Scientists . . . said yesterday that the existing public health measures had been effective in containing the [SARS] disease in many countries and should work eventually in China and Taiwan, where the disease is now concentrated" (p. 13). Ironically, SARS reportedly began in China but was contained in places as near as Hong Kong and as far away as Toronto, Canada, before it was under control in China. This is likely due to the Chinese government's initial denial of the problem. Unlike Hong Kong, China was unwilling to confront the data and face the fears associated with this epidemic. As this article indicated, "The New China News Agency reported that 31 officials in the capital were disciplined for poor performances in carrying out measures to combat the epidemic" (p. 13).

2. In February 2003, the space shuttle *Columbia* burst into flames upon reentry into the earth's atmosphere, killing all seven astronauts aboard.

The subsequent investigation revealed that a suitcase-sized chunk of foam smashed into the *Columbia*'s left wing and damaged a critical heat shield, causing the *Columbia* space shuttle disaster.

According to the Associated Press (Test, 2003), "During *Columbia*'s flight, shuttle managers rejected engineers' request for spy satellite images to ascertain the extent of damage to the left wing" (para. 19).

Although it is impossible to know what the fate of this flight mission might have been had scientists confronted the data (and their fears) early on, it is clear that they did not take this approach. By contrast, confronting the data and facing fears were critical to saving the lives of the three men on *Apollo 13*, as described in Chapter 1.

Like other organizations, school communities tend to avoid certain facts and related fears. We have entered many fine schools, for example, that pride themselves on an 85% passing rate on standardized tests, without examining who is in the 15% that are failing.

It is essential to develop the organizational norms and the personal "habits of mind" (Costa & Kallick, 2000) to dispassionately and regularly evaluate one's position relative to the ideal and to use data-based assessments as fuel for continued improvements, hope, optimism, and action.

5. Build Sustainable Relationships

In the prior "A Test of Courage" section of this chapter, we noted that each of the more than 3,000 leaders surveyed emphatically said "yes" when asked if they would enter a burning shopping mall if their child were in it. Although the "moral imperative" (Fullan, 2003a) of potentially saving children was the same in both questions 3 and 4 of this survey, the *relationship* was not. When the children in question were the *respondents'* children, there was no doubt as to whether they would risk their lives to save them.

Studies of courageous actions in war indicate that it is not so much moral purpose that lies behind putting your life on the line (although that can be a part of it), but the more tangible impact of loyalty to your buddies. "Quality relationships, in other words, are even more powerful than moral purpose" (Fullan, 2003b, p. 35).

Clearly, in this book we are not advocating that leaders or their staff put their lives on the line. The research is clear, however, that relationships are a crucial element of student achievement and school success (Barth, 2001; Bryk and Schneider, 2002; see also "Lesson 3: Relational Trust Trumps Technique" in Chapter 1). They also support courageous leadership.

The relationships we refer to are myriad and multifaceted. They include relationships among staff, between staff and students, among students, between the school personnel and the community—among everyone touched by the work of the school.

Kouzes and Posner (1999) wrote,

Leaders create relationships, and one of those relationships is between individuals and their work. Ultimately we all work for a purpose, and that purpose has to be served if we are to feel encouraged. Encouraging the heart only works if there's a fit between person, the work, and the organization. (p. xv)

It is important to understand that all of the preceding axioms interact with one another. Relationships serve to weave them together into a unified whole. Relationships support a leader in taking the risk to act from his or her *core* to create *organizational meaning.* Relationships allow leaders to maintain *clarity and constancy of purpose* and to *face the data and the fears,* though this might otherwise be too stressful, threatening, and disheartening.

In every district in which we worked toward long-term school reform prior to 2005, we spent the first year on nonacademic items such as the development of mission and vision in ways that were collaborative and relationship enhancing. It is interesting to note that although we did not focus on academics in the first year, in every instance academic achievement improved significantly during that same year. Even now, we spend considerable time on relationship building in order to more deeply and honestly address data-driven teaching practices. The Case Story in the next chapter on the Alton, Illinois, school district provides corroborating details.

Throughout this book, we share ways to enhance affinity among those in the school community. In Chapter 4, we also advocate the creation of learning communities based on relational trust. These sections provide specific strategies for developing relationships critical to the success of schools.

DEVELOP COURAGEOUS LEADERSHIP FOR ACTION

> *This culture, and we as members of it, have yielded too easily to what is doable and practical. . . . We have sacrificed the pursuit of what is in our hearts. We find ourselves giving in to doubts and settling for what we know how to do, or can learn to do, instead of pursuing what matters most to us and living with the adventure and anxiety that this requires.*
>
> —Peter Block, *The Answer to How Is Yes*

There is frequently a chasm between what we know to be the best action and what we do. The connecting tissue is often the courage to act.

In this book, we appeal to the *heart* (as well as the mind) in order to find the courage to increase and sustain levels of student achievement. Given the challenges for staff, students, and the larger community in today's environment of accountability, there is much at stake.

As mentioned earlier, courage comes from the French word *coeur,* or "heart." Effective leaders act with heart. In the final analysis, their decisions are informed by judgment but emanate from their core purpose, values, and intention. Leaders who act in this manner transcend fears of failure that would otherwise impede them; they act with a courageous leadership imperative.

When courageous leadership permeates the school community, the *how to* questions of school improvement become easier to determine and implement. Where there's a will, there is indeed a way. When the will is lacking, questions about specific techniques and tools can become an obstacle to action or any real change. Developing the CLI goes a long way toward ensuring sustained student achievement. The next chapter looks in detail at 10 other common obstacles to school change and how to overcome each.

CHAPTER 3

10 Common Routes to Failure, and How to Avoid Each

Educational change is technically simple and socially complex.

—Michael Fullan, *Leading in a Culture of Change*

Slow is smooth and smooth is fast.

—Jeff Pascal, Bicentennial East
Coast Weapons Champion, U.S. Martial Arts
Association Kung Fu Instructor of the Year, 2000

Every diaper-changing parent is likely to agree: Change is messy business. Chang*ing* is even messier!

Although people may like the eventual *change*, they often don't like chang*ing* because the *process* can be uncomfortable. Installing new solar panels on your roof, for example, may be eco-friendly and cost effective in the long run, but the disruption, chaos, and expense of the installation process are sure to give you major headaches in the short term.

Some of us are innovators and enthusiastic "early adopters" of change but most of us take a cautious approach and have genuine concerns to work through.

Like all of us, teachers are often less than enthusiastic about embracing change, especially when it is done *to* them instead of *with* them. Although they may agree with the overall *concepts* of learning communities, collaborative teaming, and differentiated instruction, getting accustomed to them can create feelings of insecurity and fear. This is especially true for practitioners who have experienced innovation overload. Questions emerge: "Why do *I* have to change?" "Haven't we done this before?" and "How exactly do you want me to find time for *this?*" If left unanswered, they can thwart any change initiative.

EDUCATIONAL MOVEMENTS COME AND GO, THE OBSTACLES REMAIN THE SAME

In the late 1980s, the HOPE Foundation began working with quality guru W. Edwards Deming, whose work formed the basis of all Japanese manufacturing processes after World War II. At that time, it became clear that Deming's approach, often mistakenly titled total quality management (TQM), was more effective in creating high-performing organizations than what was then being used in most U.S. corporations (Blankstein, 1992). Most important for us, Deming's work shed light on a potentially powerful new paradigm for education.

Not long afterward, we introduced Deming and, later, Peter Senge to the top educational leadership of the era through a series of Shaping America's Future forums, and PBS-ALSS programs. We proposed his concepts and those of total quality education (TQE) and learning communities for discussion in educational circles.

Lew Rhodes of the American Association of School Administrators asked to meet privately with Deming and a few months later began the Total Quality Network. At the same time, the Association for Supervision and Curriculum Development introduced *their* Total Quality Learning Network, with Jay Bonstingl leading the charge (Bonstingl, 2001). Powerful business groups, including the Business Roundtable, added "total quality" approaches to their current site-based management initiatives. Prominent educational authors like William Glasser (1992) began writing about total quality education. One could hear a swelling chant from the ranks of educational leaders: "TQE! TQE! TQE!"

By the end of the 1990s, however, the "movement" was dead. Only a few remnants of some of the more technical aspects of Deming's work remain. The leaders of the HOPE Foundation went on to help catalyze the next educational leadership wave—professional learning communities (PLCs)—through their publication of three works by DuFour and Eaker (DuFour, 1991; DuFour and Eaker, 1992, 1998). Many publications furthered the movement (Hord & Sommers, 2007; Blankstein, Houston, & Cole, 2008). The cycle recommences.

Creating substantive and sustainable change in education has been elusive. Here are some of the common obstacles and means of overcoming them:

Obstacle 1: We Don't Want to Change

People are often wary of new ideas, and in schools such resistance can present itself on many fronts. Teachers can tire of being asked to rethink their practice. Parents want their children's school days to be just like their own and are often reluctant to endorse new and different approaches to education.

It is possible to overcome this reluctance to change. In Case Story 1 (see Chapter 1), we saw how principal Christine Sermak phased in sustainable change at Williamston Middle School, in Williamston, Michigan. Similarly, at Kate Sullivan Elementary School in Tallahassee, Florida, then principal Nancy Duden dealt with resistance by encouraging teachers, staff members, and parents to explore change initiatives at their own pace. Duden did not force acceptance of these new ideas; rather, she provided workshops, reading materials, support groups, and community volunteers to help teachers and parents become familiar with the new ideas. Duden also supported a great deal of dialogue with teachers and parents, primarily through the PTA, which uncovered and helped to dispel anxieties about adopting new principles. By taking her time and letting individuals voice their concerns, Duden quelled much of the fear that usually accompanies change (Blankstein & Swain, 1994).

Obstacle 2: You're the Leader, Tell Me What to Do

Through our experiences as students and employees, many of us have learned that the leaders' role is to make decisions and control outcomes. In education, principals might fear that relinquishing control over every aspect of the school could hinder its effective functioning. Other members of the staff become comfortable in established roles as well and find it difficult to transcend years of experience as a "leader" or "follower."

True change requires that all individuals within an organization—administrators, teachers, staff members, parents, and students—work cooperatively for the benefit of the students. In the long run, monopolizing power inhibits individuals in these groups from viewing themselves as contributing to the overall success of the larger system.

At Kate Sullivan, Nancy Duden reevaluated her own leadership style and realized that her authoritarian role would not produce long-term commitment from her staff. Instead she decided to "diversify the leadership portfolio" by giving teachers and parents the opportunity to lead as well (see Chapter 10 on distributed leadership).

She played a support role and helped promote change, for example, by acting as a participant, rather than leader, in meetings; encouraging teachers and parents to explore new ideas, instead of moving them toward a predetermined agenda; and endorsing the changes teachers determine are beneficial for students, versus asking their opinion and then following another path.

By playing a supportive role with her staff, Duden created a nurturing environment in which *teacher leaders* were unafraid to take risks in leadership roles. Duden's commitment to changing her own leadership style allowed individuals throughout the school community to reevaluate both their roles and the concept of leadership itself.

Obstacle 3: We Have No Time for This!

This statement is, on its face, completely legitimate. There is simply no way of getting around it—the process of creating mission, vision, values, and goals statements; completing needs assessments; collecting and analyzing data; and planning for change require an investment of time. Schools also need to make time in the daily schedule for teacher collaboration and continued professional development.

At the same time, this statement can also be a smokescreen for staff who resist change. This ruse can be uncovered by asking, "Is time the only issue? If I were to assure you that you will have sufficient time to do this, would you become actively involved in the process?" The change process must be seen as *worth* the time spent. In fact, some cultures, communities, and educational systems may not value collaboration or in-depth professional development.

Among the key findings of the National Staff Development Council status report *Professional Learning in the Learning Profession* (Darling-Hammond, Wei, Andree, Richardson, & Orphanos, 2009) is this:

Key Finding 15: American teachers spend much more time teaching students and have significantly less time to plan and learn together, and to develop high quality curriculum and instruction than teachers in other nations. U.S. teachers spend about 80 percent of their total working time engaged in classroom instruction, as compared to about 60 percent for these other nations' teachers.

Rethinking the school culture and the importance of continual, embedded professional development is key for long-term success. Beyond this comes the practical issue of finding time. Here are some examples of how schools have addressed this issue:

- *Provide Common Planning Time.* Schedule several classes for the same activity at the same time to free classroom teachers to work together (e.g., all third-grade art classes or seventh-grade PE classes meet simultaneously).
- *Involve Students in Community-Based Service Learning.* At Central Park East Secondary School, eighth-, ninth-, and tenth-grade students spend one half-day of each week away from school, working in various community-service programs. Teachers use the time for collaboration (Pardini, 1999).
- *Create Banks of Time.* Add a few minutes of teaching time to each class in a particular period daily for four days. On the fifth day, the class is cancelled or shortened by the number of extra minutes accumulated. Students are provided with an alternative activity, and teachers use that time to meet in teams.

There are many ways to deal with the issue of time. An additional 12 ideas can be found in Resource 7. We suggest that the ideas on this list be used as starters to stimulate brainstorming within your own school. Each teaching staff must develop approaches that *they* believe will work and that they are invested in implementing.

Obstacle 4: Carrots and Sticks Don't Work

For many years, the operation of American schools was modeled on the same assembly-line method that first permitted mass production of automobiles. In this fear-driven system, which requires employees to meet quotas and product specifications, workers compete with one another for promotions and bonuses that are parceled out to a few "winners." The internal strife and long-term demotivation this system causes is well documented. Yet educators persist in using grades, class ranks, and even merit pay to the same end.

This extrinsic approach to motivation implies that if individuals are not rewarded, punished, or pitted against one another in competition, they will fail to "perform." In fact, in our current system, "performance" is the best possible outcome. Unfortunately, children learn to simply get the "right answer" instead of going on a road of discovery, which often leads to "wrong" answers, but enhances "true" learning.

Deming, in contrast, bases his philosophy on the opposite premise: that individuals have an *intrinsic* drive to learn and do well and that they do not want to fail. He maintains that if allowed to pursue this natural drive, people will strive to reach their potential without any need for external motivators such as competition or fear. The role of the education system, given such an assumption, is one of guidance and evaluation in an environment of continual learning.

At Kate Sullivan, Nancy Duden provided constructive alternatives to extrinsic rewards such as grades. Portfolios of students' work and parent/teacher conferences to help parents gauge their children's progress replaced report cards with self-evaluation. These and other processes have allowed teachers, parents, and students to work together for constant improvement, one of Deming's principles. Attaining the grade is no longer the goal. Now the goal is continually learning and growing. (We will discuss assessment for learning in Chapter 8.)

Duden also replaced motivation by fear with motivation toward a common vision. Administrators, staff members, parents, and community volunteers refined this vision over three years. The school supports such a vision with a set of core values developed by a task force: Individuals are valued, teachers are professional educators, parents are partners, decision making is shared, and teachers are team members.

Obstacle 5: Students Must Be Tested and Graded

Accountability for teachers and school leaders has its analogue in grades and high-stakes test scores for students: both can crowd out innovation, student engagement, and profound learning. Legislators pressure schools to raise student test scores, and parents can be even more insistent on the need for grades because, unlike legislators, they have the added fear that their children's future in higher education or the job market will depend on grades. But as many educators now realize, grades and test scores do not reflect what children are really learning, for many reasons, including poorly constructed assessments. (See Chapter 8.)

The Kate Sullivan staff struggled for years with the transition to a nongrading system and the struggles continue. Even when student work samples, portfolios, and conferences replace grades in the early years, intrinsic motivation may be driven out when children receive grades for the first time. One Kate Sullivan parent relates the devastating impact of her daughter's first report card. Until third grade, the girl had been motivated and interested in learning. When she received her first traditional report card, the student shifted her energy toward getting a better grade on the next report card. This child's intrinsic motivation to learn and do well had been replaced by an external motivator: grades.

Obstacle 6: The Mandates Are in the Way

Even if a school successfully overcomes all of the internal barriers to change, external barriers still exist. State, provincial, and federal mandates dictate funding and often provide powerful stumbling blocks to truly transforming a school. At Kate Sullivan, Duden needed courage, data, and persistence when the school decided to object to top-down mandated teacher observations. Eventually, she succeeded and obtained permission from her school district to provide data on teacher performance based on the school's principles of learning.

Obstacle 7: We Like Last Year's Silver Bullet Better

Unquestioned belief in and adherence to PLCs, TQE, differentiated instruction, or this year's newest miracle cure will not significantly alter learning for students or improve the efficacy of the staff. Deploying mechanical techniques cannot become a substitute for understanding why we're doing what we're doing. The outcome would simply be more of the same, with an "exciting" new label. When a school finds itself cycling through initiatives, it is important that the staff clarifies intentions, beliefs, values, and mission to assure alignment. (See Chapter 5 on Common Mission, Vision, Values, and Goals.) Any new initiative will need to clearly align with core beliefs, values, and the mission of the school in order to be effective. Moreover, it must become a well-planned and assessed means of reaching the school's SMART goals.

Obstacle 8: We Don't Know What We Want, What We Need, or the Difference Between the Two

This list of 10 roads to failure does not apply equally to all schools—nor does *any* single approach to school improvement. For example, whereas some schools are "cruising" based on past successes and not yet willing to recognize and reveal their own areas for improvement, others have hit bottom and are desperate for *anything* that offers new hope (Stoll & Fink, 1996).

Without a clear picture of the *needs* of the school community, it is easy to be like a kid in the candy store when pursuing the appropriate means of enhancing and sustaining student achievement. Whatever speaker or program is the most enjoyable, interesting, or popular in the neighboring school district wins!

The quick self-assessment provided in Resource 8 will allow school teams to get a clearer picture of where they stand. Completing this assessment will help to focus all school efforts, guide the school improvement process, and maximize the benefits of this book.

Obstacle 9: We Can't Agree

Understanding and empathizing with people's legitimate concerns and fears goes a long way in helping to overcome them. At the same time, we often find too much attention paid to a few holdouts to an overwhelming consensus for a particular schoolwide reform effort.

Gaining consensus on the definition of consensus is a critical first step. Here is one that may work for your school: (1) All points of view have been heard, and (2) the will of the group is evident, even to those who most oppose it (Eaker, DuFour, & Burnette, 2002). Once the school community has had ample time to reach consensus on an improvement initiative, it is better to spend time reinforcing those leading the change than on those trying to hold it back. "Water the flowers, not the rocks in your garden!" (See Resource 9 for more strategies for dealing with resistance.)

After there is general consensus, the leaders need to confront behaviors that are inconsistent with the mutual agreement while broadly touting and celebrating successes (see Chapter 5 on celebrating success).

Obstacle 10: We're Waiting for the Dream Team

The many nuances of creating meaningful change defy formulaic approaches. What works in a wealthy suburb may not work in an urban center or a region of rural poverty. Even if the change processes are equally applicable, the implementation is sure to vary. School staff members would likely lack commitment to any "imported" initiative. And becoming too attached to a given charismatic speaker, buzzword, or program is inherently contrary to developing ownership.

We have seen leaders *wait* to begin a new initiative until the sage of that particular program arrives to give a keynote speech or daylong workshop. Similarly, some school leaders, having had many of their past efforts thwarted by a new district leader, opt to wait before making changes so that their current superintendent can retire and the incoming leader can set the new direction!

While having districtwide alignment exponentially enhances outcomes for schools, taking leadership at any level—in the classroom or building—can still contribute to student success. The ideal response to a void in leadership is to fill it.

CASE STORY 2: ALTON OVERCOMES OBSTACLES TO CHANGE

These kinds of obstacles to change were addressed courageously by Nancy Duden in our examples from the Kate Sullivan school. Being clear about who she was and why she was there made this possible. She carefully laid the foundation to sustain the changes and have them endure beyond her retirement. How to develop the kind of clarity, focus, and fortitude necessary to sustain student success was the thrust of Chapter 2.

The following Case Story provides an example of how one school district grappled with fundamental changes and overcame many of the obstacles discussed in this chapter. It provides a picture of progress since the beginning, in 2000, and at various points up to the present. Which solutions were most effective? Which are closest to your situation?

CASE STORY 2

Alton Community School District Chooses a New Direction

Part 1: Recognizing the Need for Change

James Baiter, Superintendent, Alton Community School District 11

On July 1, 2000, I became superintendent of Alton Community School District 11. Having been employed in the district for 30 years, I felt I had a clear understanding of the challenges and opportunities ahead of us. In the spring of 2000, the board of education approved a plan for reconfiguring the district to reduce operational costs. The plan included the closing of four elementary schools, the consolidation of three middle schools into two buildings, and the reassignment of several employees to become effective in August 2000. The district also needed to address the need to improve the academic achievement levels for all students. It became our goal for each of our schools to strive for continuous improvement.

James Scaife, Principal, Lovejoy School

"We've heard a lot of this before." "This is the same old thing presented differently." The reactions were negative at first. This was what I expected to hear from veteran staff when we started a new comprehensive school reform model now called Failure Is Not an Option (FNO). We had just begun to create some momentum in improvement of test scores the year before and were faced with an ultimatum from the state and the district to improve our low scores on state standardized tests (ISAT).

Failure to meet specific targets for these scores would result in our being placed on the Academic Watch List, with serious consequences for the school and district. We were forced to meet almost weekly to come up with effective strategies to improve our scores. Faculty had been required to attend these meetings and would not be happy about another initiative that would require additional time.

Debra Pitts, Former Teacher and Assistant Principal, Alton High School

"How can this model help our students? Our school? Our community?" "How will our faculty react?" "How will we get the time?" My biggest challenge was getting my high school faculty to understand the new model and to believe that it wouldn't be just another "here today, gone tomorrow" model. After 26 years in education, I had the same reservations myself.

Nancy Shin, Executive Director, HOPE Foundation

Alton was still recovering from a massive reorganization that had taken place the year before we arrived. Leadership and faculty were all rearranged. People were very upset. In addition, the staff was asked to undertake major school reform. I was asked: "How much time will it take? How will we get that time from the union? How will we convince others that *this* effort will work?" Within two years of beginning our change effort, we lost the administrator who began this initiative and an additional six building principals, more than half of the entire group with whom we had begun the process.

(Continued)

(Continued)

Mary Pat Venardos, Principal, Mark Twain School

When the HOPE Foundation team showed up to do their initial on-site evaluation, I remember thinking, "Yes, this is what we have needed for a long time!" I was excited to be working toward common goals throughout the district. It is very exciting to be able to discuss similar topics concerning mission, vision, values, and goals with other administrators in the district and to have central office support along the way.

I had been involved in a previous school reform model that had not been successful in increasing academic achievement, and I had allowed a few individuals within the school to control decision making. Having gone through that experience, and knowing the attitudes of those in my building, I knew that getting the staff to buy into a model that included everyone in decision making would not be easy.

My biggest challenge was helping the leaders of the previous reform model understand why we needed to look at something new.

Part 2: Responding to the Challenge

Mary Pat Venardos, Principal, Mark Twain School

I turned to the data and, before presenting them to the faculty, talked with a few key individuals about the FNO process. We discussed how it would incorporate elements of the prior model, include all our stakeholders in collaborative teaming, and lead to increased student achievement. I wanted their support before I went to the whole faculty.

I then presented the data to the entire faculty for discussion. The data clearly showed that the previous model had not been effective in increasing student achievement. We discussed the new process and how we would be collaborating in grade-level teams involving all faculties, basing all decisions on data.

I called upon the resisters to join the leadership team. They declined. I asked for their advice on how to improve the process as we began to set up our teams and start looking at learning issues in the building. They continued to resist but as our leadership team and grade-level teams began to experience the process and understand how it would impact student achievement, building support began to grow.

James Scaife, Principal, Lovejoy School

Because I also had a large number of young staff and a large number of young teachers, I was concerned that bringing in a new approach would create a division between new and veteran teachers. I recruited several veteran teachers to become a part of our leadership team. They were skeptical of "yet another program," so I set up a meeting with the HOPE Foundation representatives so they could ask all their questions face to face. When they were treated respectfully and believed that their input was truly going to be valued, they became advocates for the process. Surprisingly, other veterans whom I expected to actively block efforts to set up collaborative teams turned out not to be a problem. I believe that being given the opportunity to participate in the decision-making process satisfied their need to be heard, and although they did not become cheerleaders for the initiative, they also did not oppose it.

Part 3: What the Outcomes Looked Like in 2004

James Scaife, Principal, Lovejoy School

As we began our leadership team meetings and our grade-level team meetings, teachers were called upon to collaborate and plan together. After a few meetings, collaboration started to become accepted as commonplace and negative tension began to subside. The teachers started seeing some positive effects of this approach and they began to share with each other.

When the results of the ISAT came back at the beginning of the following year, our work and collaboration had paid off. We went from 38% of our students meeting expectations on the test to nearly 50%. We easily surpassed the percentage needed to keep us off the Watch List. We still had a lot of work to be done, but collaboration had put us on the right track.

Mary Pat Venardos, Principal, Mark Twain School

As the building leader, I was challenged to walk the walk and talk the talk. Terms like *data-driven, collaboration, research-based, mission, vision, values,* and *goals* became second nature to me. I learned to guide the leadership team in decision making by using data-driven processes. The leadership team and I began to support one another. I feel more like an instructional leader in the building than I had prior, and I like that shift.

If you visit Mark Twain today, you will observe

1. Leadership team members taking turns leading committee and schoolwide meetings;
2. Grade-level teams all using the same format for meetings, and minutes are distributed to the whole staff;

(Continued)

(Continued)

3. Meetings organized with timekeeper, recorder, and agenda;

4. Use of a "parking lot" to defer items not on the agenda;

5. Each staff member has a folder with sections for minutes from schoolwide and grade-level meetings as well as meetings of the MVVG (mission, vision, values, and goals) committee;

6. All decisions are data based;

7. Our school improvement plan is aligned with the FNO process as well as the district's soon-to-be-finalized mission, vision, values, and goals;

8. We meet monthly with district principals to discuss FNO issues, topics, and challenges and strategies to overcome them;

9. FNO consultant meets regularly with principal and building staff;

10. Language arts curriculum is aligned to standards; and

11. We have built a pyramid of interventions by the end of the school year to be used districtwide for all primary buildings. (See Chapter 6 on how to build the pyramid.)

We know FNO is working because we have seen that

1. Language arts developmental reading assessment scores significantly increase;

2. Discipline referrals are down;

3. Staff can be observed collaborating in grade-level and committee meetings;

4. Minutes of grade-level meetings reflect the PDSA (Shewhart cycle—plan, do, study, act) plan (see also Chapter 8);

5. We achieved our SMART (strategic and specific, measurable, attainable, results-oriented, and time-bound) goals for increasing student achievement at each grade level (see Chapter 5 on creating SMART goals);

6. We can observe that teachers' respect for one another is reflected in the ways students, in turn, respect each other; and

7. We are proud to have a warm, family atmosphere at school that promotes this climate with students, staff, and visitors.

Debra Pitts, Former Teacher and Assistant Principal, Alton High School

This is the first time in my 28 years in education that I have witnessed teachers collaborating and looking at data to determine where students are achieving and systematically looking at ways to move them forward. Since we began this process, I've noticed change from the top down—our superintendent, assistant superintendent, and principals. We're all talking the same language: *student achievement!*

Nancy Shin, Executive Director, HOPE Foundation

We created a closely knit group of principals and leadership teams early on. This group, along with our support team, enabled us to endure the many leadership transitions and move forward toward increased student achievement. At the end of the biggest year of transition for us (year one), the Alton schools performed better than the state average on 10 of 13 indicators on state standardized achievement tests (ISAT).

James Baiter, Superintendent

Completing the second phase of our reconfiguration plan required the passage of a bond referendum by the voters. Our first attempt in April 2001 was unsuccessful. Shortly after the final results were in, the citizens' group announced they would begin planning for the next referendum in March 2002. This time, we were successful. The voters approved a $38.2 million bond issue.

Disaster struck again as the economy worsened, resulting in a loss of revenue in fiscal year 2003 in excess of $2 million. The board of education approved budget reductions of approximately $2.8 million for fiscal year 2004, resulting in the reduction of 81 certified and support positions.

Part 4: What the Outcomes Look Like in 2009

Nancy Shin, Executive Director, HOPE Foundation

By 2004, the culture in the district, typified by Alton High School, has clearly become collaborative in significant ways, a noteworthy accomplishment in a school with more than 100 faculty and 2,000 students. When the high school received a Bill and Melinda Gates Planning Grant in 2004, their focus shifted away from collaborative learning communities toward building a freshman academy, followed by a three-year Gates grant for

(Continued)

(Continued)

Career Academies. Barbara Gillian became Alton High School's assistant principal in 2006. She was given the reins in spring 2008 by then principal Philip Trapani, who was heavily involved in the FNO process early on.

Barbara Gillian, Principal, Alton High School

We found out that we tried to do too much too fast. We were in the process of once again reconfiguring the entire district, moving to a new high school building, consolidating the middle schools at the old high school, and restructuring the elementary schools. It became apparent that the curriculum development was not moving along because we weren't communicating—we needed to return to what we learned about PLCs to pull our improvement plans together.

Nancy Shin, Executive Director, HOPE Foundation

The hard work of 2000–2007 made it possible to return to the PLC constructs they once had within a year, including additional school improvement teams and book studies initiated by the principal. In math, for example, there is now an Algebra Concepts team that meets every two weeks. They can now identify students who are failing in math (24 out of 513 freshmen this year) and create appropriate interventions to focus on and help them succeed.

Three years ago, they noticed that English I classes were populated mostly by nonwhite students, while honors English classes were mostly white. When the faculty teams and department chairs took a closer look at the data—printing out course rosters with race codes—they were appalled and set out to change the landscape.

They began by eliminating English I, putting *all* students into CP (college prep) English I, the middle-of-the-road course. What they already knew but hadn't documented was that the freshmen coming from middle school were not prepared for ninth-grade reading. Consequently, for students at sixth-, seventh-, and eighth-grade reading levels, they implemented English lit and comp using Read 180 to focus on reading and writing for one hour a day, moving to a daily 90-minute block in year two. This year, they have advanced 18 students from that class to honors English.

Last year, they followed suit in science by eliminating science survey, the lower level science course, and requiring *all* students to take biology. This was a struggle for teachers accustomed to working only with high achievers, but they are now focusing on getting *everyone* to pass. The challenge is to retain the rigor. Ongoing professional development oils the wheels of continuous improvement, supporting instructional improvement via professional learning communities.

Barb Gillian, Principal, Alton High School

We have to be committed to ongoing learning ourselves, as leaders, to keep current with effective instructional strategies. We need to teach kids not just content but also how to learn.

Nancy Shin, Executive Director, HOPE Foundation

Alton has been looking at data for more than a decade now. They began with Positive Behavior Intervention and Support (PBIS), but recently, they've gone deeper into the data. They came to understand that there is no correlation between the elementary standardized test (ISAT) and the Prairie Standard Achievement Examination (PSAE) and they needed additional tools to know how to prepare their students. By studying the data, they have gradually increased their standardized testing to follow each student for four full years with nationally normed assessments. As a result, their ACT scores have gone up consistently each year since they started tracking this way. The staff asked the students and found out that they could do the work but not in the time period allowed, so the faculty focused on students' proficiency in order to increase their speed. The table below illustrates Alton's students progress.

Alton High School Data Compared to the State of Illinois: Percentage of Students Who Meet or Exceed Standards in the Prairie Standard Achievement Examination (PSAE)

	2001	*2008*
Reading		
Illinois	58	53.3
Alton	55	66.9
Math		
Illinois	54	52.7
Alton	51	67.4
Science		
Illinois	50	51.2
Alton	49	59.0

Source: Used with permission of Nancy Shin, Mary Pat Venardos, Barb Gillian, James Scaife, and Debra Pitts.

CONCLUSION

The next chapter provides the research base for the rest of this book. It explores how relational trust provides a foundation for a true learning community: one that is likely to be sustained through many challenges, including change of leadership.

Chapter 3 Resources

Resource 7. Strategies for Making Time

Resource 8. Self-Assessment

Resource 9. Strategies for Dealing With Resistance

These Resources for *Failure Is Not an Option,* Second Edition can be found

1. At the HOPE Foundation Web site at www.hopefoundation.org.

2. In the *Facilitator's Guide* to *Failure Is Not an Option,* Second Edition (ISBN 978-1-4129-8174-3) available for order at www.corwinpress.com.

CHAPTER 4

Relational Trust as Foundation for the Learning Community

The relationship among the adults in the schoolhouse has more impact on the quality and the character of the schoolhouse—and on the accomplishments of youngsters—than any other factor.

—Roland Barth, *Learning by Heart*

In the past, the technical aspects of a given model (like total quality management) or process for shaping cultures (like professional learning communities) have gained widespread acceptance. The relationships and human side of change, however, are often left to chance (Barth, 2001; Kruse, Louis, & Bryk, 1994). The following section is focused on recent data that correlate "relational trust" with student success. In essence, every effective, sustainable, professional learning community (PLC) that we have worked with in the past 20 years was founded on a consensus of what it meant to be such a community and on relational trust. The next section addresses the meaning, importance, and development of *relational trust*.

RELATIONAL TRUST

The report by the American Institutes for Research and the U.S. Office of Educational Research and Information (OERI), based on in-depth research on student success at 12 model and 6 replicate schools nationwide, states:

> We noted several attributes of *interpersonal relations* in schools that were associated with effective programs or periods of program effectiveness. Students felt cared about and respected, teachers shared a vision and sense of purpose, teachers and students maintained free and *open communication,* and all parties shared a *deep sense of trust.* (in Rossi & Stringfield, 1997, p. 3)

Relationships are at the core of successful learning communities as well as student success (Bryk & Schneider, 2002; Ferguson, 2002; Haynes, Emmons, & Woodruff, 1998; Kruse et al., 1994; Meier, 1995). This is particularly true for students who are "minorities" in their schools (Ferguson, 2002). In its *Set for Success* report of 2002, the Ewing Marion Kauffman Foundation summarizes, "Stated simply, positive relationships are essential to a child's ability to grow up healthy and achieve later social, emotional, and academic success" (p. 2).

Those positive relationships begin with the adults in the school building and district. The personal rapport among teachers, students, and parents influences students' school attendance and their sustained efforts at difficult school tasks (Bryk & Driscoll, 1998; Bryk, Lee, & Holland, 1993; Bryk & Thum, 1989). The history of relations between the principal and the teaching staff determines teachers' willingness to undertake new reforms (Fullan, 1991), and the relationships among adults in the school greatly influence the extent to which students in that school will succeed academically (Barth, 2001; Bryk & Schneider, 2002). In essence, if the adults in the building get along, so will the students.

The relationship among adults is an area for potential improvement in a great many schools. While it is relatively easy to install the technical aspects of a PLC—systems to collect data, time for teams to meet, and so on—the tough part is subtler, less scripted, and more human (Blankstein, 2007).

> Human resources—such as openness to improvement, trust and respect, teachers having knowledge and skills, supportive leadership, and socialization—are more critical to the development of professional community than structural conditions. . . . The need

to improve the culture, climate, and interpersonal relationships in schools has received too little attention. (Kruse et al., 1994, p. 8)

Building meaningful and productive relationships with people is complex; people are less predictable, and their emotions can be scary! How many school leaders have been trained in the many nuances of dealing with an angry parent, a disgruntled staff member, or a crying teacher? Where is the how-to manual for these tasks? Moreover, who has time for these things when the "real" work of increasing student achievement awaits?

As stated earlier (and throughout this book), relationships *are* the real work of school improvement! Without people, whom exactly will administrators be leading, and how far will followers be willing to go?

The concept of "relational trust" came from a 10-year study of achievement in math and literacy in 12 Chicago public schools by the Center for School Improvement at the University of Chicago. As discussed in Bryk and Schneider (2002), these systematic case studies were augmented by researchers' clinical observations and field notes. The summary of research results is as follows:

Schools reporting strong positive trust levels in 1994 were three times more likely to be categorized eventually as improving in reading and mathematics than those with very weak trust reports. . . . Schools with weak trust reports in 1994 and 1997 had virtually no chance of showing improvement in either reading or mathematics. (p. 111)

There are several preestablished bases of trust, including contractual trust, which focuses on material and services exchange. The concept of *relational* trust in schools, however, focuses on distinct role relationships and the obligations and expectations associated with each. When these expectations are met, trust is enhanced. When a person's expectations of another person are not met, trust is diminished.

There are four components of relational trust:

1. *Respect* for the importance of a person's role, as well as their viewpoint. Listening carefully augments a sense of respect and builds trust.

2. *Competence* to administer your role. This includes one's ability to act on what was heard. On the building level, it is also associated with having respectful discipline, an orderly and safe school, and meaningful instruction and assessment.

3. *Personal regard for others* is highly associated with reducing others' sense of vulnerability and with general caring. This is especially demonstrated by extending oneself beyond the requirement of one's role or normal duties—finding out about a staff member's personal challenges, helping teachers develop their careers, and so on.

4. *Integrity* in this context means alignment of words, actions, and ethics. Does this person keep his or her word, and are the intentions ethical? (Bryk & Schneider, 2002, pp. 23–26)

CASE EXAMPLE

 ### Relational Trust and Hiring Decisions

Shambaugh is a "family" and trust is embedded in the culture. Teachers and staff here have been together for upward of 10 to 20 years. Being the new guy, I was going to have to earn this trust from some, and of others it was expected because I was the principal and it was just the "way we do things around here." However, I was still the new guy and there is no mistake that what I said, did, and encouraged was going to be watched, judged, and rated in some way or another.

Trust is important in every way. The only way I knew this piece was going to be embedded into what I wanted to accomplish was to do two things: (1) Build relationships. Relationships are key to the trusting component. My Area Administrator says it very plainly. Relationships lead to trust, trust leads to influence. (2) Be honest. I promised I would not hide what I felt, and I would praise where it was needed. I expected others to be honest with me. I expected to know when I was stepping on toes, when I was going in a direction too quickly, which made teachers uneasy. With those two things in mind, we were going to be able to make the gains and meet the expectations I made clear at the beginning of the year.

At times, trust is only measured when you can see it has been broken. At the end of the year, I had hired an employee for a different position than what she currently held. Another current employee had also applied for this job. One employee was new to the building and the other had been here longer and had the trust built in the building, and she is loved greatly. When the new employee had been hired over the veteran, there was one member whose expectations were not met and therefore felt the trust factor had been broken. Sometimes "trust" is based on people's personal perceptions. It is important to continually communicate, clarify, and allow the trust factor to grow over time versus assuming it will be given to you just because you have the office.

Source: Used with permission of Shawn Smiley.

In general, the effective leader will create relational trust through showing a genuine regard for the professional role, interest in the concerns of others (respect), awareness of their personal interests (personal regard), and a willingness to act on those concerns (competence) toward an ethical outcome (integrity). If action on someone's concerns is not feasible, the leader will be truthful as to why such action will not be forthcoming (integrity).

When we combine this information with the list above, we can see that the challenge often comes in *listening* to others (respect) and their beliefs about your behavior (competence, personal regard, and integrity). For this reason, it is best to check in with people to determine their perspective of a given situation.

CASE EXAMPLE

 Time Builds Trust

Each time I have taken a new administrative position, no matter how effective and successful I was at my last position, I started at the bottom on the trust scale and had to work my way up. The more informal information exchanged between individual staff members and me, the more I listened and took notes, the more I observed and confirmed the importance of each person at the school, the closer I came to a bit of trust. Time builds trust, walking the talk, and being visible and interacting with children builds trust. Calling parents to share the good news about their children builds trust. Without trust, complaints go directly to the superintendent, teachers call the union, and children do not feel anyone cares about them. With trust, parents call when they have an issue or stop me in the hallway; teachers know an open door means open, honest dialogue; and the union will call me in order to help my year be successful. Relationships are the key to success. Relationships build trust. Effective communication builds relationships.

The following question was presented to a staff that functioned as a successful professional learning community: What can the new principal do in order to begin to fit into the culture of this school? The answer was to visit the classrooms, observe, and ask questions. This way, the principal will gain understanding of the program and how the teachers view the children. Through dialogue, we will move forward together.

Source: Used with permission of Carolyn Powers.

STRATEGIES FOR BUILDING TRUST

Building relational trust with the staff is a precursor to sustainable success. In our work in thousands of schools and districts, this trust has been built by the leader using various approaches:

- *Listen first.* As the example above indicates, everyone wants to be heard. The new-leader syndrome, however, often entails changing things quickly to establish authority. Many veteran leaders, on the other hand, may feel they already know what is best and may move forward without building consensus. In both cases, the "slow" part of going fast—listening—is cut out of the process and initiatives are short-lived.

- *Over communicate.* As the case story above indicates, it is best to do a lot of listening in the relationship-building process, and as the first case in this chapter points out, checking in with people to align their perceptions and your intentions as a leader is also critical. To that end, it helps to clearly communicate one's own perspective or point of view—and to do it often. If this is vague for people, or if there is a void of communication, it is often filled in with others' fears, worst-case scenarios, and rumors.

- *Confront inappropriate behaviors.* In Chapter 1 (in the section "Lesson 3: Relational Trust Trumps Technique"), there is an example of using data in a neutral manner to confront behaviors that are not in keeping with the school's mission and values. There is little that will undermine a leader more than to ignore inappropriate behaviors. While it enables people to avoid a short-term conflict, it also erodes trust in the leader. The outcome is that respect for the leader and confidence in the school community's ability to succeed is diminished among those who *are* adhering to the agreed-upon norms.

- *Create fail-free zones.* While confronting behaviors is necessary, so is indicating in advance the rules by which people will be judged. Failing in a pilot project or doing poorly in a new instructional practice, for example, should be off limits. Refusing to be coached, to collaborate, or to modify one's instruction when data reveals the need to do so, by contrast, may be among the areas in which a learning community might agree would require intervention.

• *Engage staff on a voluntary basis initially to gain support and build capacity.* The first case story in Chapter 1 demonstrates how one leadership team decided to introduce learning walks in a non-threatening manner beginning with volunteers, calling it peer-to-peer, and avoiding any formal evaluations initially. Here is a closer look at that example.

 Peer-to-Peer Observations

We have a staff that has always worked well together. As we discussed peer-to-peer observations, the benefits were numerous. We had the opportunity to learn from each other and become engaged in relevant conversations about instruction and learning. The challenge, at times, was making sure there was a desirable comfort level and trust as teachers came into classes to observe, learn, and begin conversations. We wanted to ensure that these observations were not seen as evaluative. This was not a situation where teachers were evaluating and "scoring" other teachers. To overcome this challenge, our first step was to simply ask each member of the staff to observe another teacher for a short time and e-mail the positive practices and strategies observed in the classroom. Not only did this let teachers share the good things occurring in classrooms, it also developed a high level of trust within the staff and let them know that this was a process designed to benefit staff and students. As the observations have evolved, we now spend more time in classrooms and take time to ask reflective questions that improve our practice.

Source: Used with permission of Duane Thurston and Reggie Rhines.

Another example of going slow to later go fast is to develop the staff's capacity for making the change by creating a common language and knowledge base. This is indicated in the following case example.

Collaborative Book Study Groups

Principal Jo Ann Pierce reports from Mark Twain Elementary School in Duncan, Oklahoma, that an FNO book study group was part of their job-embedded staff development.

Twenty-one of us assembled in our school's library in a big circle and combed the contents page to come up with an action plan. We decided to read the first three chapters on our own and then divide into six small groups to jigsaw Chapters 5 through 10 on a day our district had set for site-based staff development.

The teams set ground rules, but their most important goal was to address problems with state-mandated tests in third, fourth, and fifth grades. "Those three discussion meetings tore down years of isolation and loneliness," says Pierce.

Sometimes we laughed at ourselves; sometimes we got really quiet as we discussed the courage we would need to change and ways that we could avoid the routes to failure in Chapter 3. Heartfelt stories of our lowest scoring students and their needs made us cry and seek to understand more clearly.

As the teams worked together to align their faculty notebooks to the six FNO principles, they clarified their vision, "As a school, we *aspire higher!*"

Source: Used with permission of Jo Ann Pierce.

DEFINING A TRUE "LEARNING COMMUNITY"

School districts should not try to simply build a learning community that has as many definitions as there are people defining it. The emphasis should be on restructuring how people work together. That's what ultimately has an effect on the classroom.

—Nelda Cambron-McCabe,
The School Administrator

For more than a decade, a growing confluence of research and practice has indicated that our best hope for success in schools is through the creation of PLCs (Bryk, Easton, Kerbow, Rollow, & Sebring, 1994; Darling-Hammond, 1996; Fullan, 1993; Louis, Kruse, & Marks, 1996; McLaughlin, 1993; Newmann & Wehlage, 1995). This is very good news indeed. It seems to provide clear direction for educators who are contemplating substantive school change. At the same time, it invites as many questions as it answers.

- What is a learning community in practice?
- What are the key elements for making such a community succeed?
- How do I know if I have succeeded in creating such a community?
- What are my next steps in the process of creating and sustaining a learning community?

There are many definitions of a *professional learning community*. We include a summary of these, as well as a brief background on the rise of interest in this area, in the next section.

Trust and the Learning Community

How do you know if you are working in a professional learning community? Consider (with a smile) these possible indicators:

You know you are in a learning community when . . .

- You enter the school building and are warmly greeted by a parent volunteer.
- You see articles with highlights all over them posted in the teacher lounge.
- You are actually *happy* to see another teacher or an administrator visiting your classroom to observe instruction.
- Colleagues stop by your home on the weekend . . . to talk about work!
- Enhancing student learning is the primary focus of team meetings, and best practices for enhancing their achievement drive decisions.
- SMART goals (see Chapter 5) are set, regularly assessed, and achieved.
- Last year's worst behaved fourth grader is tutoring a second grader this year.
- During professional development days, the *last* rows of seats are the ones left empty.
- The principal says, "I don't know. Let's research this together."
- When the final bell rings, the teachers and principal aren't the first ones out the door!

More important than the use of one definition or another, however, is the common understanding of what such a community looks and feels like, how one behaves in this context, what the mutual commitments are, and how all of this affects students in general and their academic achievement in particular. It is more common to find school professionals who say they are part of a "learning community" than it is to actually find a PLC in operation. In fact, a shadow version of true learning communities, "performance training sects" (Hargreaves, 2003, p. 176), provides intensive pressure and support for teachers in a limited number of instructional priority areas. While student performance is enhanced, it is rarely sustained and comes at the expense of other instructional areas (Hargreaves, 2003). Moreover, the research indicates that teachers dislike such highly prescriptive programs (Datnow & Castellano, 2000), which often diminish their long-term commitment to their work (Galton, 2000). There are many possible reasons for the disparity between the number of schools that *see* themselves as PLCs and those that actually are.

As we saw in the previous chapter, making fundamental changes and shifts in assumptions, beliefs, and actions is difficult. It is far easier to make slight modifications to old behaviors and then give the effort a new name. Moreover, this can be reinforcing, because some of these modifications actually *do* bring about modest changes. For example, it would be easier to create times when teams meet than to build a true collaborative culture in the school (see Chapter 7). One is structural, easily implemented, and *may* still have the benefits of creating a more motivated staff. The collaborative *culture*, however, would require more time, an effective school mission (defined in Chapter 5), and deeper conversations about the meaning and focus of the collaboration. This collaborative culture would also require discipline to maintain a focus on student learning.

Clarifying terminology *alone* requires time and effort. W. Edwards Deming (1986) wisely called for developing "operational definitions" before undertaking a new project. He would say, for example, "Is this table clean? How could one answer the question without knowing for what purpose or use the table would need to be clean?" (i.e., defining *clean* in operational terms). "If this is to be used to eat on, it may well be clean. Yet this would not be clean enough to place a patient upon for an operation" (personal communication, 1989).

Many schools striving to become PLCs, for example, are challenged to come to a common understanding of the word *community*. This is particularly true of both moderately high-performing "cruising schools" and low-performing "sinking schools" (to determine your school's profile, see

Resource 8). In these schools, it is more likely to find changes occurring in *professional* structure (e.g., time for collaborative teaming) and even in a *learning* focus (focus on adult pedagogy and student learning). Richard Elmore (2002) describes the challenge:

> The schools that I have observed usually share a strong motivation to learn new teaching practices and a sense of urgency about improving learning for students and teachers. What they lack is a sense of individual and collective agency, or control, over the organizational conditions that affect the learning of students and adults in their schools. (p. 24)

This sense of *collective* agency and control over organizational *conditions* is embodied in the *community* of PLCs. Many schools—especially high schools—lack these qualities. These schools do not often benefit from the deeper meaning implied in the term *community.*

COHESIVE COMMUNITIES

There are several definitions of the word *community.* Here are two:

1. Common character, similarity, likeness, as, *community* of spirit.

2. The people living in the same district, city, etc., under the same laws.

The second definition is more commonly used. It is easier for a group of school professionals to achieve this definition since they generally work together, under the same rules, in the same location.

The first definition, however, is closer to how we would describe the ideal school community—one that leads to sustainable student achievement. "Community is concerned with the deep-structural fabric of interpersonal relations" (Gardner, 1991). "Soundly woven, this fabric permits a shared frame of reference and supports mutual expectations" (Rossi & Stringfield, 1997, p. 3).

Relationships and trust are the glue that holds this kind of community together. A professional community is built on more than a pay-for-service contract in which adults and children run for the exits when the final school bell rings. It is built on more than common geography. It goes beyond symbiosis, common rules, or policies that bind all to *minimum* behaviors. This kind of community is founded on mutual respect, concern, caring, reliability, and commitment to a common, larger cause. In short, it is founded on relational trust described in the previous section.

Creating common understandings, therefore, is hard work. Getting commitment from the school community is even more difficult. And changing fundamental assumptions or beliefs is harder still. Yet, these are the challenges inherent in building a true learning community, and the payoff for doing so is enormous. The chapters on building a courageous leadership imperative and overcoming common pitfalls provide a foundation for beginning an enduring, sustainable learning community. The next sections of this chapter indicate the evolution of learning communities and more definition around the terms using in defining such a community.

ORIGINS AND DEFINITIONS OF THE "LEARNING COMMUNITY"

Peter Senge (1990) first used the term "learning organization" in his best seller, *The Fifth Discipline*. Though Senge was writing for the business community, soon thereafter the term made its way into the education literature. Thomas Sergiovanni (1992) translated one of Senge's five principles—"team learning"—to an educational context: "The idea of school as a learning community suggests a kind of connectedness among members that resembles what is found in a family, a neighborhood, or some other closely knit group." This and "building shared vision" are two of Senge's original dimensions that have been embraced by the education community.

The concept of a "school-based learning community" was understood to include

1. Reflective dialogue among teachers;

2. Deprivatization of practice;

3. Collective focus on student learning;

4. Collaboration; and

5. Shared norms and values. (adapted from Kruse et al., 1994)

In their landmark study of school reform and restructuring, Newmann and Wehlage (1995) determined that there were four "circles of support" that determined successful outcomes for schools and students: student learning (focus), authentic pedagogy, school organizational capacity (including the creation of professional communities to support the first two items), and external support. The report stated, "The most successful schools were those that used restructuring tools to help them function as professional communities" (p. 3).

These communities were defined as having three general features:

1. Teachers pursue a clear, shared purpose for all students' learning.

2. Teachers engage in collaborative activity to achieve their stated purpose.

3. Teachers take collective responsibility for student learning.

The National Education Association's KEYS 2.0 is used in school districts working to improve the culture of schools by fostering open communication, using data for decision making, and developing programs and projects specifically designed to meet student needs. KEYS focuses on climate, communication, and commitment of a learning community:

1. Shared understanding and commitment to high goals

2. Open communication and collaborative problem solving

3. Continuous assessment for teaching and learning

4. Personal and professional learning

5. Resources to support teaching and learning

6. Curriculum and instruction (National Education Association, 1995. Keys to Excellence for Your School—KEYS 2.0)

In 1997, Shirley Hord coined the term *professional learning community* (Hord, 1997a and b). Her research through the Southwest Educational Development Laboratory (SEDL) led her to describe these communities as having five characteristics:

1. Supportive and shared leadership

2. Shared values and vision

3. Collective learning and application

4. Shared personal practice

5. Supportive conditions (including human and physical or structural capacity)

Another derivative of these earlier works, by DuFour and Eaker
(1998), also termed *professional learning community,* borrows as well from
business models to include shared mission, vision, values, goals; collective
inquiry; collaborative teams; action orientation and experimentation;
continuous improvement; and results orientation.

In a related area, the standards for leaders developed by the
Interstate School Leaders Licensure Consortium (ISLLC) have become
another guiding polestar for enhancing school effectiveness. Developed
with the Council of Chief State School Officers, the standards are used
throughout North America to influence leadership, development,
licensure, and academic leadership. Its principles state, "A school
administrator is an educational leader who promotes the success of all
students by"

Principle 1. Facilitating the development, articulation, implementation, and stewardship of a vision of learning that is shared and supported by the school community.

Principle 2. Advocating, nurturing, and sustaining a school culture
and instructional program conducive to student learning and staff
professional growth.

Principle 3. Ensuring management of the organization, operations, and resources for a safe, efficient, and effective learning
environment.

Principle 4. Collaborating with families and community members,
responding to diverse community interests and needs, and mobilizing
community resources.

Principle 5. Acting with integrity, fairness, and in an ethical manner.

Principle 6. Understanding, responding to, and influencing the larger
political, social, economic, legal, and cultural context. (Murphy, Jost,
& Shipman, 2000)

Table 4.1 summarizes this history.

| Table 4.1 | Development of the *Learning Community* Concept |

Date	Author	Terminology	Guiding Principles
1990	Peter M. Senge	Five disciplines	1. Systems thinking 2. Personal mastery 3. Mental models 4. Team learning 5. Shared vision
1994	Sharon D. Kruse and Karen Seashore Louis	School-based learning community	1. Reflective dialogue among teachers 2. Deprivatization of practice 3. Collective focus on student learning 4. Collaboration 5. Shared norms and values
1995	Fred M. Newmann and Gary G. Wehlage	Circles of support	1. Student learning 2. Authentic pedagogy 3. School organizational capacity 4. External support
1995	National Education Association	Keys to Excellence for Your School—KEYS 2.0	1. Shared understanding and commitment to high goals 2. Open communication and collaborative problem solving 3. Continuous assessment for teaching and learning 4. Personal and professional learning 5. Resources to support teaching and learning 6. Curriculum and instruction
1997	Shirley Hord	Professional learning community	1. Supportive and shared leadership 2. Shared values and vision 3. Collective learning and application 4. Shared personal practice 5. Supportive conditions
1998	Richard DuFour and Robert Eaker	Professional learning community	1. Shared mission, vision, values, and goals 2. Collective inquiry 3. Collaborative teams 4. Action orientation and experimentation 5. Continuous improvement 6. Results oriented
2004	Alan M. Blankstein	Failure Is Not an Option	1. Shared mission, vision, values, and goals 2. Prevention and intervention 3. Collaborative teams

(Continued)

Table 4.1   (Continued)

Date	Author	Terminology	Guiding Principles
			4. Data-based decisions
			5. Family and community engagement
			6. Sustainable leadership capacity
2000–2008	Interstate School Leaders Licensure Consortium (ISLLC)	Standards for educational administration	Promotes the success of all students by 1. Facilitating the development, articulation, implementation, and stewardship of a vision of learning that is shared and supported by the school community. 2. Advocating, nurturing, and sustaining a school culture and instructional program conducive to student learning and staff professional growth. 3. Ensuring management of the organization, operations, and resources for a safe, efficient, and effective learning environment. 4. Collaborating with families and community members, responding to diverse community interests and needs, and mobilizing community resources. 5. Acting with integrity, fairness, and in an ethical manner. 6. Understanding, responding to, and influencing the larger political, social, economic, legal, and cultural context.

Source: HOPE Foundation, *Failure Is Not an Option* Success Series.

Synthesizing the research from the above sources, and factoring in research on effective schools, the U.S. Department of Education's criteria for excellent schools, and our own practice in the field, we have distilled the essence of PLCs into the following six principles:

Principle 1. Common mission, vision, values, and goals

Principle 2. Ensuring achievement for *all* students: creating systems for prevention and intervention

Principle 3. Collaborative teaming focused on teaching and learning

Principle 4. Using data to guide decision making and continuous improvement

Principle 5. Gaining active engagement from family and community

Principle 6. Building sustainable leadership capacity

These principles encompass the focus on student learning and collaboration emphasized in the above research. In addition, as with Shirley Hord's (1997b) definition, the ISLLC (2000–2008) standards, and the larger body of research of Newmann and Wehlage (1995) summarized earlier in this section, our sixth principle explicitly calls for the development of sustainable leadership capacity. Given the extraordinary rate of turnover in educational leadership and the tendency toward "launching" versus "sustaining" learning communities, we have found this principle to be critical to the success of our work with schools throughout North America.

Similarly, as cited in Newmann and Wehlage's (1995) "circles of support" research and the ISLLC standards (see Murphy, Jost, & Shipman, 2000), we have found that actively engaging family and communities (our fifth principle) is essential for long-term support and sustainability of school initiatives. This has been particularly true in times of great change, economic downturn, or intense media pressure on schools. Chapter 9 provides an abundance of research correlating enhanced student achievement and family support.

The prior synthesis of research and our own relevant experiences are presented as an explanation of how we arrived at these working principles for PLCs. Having "one best definition" for this or any other school improvement effort is counterproductive and defies all that we know about change efforts. In fact, there is danger in becoming too attached to one certain speaker, program, or set of principles. It is far more important that whatever is practiced is internally aligned, consistent with the research, and focused on student success.

Taking a cue from the medical profession, it is advisable to continually scan for new best practices and to stay current with changes in the research:

> Here on our first day of med. school, we were presented with the short white coats that proclaim us part of the mystery and the discipline of medicine. During that ceremony, the dean said something that was repeated throughout my education: "Half of what we teach you here is wrong—unfortunately, we don't know which half." (Sanders, 2003, p. 29)

CONCLUSION

This chapter was meant to serve as a final checkpoint. We have defined purpose as *sustaining student success because failure is not an option* (Chapter 1); anticipated and sidestepped common obstacles to success (Chapter 2); developed a courageous leadership imperative (Chapter 3); and, in this chapter, determined the framework and system for moving forward. Now, you are prepared to take action. The rest of this book will emphasize specific processes for building such a sustainable learning community, beginning with the next chapter on creating common mission, vision, values, and goals.

CHAPTER 5

Principle 1

Common Mission, Vision, Values, and Goals

You cannot have a learning organization without shared vision.

—Peter Senge, *The Fifth Discipline*

The core values of a firm give it long-standing [sustainability].

—Marianne Jennings, *Business:
Its Legal, Ethical, and Global Environment*

The key to creating a school where failure is not an option is this: transforming the school culture. Some schools have productive cultures; others have problematic ones. But *every* school *has* a culture, whether one is aware of it or not. Does this sound familiar?

Take a look at these test scores from my history class. They're just terrible. Quite a few Fs . . . most of them got Ds. We've been over and over this material, but they just don't seem to care. They don't do their homework, they don't participate in class. I have *no* family support. I don't know what more to do!

We have worked with many schools that have a culture of blame and hopelessness. One high school staff was asked to analyze a situation in which 25% of their students were not passing state tests. After much deliberation, the staff reached a consensus: *It's that middle school! They were sending us students who were unprepared!*

A corollary to a culture of blame is a shift in responsibility for ensuring student learning. Consider the following often-heard statements:

- It's not *my* job to ensure that students *learned* the lesson—my job is to teach it!
- We believe all students can learn, but some learn better than others.
- In general, all students will learn, but *those* kids from *that* neighborhood aren't as smart or as motivated as the rest.
- If we had more _____ (discipline, resources, time, parental support, and so on), *then* I would be successful!

What these statements have in common is that they shift accountability *away* from school professionals. What could be more demotivating for a school community than to believe that they have no power and that what they do makes no difference? The research shows that the belief systems of teachers affects student success (see Chapter 2).

In this chapter, we provide direction for transforming the school culture by addressing some often-held beliefs. We do this through a discussion of the four pillars of any organization: mission, vision, values, and goals (MVVG). Together they establish the common base upon which all of our efforts will be built. The six principles of Failure Is Not an Option act as a system (see Chapter 1) and are not implemented in concrete sequential manner. Thus, the way in which the MVVG are created can also serve as a means of developing leadership capacity. In addition, in our Beacons of Hope districts, the school and district MVVGs are mutually supportive.

THE MISSION

The mission of an organization is essential to its success. A mission statement should be created and published as a means of giving those involved with the organization a clear understanding of its purpose for existence.

Mission statements are found everywhere—in schools, big businesses, small businesses, nonprofit organizations, organized religion, and all levels of government. They are a popular management tool used by corporations to motivate stakeholders and keep everyone on the same page. A quick survey of mission statements reveals a common pattern: They use superlatives and absolutes. Such an approach leaves people feeling as though they had cotton candy for lunch: happy but still hungry for the real meal! Phrases like *world's best, premier, largest,* and *first choice of customers everywhere* abound. How "premier" status will be attained and how "best" will be measured are rarely clarified or discussed.

Schools and school districts also have mission statements—and they should. Unfortunately, education is not exempt from the tendency toward generic, vague, and meaningless mission statements.

The typical mission statement of schools is going to sound very familiar, regardless of what part of the country or what part of North America we are talking about. In essence, we've all written the same mission statement. It's all based on this premise of learning for all. We want all of our students to become responsible, productive, and so on. I think what effective schools do is move beyond that sort of generic "here are our hopes for students," and they ask the critical corollary questions—that begin to translate those hopes into reality. (DuFour, quoted in HOPE Foundation, 2002)

The four critical questions to be addressed in the mission statement are, by and large, *not* new:

1. If we expect all students to learn, *what* is it we expect them to learn? (Tyler, 1949)

2. *How* will we know if they are learning it? (Tyler, 1949)

3. *How* will we ensure an engaging, relevant pedagogy? (Blankstein, 2004)

4. What will we do when they *don't* learn?

An effective mission statement must be specific enough to answer all four of these questions. If it does not, it will lack resonance for staff members, and it will quickly be forgotten or written off as meaningless. Because most schools already have a mission statement, it is best to review the statement in light of these criteria. More expansive missions could involve creating the school as hub of the community (see Chapter 9) or, as is done in Mattoon, Illinois, ensuring successful student transitions from high school to careers and/or higher education.

In the Case Story that follows, we'll accompany a school administrator as she puts the power of a school mission into action in two very different schools with widely varying demographics.

> ## CASE STORY 3
>
> ## Confidence, Commitment, and Culture
>
> **Middle School Mission: "Rising Stars, Reaching Academic Excellence"**
>
> Having spent four years as a successful elementary principal in the inner city, I was excited the new challenge as principal of an elementary/middle school. As I walked from the curb down what seemed like a mile to the front door, the students asked many questions. "Are you our new principal?" I knew the answer to that question. "Yes," I responded. "Have you been a principal before?" I knew that answer, too. "Yes." I guess, having successfully met their requirement, I qualified for the next series of questions.
>
> A tall, handsome young man stepped forward. "Hi, I'm in the middle school. Can you have the middle school name added to the front of the building?" As I gazed at the top of the building, I realized this young man was absolutely right. The name of the school was incomplete. Three years ago, the elementary school was extended to include the middle grades. It was a matter of pride for the students to have "middle school" added to the existing elementary name. Feeling confident, I agreed to honor this request. Relieved, the student launched another question. This one caused me to pause, reflect, and think of the reason behind the question. He asked, "Am I in the slow class?" By this time, we were approaching the front door of the incompletely titled school.
>
> The students had graciously carried my book bags, and we were already beginning to bond. I could not start off on the wrong foot. This precious jewel needed to know, in essence, if I could change the mission, vision, values, and goals of this school. "What makes you think that you are in the slow class?" When in doubt, I always answer a question with a question. This gives you time to think! "Well," he said, "I got into trouble a lot last year. I barely passed. I missed a lot of days from school. I didn't want to come to school because I would just get into trouble. My report card was not good. And, I'm in 08-03. That's the last class of the eighth grade. So, am I in the slow class?" Everything that he said made me think he definitely qualified to be in the "slow" class. Suspensions, poor grades, and poor attendance—any principal's nightmare.
>
> I hadn't even entered the building and I was holding an unofficial "press conference" with my most important constituents. What could I say? In an instant, my entire educational philosophy came to me. What is my mission? Why do I exist? The reason I entered the field of education hung in the balance. The student looked at me to see if I believed in his

capacity to learn. He looked at me with hope in his eyes. He looked at me as if to say, "Are you the one for such a time as this?" Pausing, looking him face-to-face, eye-to-eye, I replied, "No, you're not in a slow class! In this school, everyone is smart! Everyone is a star! Whatever kept you from learning, whatever caused you to miss school, whatever made you get suspended, will change."

Were these just words filled with hot air? Were my words just another cliché? Did I believe? I asked for his help. "Will you help me? Will you help let everyone know that we are going to succeed?" With a smile on his face, he said, "Yeah, and by the way, what's your name?" I entered the school feeling empowered, directed, on a mission. He had given me a job to do.

That year was most unusual. It would be like no other year in my career. The year began with creating the mission statement and a clear vision of how we would get there. "Rising Stars, Reaching Academic Excellence" would be posted everywhere! Two thousand stars of all shapes, forms, and colors appeared almost overnight. We discussed and documented things that we valued as a school and how those commitments would change our behavior and define our steps to reach our mission. We committed ourselves to deny sorting and selecting as a way of determining who would succeed. We made commitments to succeed in improving the culture through collaboration. We used the budget to make our commitments a reality. Resource teachers were hired to provide team collaboration time during the day. Each grade-level team met twice a week for 45 minutes. Team leaders were identified and taught how to conduct team meetings. Team leaders completed team-meeting log sheets and received feedback concerning issues raised. As the principal, I spent 50% of my day in the classrooms serving as the instructional leader. The secretaries could only call me to the office if it was one of the "Three Bs." The Three Bs meant:

1. Boss (Board)

2. Boys in Blue (fire, police, ambulance)

3. Beloved (family)

Adhering to the Three Bs allowed me to focus on classroom instruction and ensure that we were "flowing mellifluously" and "honoring time." Flowing mellifluously and honoring time meant that teachers would be mindful of time wasters (late starts, transitions, etc.). Teachers received daily feedback "love notes" concerning instructional strategies seen during the day. Intense job-embedded professional development was planned based on the love notes. In addition to their regularly scheduled team meetings,

(Continued)

(Continued)

teachers routinely collaborated about student work before school and during lunch. Conversations during evening socials were also the norm.

It took three months for the 750-member student body and 40-member teaching staff to realize that they were all smart and that they could get smarter through collaboration and hard work. Walking into classrooms, asking for the smart students to raise their hands grew from one student to ultimately everyone raising their hand!

Adhering to the mission statement was a task. But it was a task that had to be done for everyone in the school. When your mission and vision are intact, then you can focus on goals for success. The entire school year was spent learning how to succeed, step-by-step, and celebrating every evidence of success.

By changing the belief system, we changed the way we operated and we changed student and staff expectations. No longer could students enter the building with a notebook rolled up in their back pocket. They now proudly walked through the neighborhood with a book bag, notebook, textbooks, and all the tools for success. Getting by was no longer the norm, and "getting smart" no longer meant being a nerd. No longer was lateness tolerated. No longer could students wear their shirts outside of their pants and their pants down to their knees. They had to dress for success: shirts in, belts on, pants up! No longer was fighting a response to every altercation: "Thoughts determine actions!" Through this step-by-step process, students and staff acquired the skills necessary to have a high quality of life. "Smart is what you get if you work hard!" The words "Never Say Never" were instilled through the school song. The key to success came in the form of an educational rebirth. Staff and students were taught to believe and succeed.

Individual success was transferred to the entire staff and student body. Because of the change in the culture (now collaborating and learning) the staff believed that they could succeed. An environment that was once marred with graffiti was transformed. The students believed that they could succeed. The physical plant received a face-lift. Students and parent volunteers helped to repaint the school. We instituted performance-based instruction, coach classes, and a Saturday academy. At the end of the year, the 435 suspensions of the previous year were reduced to 43. Student attendance increased from 94% to 95%, and staff attendance increased from 94% to 96%. Test scores? A three-year decline ended. State test scores increased from 24% to 34% of the students scoring 70% or better. Parents cried at year-end closing exercises. Students crossed the stage determined to move forward. They overcame a stigma, a label of inferiority that's placed on students early in life.

All of these changes only required confidence in the established mission vision, values, and goals of the school. Confidence in their capacity to believe that they had what it took to grow and develop. Teachers had confidence to believe that they had in their repertoire what it took to find the strategies for student success.

High School Mission: Every Student Goes to College

Four years later, wealthy suburb, new school, and I'm now the central office administrator introducing myself by walking the halls and visiting classrooms to make sure everyone knows the former principal has been removed.

Just one week prior, students were refusing to go to class. They were in an uproar because their annual Rally had been cancelled in response to poor behavior: roaming the halls, cutting class, leaving campus during closed lunch periods, and so on. Teachers and administrators enforced consequences, with the hopes of curbing the negative behaviors, by calling the city police, spraying students with mace, and giving them the ultimatum to go to class or go home.

Parents were outraged by the consequences enforced by the teachers and administrators, and this is what I inherited. To encourage students to return to class I asked them, "Where are you going to college?" They responded with the name of a college (true or not). My response was, "You can't get there from here (the hallway)!" This choice, and its outcomes, is a lesson in the value, power and capacity for positive change that principals have when they choose to implement the mission of a school.

Because of the overwhelmingly positive response by students, the first professional development session with teachers was devoted to reviewing the mission statement. Did it respond to the four questions?

1. What should students learn?

2. How will we ensure engaging pedagogy?

3. How will we know if we are achieving it?

4. What will we do to guarantee success?

In that session, commitment was reignited! The teachers rallied around the reason the school existed. The school existed (according to the mission statement) to get students into college. They rallied around the rich history of the school and the strong alumni. They rallied around the real responses to the questions and provided data to

(Continued)

(Continued)

prove that they were achieving their goal. They spent time discussing ways to guarantee success. They knew that they could not continue in the manner in which they were headed. They had lost sight of their mission. They needed someone to navigate the course again.

The teachers left that session with a determination to stay focused on the mission of the school. They each were assigned a senior student to mentor. The goal was to work with each senior and support their quest for acceptance into college. At the end of the year, the school had the highest graduation rate of all 43 high schools in the district! They announced a total of $17 million in college scholarships and financial aid. Of the 350 graduates, 2 enrolled in the armed services, the rest in either a two-year or a four-year college or university! Oh, let's not forget the lone summer school graduate!

Source: Used with permission of Deborah Wortham.

What Is Mission?

In effective schools, the mission statement goes far beyond an expression of "wishful thinking." The mission statement can serve as the vital lifeblood of the school's daily activities and policies. It should be fundamental to every decision at every level. An effective mission statement expresses the school's purpose—its essential reason for educating in the first place. It expresses why a school *exists.*

The mission serves as a polestar, or guiding principle, for a school. Just as a ship sails toward but never actually reaches its guiding star, we too strive toward but never actually fulfill our mission. Why? Because as long as the world continues to change and evolve, our students' needs will change, and we will need to develop new ways to respond.

What Good Looks Like

The best mission statements are clear about why the organization exists and what will be done to ensure that the purpose is met. The mission statement serves the organization by providing specifics about (1) what do we want to do? (2) how will we know if we are succeeding? and (3) what will we do to ensure success?

Given the three questions provided above regarding effective mission statements, which of the following would you consider effective? Mark each one with an E for effective or an I for ineffective, and note why you made the selection.

Mission 1 _____

The mission of this school district is to ensure that each and every student is prepared to succeed in life. This is accomplished in an environment of trust and respect that fosters positive attitudes toward self, others, work, and responsible citizenship. We are dedicated to maximizing individual potential and developing lifelong learners who will be contributing members in a global society.

Mission 2 _____

The mission of our school is to create and maintain an environment that ensures that every member of the school community reaches a high level of academic achievement as determined by state and national standards. We commit to a comprehensive system of support to assure this outcome.

Mission 3 _____

It is our mission as a school district to educate students to be creative, responsible, self-sufficient citizens who have the capacity and motivation for continued individual growth and who will have the ability to make a positive contribution in our society.

Mission 4 _____

We are committed to the academic excellence of every student by empowering them with the means for the successful completion of high educational standards and by challenging them to become productive members of society.

What's your analysis? Consider the following.

The examples numbered 1 and 3 above do not attempt to clearly define *success* in measurable ways. "Success in life" would demand that we wait too long for feedback on how a school community is doing in fulfilling its mission. Similarly, terms like *creative* and *responsible* are vague and hard to measure.

Example number 4 provides more specificity on both the definition of students' success and how it will be measured (by "high educational standards"). However, it lacks the clarity to answer the third question ("What will we do to ensure success?"). Number 2 does answer this question.

Only the second example above addresses all the questions. But be aware: Photocopying this statement and hanging it underneath the office clock for all to see will not improve your school. It is the process of collaboratively creating a mission and spelling out all the specifics that are not provided in a generic mission statement that will lead to school improvements and cultural shifts. Figure 5.1 summarizes some of the differences between traditional and more effective mission statements. Another example of an effective mission statement can be found in Resource 10.

Figure 5.1 Effective Mission Statements

Traditional Mission Statements . . .	Effective Mission Statements . . .
Are vague or generic	Are clear
Say all kids can learn	Are specific (what exactly are students supposed to learn?)
Do not define *learning*	Are measurable (how do we know students have learned?)
Do not address the possibility of failure	Provide for failure (how do we respond when students don't learn?)

Source: *Failure Is Not an Option* video series, HOPE Foundation, 2002.

Implementation Guidelines

Most schools have no problem creating a mission statement. A small number of people can sit down at a restaurant and hammer one out before the food arrives. The discussions leading to the final document, however, are as important as the final document itself. It is critical that the process involve representatives from all stakeholder groups—teachers, paraeducators, administrators, community members, students, and parents. It is equally important that those involved reflect ethnic and socioeconomic diversity, as well as diverse learning styles. A statement of mission has little meaning or impact unless it reflects the thoughts of the school community and is collectively embraced by those whom it affects.

There are various ways to collaboratively create a mission statement. The first step for any process should be to evaluate what already exists. Using the criteria that have been laid out, ask stakeholders to evaluate and revise the statement, using any of the following methods.

1. *Assemble a task force* made up of representatives from each stakeholder group. In this strategy, the representatives are responsible for soliciting

feedback from and accurately representing the views of their constituencies. They are also responsible for sharing drafts of the evolving statements with their respective groups.

2. *Collect the views of each stakeholder group* in a more formal way, perhaps through a written survey instrument. Convene representative focus groups, then examine and discuss the views obtained through the survey. Ultimately, the focus groups report their findings to a task force, which is responsible for drafting the statement.

3. *Small-group work* is still another approach, used successfully in Alton, Illinois, that brings stakeholders together for small-group work around the four questions (see Chapter 3). In this approach, groups of representative stakeholders are first reminded of the four critical questions that their mission statement must answer. They then form small groups of five to seven people, and each group drafts a complete mission statement. The groups' statements are posted on the walls around the room, and participants do a "gallery walk," reviewing each statement and offering feedback on sticky notes. At the end of the session, the school's leadership team collects all the drafts and sticky notes and uses them to write a statement—which then goes out for more feedback from all stakeholders.

4. *A "snowball" method* can also yield good results. In this approach, all stakeholders are paired into groups of two. After each initial pair drafts a statement, two pairs join together to share their thoughts and merge their statements into one. That group of four joins with another group of four, and the new group of eight then does the same. The process is repeated until there is one comprehensive statement that incorporates all stakeholder feedback. This statement is then reviewed by a representative group in light of the criteria for a good mission statement. The resulting statement is circulated for final approval.

In smaller schools, the above approaches can be, and ideally are, used with the entire school staff. Doing so takes longer, but it deepens the commitment to the outcome. In any case, it is vital to focus the discussion around the purpose and the three questions that ask for the necessary specifics. Collecting feedback from all stakeholder groups helps to ensure that the mission statement provides enough detail and is meaningful. Such an outcome requires plenty of time for thoughtful reflection and response—as well as time for writing, reviewing, and revising the statement. A step-by-step outline of the mission development process can be found in Resource 11.

Sustaining Success

Once you have developed an effective mission, your next challenge will be to establish it in action and keep it alive. In all schools, the entire student body is replaced every three to six years, and in a growing number of schools, staff turnover is even more frequent. How can you ensure that your mission statement remains a living, integral part of the school experience? Here are some strategies:

Think It Through . . .

Do you know your school's mission statement? Does it address what you want students to learn, how learning will be measured, and how you will respond when learning doesn't happen?

- Display your mission statement prominently within the school and in places where the school presents itself to the public, for instance, on your Web site, press releases, letterhead, and the like.
- Make sure the mission is cited as a guide whenever staff meets to set goals, plan programs, make decisions, or discuss problems. In Fort Wayne, Indiana, schoolwide plans and goals are regularly presented to other school, district, and board leaders for review and critical, friendly feedback to assure alignment of plans with MVVG.
- Coach teacher leaders in using the mission as a guiding force in their team meetings. Teachers' understanding of their role in maintaining the mission is critical for success.
- Frequently evaluate the school's policies and procedures to ensure their adherence to the mission.
- Schedule time to familiarize new staff and students with the mission. This should include in-depth discussions about the implications for how the school operates.
- Respond quickly and correctively to any and all failures to act in accordance with the school's mission.
- Formally review and update your mission every four to five years.

THE VISION

Like mission, creating a vision is another common part of the planning process in most organizations today. The word *vision* is used as an adjective (the visionary leader), a noun (a vision for the community), and even as a verb (visioning the future). But what exactly *is* this elusive vision—and where do you get one?

What Is Vision?

Whereas the mission statement reminds us of why we exist, a vision paints a picture of what we can become. Most of us employ vision in our personal lives. We strive toward a better, future version of ourselves that may be wealthier, smarter, better organized, healthier, and so forth. We use that vision to guide our behaviors on both a long-term and short-term basis.

A school's vision serves the same purpose—that is, it offers a realistic alternative for a better future. It says, "This is what we want to be." Just as our own vision guides the personal or professional course we follow, a school's vision should guide the collective direction of its stakeholders. It should provide a compelling sense of where the school is headed and, in broad terms, what must be accomplished in the future to fulfill the school's purpose. Every decision made, every program implemented, every policy instituted, and all goals should align with this vision.

Without a common vision, decisions are made randomly. At best, policies, procedures, and programs will lack unity and fail to adequately support one another. At worst, they will actually work at cross-purposes. Virtually no school lacks for new initiatives or programs; *most* schools lack cohesion and a unified effort shared between various programs and initiatives. Whereas the mission statement answers the question "Why do we exist?" the vision explains where the school is *headed.*

CASE EXAMPLE

 Vision as a Unifying Force for the District

When engaging in the school-improvement process, many schools skipped over the vision statement because they felt they had spent time on a statement years ago and it still applied. The time it would take to rewrite this statement seemed wasted. School improvement plans were created and submitted to the state on time. The plans did not raise student achievement. When revisiting the planning process the next year, teams of teachers engaged in a shared vision process with the principal. The different vision statements from schools related directly to the culture and needs of the buildings. From the shared vision, a statement of purpose was crafted for the entire district. With everyone on board, the action plans for student achievement just fell into place for the teams.

Source: Used with permission of Carolyn Powers.

What Good Looks Like

Like mission statements, a good vision statement should be detailed enough to carry meaning. The most successful vision statements are vivid and compelling; they motivate us to strive for an improved future. They provide a foundation on which we can assess the areas for improvement—and then plan. Perhaps most important, an effective vision statement describes a *collective* vision and is shared by all stakeholders.

Below are two sets of evaluation criteria for vision statements. The first, derived from Kotter (1996), says that vision statements should be

- *Imaginable.* They convey a picture of what the future will look like.
- *Desirable.* They appeal to the long-term interests of stakeholders.
- *Feasible.* They comprise realistic, attainable goals.
- *Focused.* They are clear enough to provide guidance in decision making.
- *Flexible.* They are general enough to allow for individual initiative and changing responses in light of changing conditions.
- *Communicable.* They are easy to communicate and explain.

The second, from Nanus (1992), provides a list of evaluative questions:

- To what extent is the vision statement future oriented?
- To what extent is it likely to lead to a clearly better future for the organization?
- To what extent does it fit with the organization's history, culture, and values?
- To what extent does it set standards of excellence and reflect high ideals?
- To what extent does it clarify direction?
- To what extent does it inspire enthusiasm and encourage commitment?
- Is it ambitious enough?

Using these criteria, how would you rate the following vision statements? Mark each one with an E for effective or an I for ineffective, and note why you made the selection.

Vision 1 _____

As you enter Highland High School, the level of pride and accomplishment is evident. The school is well maintained and has a safe environment, with current technology appropriate to a wide range of curricular and extracurricular activities. The learning atmosphere, which is exciting, stimulating, and success oriented, also affords students the opportunity to learn from their mistakes.

Students have access to a wide spectrum of academic and extracurricular experiences and are encouraged to widen their worldview by taking full advantage of diverse offerings. They possess a greater freedom of choice in decisions affecting their school community. The school climate engenders respect; students feel free to accept and express ideas without fear or prejudice. Adults are compassionate, competent, committed, consistent, considerate, and enabled.

Students at Highland accept their roles in education. This is evident by the way students accept responsibility for their learning, possess positive attitudes, and maintain well-rounded participation in academics and extracurriculars. Their communication is open, friendly, and caring, not only between students but also with staff. This exists because of respect among students and the adults in their lives. The students are self-motivated and excited about learning. Students have a true sense of direction, with goals and career paths clearly established.

Students possess a high sense of responsibility. Through their sense of good values, positive behavior, and high moral conscience, they hold themselves accountable for their actions. They accept the consequences of the choices they make.

Open communication exists between students and adults through mentoring; the mastering of all levels of communication, including oral and written; and the fostering of positive relationships.

Students come to school prepared, eager to participate, and devoted to their learning. They complete learning projects and assignments without hesitation and are successful because they believe in who they are.

Finally, all students work to become productive adults and contributing members of society. They aspire to be lifelong learners as they prepare and plan for the future.

The entire community embraces involvement in the educational development of all students. The parents and other members of the community demonstrate respect for education through their availability to and support for all members of the school population. Parents take an active role in their child's education by providing basic needs so their child is ready to learn. By learning values and good work ethics at home, the students are prepared to succeed at school. Mutually respectful and cooperative in school and community, parents and staff work together with the vision of helping students become productive members of Highland High School and society. Administrators and guidance counselors are visible and accessible to students.

Vision 2 _____

We envision a school where children and adults work productively toward success for all students. This would involve mutual respect, cooperation, and responsibility on everyone's part.

Vision 3 _____

Our vision is increasing reading by 6% in the next three years.

What is your analysis of these vision statements? Ours follows.

The second example fails to provide clarity. From our perspective, it is not compelling. The third example is very clear, understandable, and communicable. Yet it is not ambitious and likely won't galvanize the school community.

Although the first vision does not include any quantifiable data, it is very specific in describing a compelling future that is imaginable and feasible. This example, from Highland High School, is our preferred vision of the three.

Figure 5.2 provides a comparison of traditional and more effective vision statements.

Figure 5.2 Effective Vision Statements

Traditional Vision Statements . . .	Effective Vision Statements . . .
Are vague or unimaginable	Are realistic, clear, and compelling
Are created by a select group	Have broad-based buy-in
State hopes and wishes	Describe intended change
Are soon forgotten	Guide action

Source: Failure Is Not an Option video series, HOPE Foundation, 2002.

Implementation Guidelines

Roland Barth (2001) notes that there are eight ways by which an organization can come to have a vision. Following is an adaptation of his list of methods (pp. 197–204), along with associated advantages and disadvantages (see Table 5.1).

Table 5.1	Eight Ways by Which an Organization Can Come to Have a Vision		
Method	*Definition*	*Advantage*	*Disadvantage*
Inherit a Vision	Use what's already there.	There is no need to go through the periodic, introspective turmoil of crafting a vision.	The vision was engraved in the granite of the past, whereas faculty come from the present and the students must be prepared for the future.
Explicate a Vision	Make overt what has been covert by putting it in writing.	The vision is comfortable, genuine, and already existing.	This doesn't ask, "What would we like to be doing in the future?" Waking a sleeping baby often causes noise—we uncover what we don't want to hear.
Refine a Vision	Take inventory of past practice, present aspirations, and tune up for the 21st century.	The vision is pragmatic; has something in it for everyone.	This can become an exercise in putting new patches on a defective tire.
Buy a Vision	Use one from a "model."	Most are rich, coherent, and fundamentally different from business as usual; those who don't like it can "shoot" at the creator rather than each other.	Looking outside reinforces the belief that those inside are unable to get their own house in order, perpetuating a sense of helplessness.
Inflict a Vision	A person or office outside the school supplies the vision.	It can come quickly and be uniformly and impressively portrayed throughout the district.	Teachers and principals are gifted and talented at offering superficial compliance to an imposed ideology while at the same time thwarting it.

(Continued)

Table 5.1 (Continued)

Method	Definition	Advantage	Disadvantage
Hire a Vision	When things aren't going well, get a new principal with a better vision.	Change in leadership may bring a change in culture.	The principal's vision equals the school's vision, which sustains the paternalistic feeling that "This is the principal's vision, not ours."
Homogenize a Vision	Invite major constituencies to reveal their personal mission; common elements become the school's mission.	There is little in the final vision not in the vision of each contributor; little is unfamiliar or threatening.	People feel there is much in their personal vision that is not in the school vision and so lose interest; the least common denominator excludes out-of-the-box thinking (often the fresh, innovative, and most promising ideas of a few individuals).
Grow a Vision	Members of the school community devise a process for examining their school, then create together a vision that provides a profound sense of purpose for each of its members. The collective vision emerges from the personal visions of each member.	It enlists and reflects not the common thinking, but the best thinking, beliefs, ideals, and ideas of the entire school community.	It is time consuming; individuals must dig deep to come to grips with personal vision.

Source: Adapted from Barth, 2001.

Of the eight possible ways to come up with a vision, it is clearly the last one—growing a vision—that is most meaningful and effective. Like mission, vision is not something that can be handed down from on high. It must be cocreated by the entire learning community in order for it to have shared meaning.

Should the vision be developed at the school level or district level? Ideally, both the district leaders and the schools they oversee should have a role in the process.

Should the development process involve only school personnel, or should it involve the larger community? Hargreaves's research (2001) calls for (1) developing (emotional) depth or connection to the effort, (2) breadth in terms of who is involved, and (3) sustainability in terms of leadership transition plans for best results. In light of this, school leaders gain the best long-term outcomes by deeply involving the broader school community in creating the vision.

The vision should also be rooted in research on best practices and reflect the school's history and existing culture. Ideally, the following information would be gathered in preparation for creating a vision:

- Relevant information about the school or district, that is, data on parent and student perceptions and engagement, student success, and staff and faculty performance; copies of prior vision or values statements, internal and external factors affecting the school or district, findings of visitation teams who evaluated the school and district for accreditation purposes, longitudinal achievement data, and community survey results
- Research on school culture
- Research on characteristics of high-performing schools and districts
- Research on school change and reculturing
- An honest assessment of the current conditions in the school or district

Once stakeholders have had an opportunity to review the background information referenced above, they or a subset of the school leadership team can begin drafting the vision. Vision statements tend to be thoughtful, fairly lengthy documents that encompass many aspects of a school. For example, a school's vision might be divided into such sections as "curriculum," "attention to individual students," "personnel," "leadership," "students," "climate," and "community partnerships." The organization of the statement is not important, but the vision should include the ideas of all stakeholders and should touch on all aspects of the school deemed significant to realizing the ideal.

One method, used successfully by Linda Jonaitis, principal of Highland High School in Highland, Indiana, involves having all stakeholders make lists of the things that they think are important for a good school. The stakeholders then form groups of eight to ten people, combine their lists, and collaboratively agree on the top 10. The school improvement team takes the top 10 lists from all the groups and clusters the statements by common theme. The school improvement team divides into groups, with each group taking one of those common themes, and writes a paragraph that captures all the statements in that theme.

A similar approach requires participants to write their initial statements—as many as they wish—on sticky notes. Participants then work together to group the notes into clusters. Each cluster is assigned a name, which is used as a vision category. As with the previous method, small groups take the various categories and draft minivisions. Ultimately, all the minivisions are combined into a single statement and sent to stakeholders for feedback.

The process described in Case Story 1 ("Six Lessons Exemplified Across a Region") for tapping ideas throughout multiple districts to create value statements could also be used in developing the vision. A step-by-step process for developing the vision statement may be found in Resource 11.

> **Think It Through** . . .
>
> Does your school have a vision statement? If so, is it detailed enough to paint a vivid picture of a better future? Does it capture a future that motivates all stakeholders? Who in the school community knows what your vision is? Who created it and how? How does it align with the entire district?

THE VALUES

Research indicates that in both business and education, an established set of shared values is a key factor in an organization's success (Champy, 1995; Sergiovanni, 1994). Values are "the most important structural element" in any organization (Sergiovanni, 1994). And Sergiovanni emphasizes the need for schools in particular to come together around shared values and ideas.

What Are Values?

Values are the attitudes and behaviors an organization embraces. They represent commitments we make regarding how we will behave on a daily basis in order to become the school we want to be. They are established and articulated guidelines we live by. "Values are best described in terms of behavior: If we operate as we should, what would an observer see us doing?" (Senge, Ross, Smith, Roberts, & Kleiner, 1994).

Values endure. They do not fluctuate with staffing changes, funding shifts, or trends in instructional methodology. They are never compromised for a short-term gain or a quick solution to a problem (see Case Example: Two Approaches to High-Stakes Testing in Chapter 10). Values express a *shared* commitment to certain behaviors; they do not result from a top-down dictate—that is, they start with "*We* will," not "*You* will."

Ideally, values reflect the attitudes and beliefs of the school community. Ultimately, after they are created, value statements guide the behavior of everyone in the organization.

School leaders cannot read minds or respond to perceptions of what people in the organization *believe.* Leaders can inquire as to staff members' beliefs on a given topic, but responses may or may not be forthcoming. At the very least, however, after having collectively created values, it is the leader's role to hold people to *behaviors* that mirror those values (as opposed to *beliefs*). In high-performing schools, eventually the school *staff* will also help bring individuals' behaviors into line with stated values. Acting in accordance with these stated values becomes part of the culture. Lateral accountability for shared commitments and agreed upon behaviors becomes the province of the entire school community. In a "paired school" model we helped develop in one high-performing district, the entire staff of one school became responsible for and committed to the success of the staff of two other schools (Hargreaves, 2005; see also Chapter 1 on networks).

Without a shared commitment to a core base of values, schools fall into the "my belief versus your belief" pattern. These schools may have certain individuals or factions that operate as "rogue agents," taking actions that run counter to the school's mission and vision. For example, imagine a school with a mission that states that all children can achieve at a high level and that it will provide an environment to make that happen. Yet many classrooms in that same school have long lists of prerequisite criteria—many of which are quite subjective—that students must meet in order to access the more rigorous curricular offerings. Clearly, such behaviors do not support the school's mission. Therefore, it lacks a *functional* set of values—a schoolwide statement that dictates *all* behavior.

What Good Looks Like

A successful statement of values touches on the most pertinent, pervasive principles shared by a school's stakeholders. The statement goes to the core of our belief and the depth of our commitment. Note that this does not mean identifying what stakeholders *should* commit to; we cannot set values and insist that others embrace them. Jim Collins (1996) points out that "core values are not something people 'buy in' to. People must be predisposed to holding them" (p. 19). He outlines an in-depth process for "getting to the core," which can help to create values that are enthusiastically endorsed by stakeholders.

A statement of values that captures only core beliefs should be relatively brief. It may contain as many as 10 values—but 5 or 6 is a more manageable number. Each value should be simply stated, so that the general meaning is easy to grasp and remember. It should also relate directly to the vision statement.

The question to consider when articulating values is not just what values are appropriate for our school, but what values *specifically support* our vision statement and are aligned with our mission. For example, the value statement "We will give students multiple opportunities to learn and to demonstrate their accomplishments" is consistent with a mission that states "All students will learn at high levels, in accordance with state standards." If a teacher is failing half of the students in his or her classroom year after year, that behavior will not be in line with the school's values or mission.

The values of a school articulate what "we will" *do* and how "we will" *behave* (i.e., "We will model," "We will support," "We will provide")—not what we *believe.* Although a statement of beliefs might be useful in some circumstances, it lacks the critical element of prescribing action—of telling us what we need to *do* to make our vision a reality.

Effective values are

- Few in number;
- Direct and simply stated;
- Focused on behaviors, not beliefs; and
- Linked to the vision statement.

Implementation Guidelines

Some view the establishment of a set of values as the most challenging component of a school's foundation because it requires a commitment to changing behaviors. It can be difficult to convey the full significance of values to staff members and get them to truly grapple with their beliefs and their perceived roles in the teaching and learning process. We must all "live into" our values by evaluating our behaviors over time.

In order for serious discussions among stakeholders to be successful, schools must invest time. As with developing mission and vision, it is best to start the process by breaking up into small groups. This helps engage participants and fosters honest, genuine dialogue. One easy approach is simply to review the school's vision statement with participants and then ask, "How do we need to behave to make this happen?" Allow time to discuss and draft answers to such questions. Then continue to consolidate lists using the snowball technique described earlier, or have a task force collect the responses and use them to draft a statement of values.

Another approach is to have participants divide into pairs. Have the pairs ask each other, "What are some of the behaviors that we [some, or all of us] engage in that are not consistent with our mission and vision?" After they have identified what they would like to see changed, have them ask each other, "What will you commit to doing, starting today, to change that?" Have participants write down their list of commitments. The facilitator can then ask each person to report out as he or she consolidates the comments onto one sheet of paper. Or the facilitator might collect the lists and consolidate them into a master list. In either case, it is best to go back to the staff to ask for a collective commitment to the final list.

Whatever process you use, be sure participants know that it is not trivial. Although it may be easy to get a list of values that everyone says they agree to, it is far more difficult to arrive at a list of values everyone will actually be willing to *live* by. One way to partially safeguard against abuses of the collective values is to go down the list and pose scenarios that might lead to someone bypassing a given value. Discuss the scenario and then ask participants to propose alternatives to behaving counter to the values.

The more energy and time you put into the process, the more effective your values will be at guiding day-to-day decision making. More information about the development process can be found in Resource 11.

Think It Through . . .

What are the prevailing values in your school right now? Which of those values accord with your mission and vision? Do any detract from your mission and vision? Are other people's behaviors consistent with your value statement?

THE GOALS

We must replace complex, long-term plans with simpler plans that focus on actual teaching lessons and units created in true "learning communities" that promote team-based, short-term thought and action.

—Mike Schmoker, "Tipping Point: From Feckless Reform to Substantive Instructional Improvement"

The three components of a successful school's foundation discussed thus far are meant for long-range planning. A school's vision, for example, may take five years or longer to reach. Values are also ongoing; we commit to them for as long as we are part of the organization.

But we also need short-term successes to help us stay focused and motivated. It is very difficult to commit to and work toward something that has no definite "success point" or preidentified benchmark that will allow us to take a deep breath, pat ourselves on the back, and look with pride at a job well done. Most of us need to feel that we are making progress and getting things done. It is through the judicious use of well-written goals—the fourth component of our foundation—that this need can be met.

Strong goals are particularly important in school cultures with little previous record of success. The process of setting, committing to, and accomplishing short-term goals builds credibility and trust. It can also serve as the beginning of positive momentum toward change.

What Are Goals?

If our vision is the grand target—a distant ideal that we are striving for—then our goals are the short-term minitargets that we aim for along the way. They break our long, winding journey toward school improvement into manageable, measurable steps. Goals provide intermittent reinforcement for our efforts and provide us with feedback on our progress toward the larger vision.

Goals also serve a more pragmatic purpose. They provide a detailed, short-term orientation for us in relation to our vision. They identify priorities and establish a timeline for our process of change. Equally important, goals establish accountability for stakeholders, ensuring that what needs to happen actually *does* happen.

What Good Looks Like

Goals, like the other foundational components we've discussed, are often too vague. A goal that is too vague to be measured is, essentially, worthless. After all, how will you ever know if you reach it? How will you know when to set a new goal?

Effective goals are both specific and measurable. They clearly identify the evidence that must be monitored to assess progress. They also set a time frame for completion. For example, "We will increase our students' average provincial test score by 20% this academic year" is a good, specific goal. "We will help all kids become lifelong learners," on the other hand, is too vague to be useful.

Goals should also focus on the results rather than on the process or the task. It's not uncommon for a school to have task-oriented goals, such as "We will adopt a new curriculum" or "We will have team meetings weekly." Although these are perfectly legitimate *inputs*, a SMART (criteria for SMART goals are listed in Figure 5.3) goal specifies the desired *results* of these actions in terms that are aligned with the school's mission and vision. To be SMART goals, these subgoals must go a step further, to answer the *so that* question: "We will adopt a new curriculum *so that we . . .*"

Ultimately, answering this additional question should get us to the *real* goal for student learning.

Implementation Guidelines

Developing goals for a school requires asking, "What steps do we need to take, in what order, to create our ideal school?" After identifying these steps, we must set a time frame or deadline for completion. To be most effective, every stakeholder in the school or district should help to set the goals for which he or she will be responsible. For example, third-grade teachers should set goals for the third-grade team. At Williamston Elementary School, for example, principal Christine Sermak and her leadership team developed SMART goals aligned with the district's goals for student success: "(1) By the end of the year, all teachers will incorporate writing using a common graphic organizer, editing tool, and rubric; and (2) We will develop the whole child (physical, emotional, and behavioral aspects included)" (see Chapter 1).

Figure 5.3	SMART Goals

SMART Goals Are . . .

Specific and Strategic. In this sense, *specific* relates to clarity. *Strategic* relates to alignment with our mission and vision.

Measurable. In most cases, this means quantifiable.

Attainable. People must believe, based on past data and current capabilities, that success is realistic.

Results Oriented. This means focusing on the outcome, not the process for getting there. This refers to our desired end result, versus inputs to the process.

Time Bound. When will the goal be accomplished?

Source: Failure Is Not an Option video series, HOPE Foundation, 2002.

How do you choose a goal? How do you decide what will make it measurable, attainable, results oriented, and time bound? An earlier vision statement example cited a 6% increase in reading scores. One might ask, "Why 6%? Why not 10% or 20%? Are folks lazy? Are they overly ambitious?"

There are different ways to begin goal setting.

- A school may be in academic trouble and have a bottom line that must be achieved.
- A school may look at last year's outcomes and then estimate how much better the school or district can do this year, based on improved processes, technology, or pedagogy.
- A school may start with the long-term vision and determine what needs to be accomplished each year to reach it and then dedicate the resources necessary for the annual improvements.

Regardless of where you begin in the process, it is essential to look at past data, new circumstances, and processes that can be modified to improve results. What will be done *differently* this year from last? How and when will we evaluate whether we are on target? Heed the warning implied in the statement "If you do what you've always done, you'll get what you've always got!"

After SMART goals are defined and implemented, they should be monitored continuously and evaluated over time. If clear evidence emerges revealing that the goal or means of achieving it is not bringing about the desired results, then one or both of these should be amended or abandoned. If goals are well chosen, and the means of achieving them are effective, then a careful analysis of the outcome should be made to determine how to continue and maintain the improvement over a longer period of time. More information about the goal-setting and monitoring process can be found in Resource 11.

Think It Through . . .

What goals are guiding your school's plans and actions right now? Are they consistent with your mission and vision? Are they SMART? How do they align with district goals? How can you use peer feedback across the district to align and assess goals?

Celebrating Successes

Many schools are reluctant to avail themselves of one of the best strategies for building positive school culture: celebrating success. In addition to concerns about lacking time, some school leaders are reluctant to single out individual achievements. Indeed, some school cultures are committed to mediocrity or egalitarianism to the point of hiding or ignoring successes!

But regular celebrations have the power to make the school's overall values increasingly positive. Moreover, celebrations help mark milestones and build motivation in the long journey of school improvement.

Here are some guidelines for celebrating success:

- Take steps that help assure the celebrations are deemed fair. This involves clarifying in advance exactly what constitutes success for all involved. (See SMART goals in Figure 5.3 for additional guidelines.)
- Tie celebrations explicitly to organizational vision, values, and goals. This provides an opportunity to reinforce these organizational pillars while providing more clarity, credibility, and rationale for the celebrations.
- Design celebrations that are attainable by all staff members. Having only one celebration with one winner per year can alienate a majority of your staff.
- For formal celebrations, communicate in advance the likely outcomes for success. This affirms the fairness of the approach.
- Make the celebration widely accessible. Involving more people heightens the impact of your school's values and goals for everybody.
- Arrange for both formal and informal celebrations. For example, simply using a staff meeting to congratulate a teacher on his or her excellent job in researching and recommending a new teaching methodology will go a long way toward encouraging others to do the same. Sometimes informal celebrations are needed to provide *timely* encouragement of people's efforts.
- Do not use celebrations to make direct or indirect comparisons between high- and low-achieving staff members. Focus on the positive results you are celebrating.
- Be specific about the nature of the success. "Eleanor actually took the time to visit the home of her most improved student, James," is far better than "Eleanor always helps her students."
- Use stories and be human.
- Build sustainability and community into the celebratory process by allowing staff and students to eventually take it over. Schools can begin early on by involving others in selection committees.

This chapter has outlined specific processes for building the foundation of a professional learning community. That foundation rests on four pillars: mission, vision, values, and goals. Creating a "product" for each of these pillars is technically simple. But the real gains in doing this come from the *process* and the *relationships* that are shaped along the way. Thus, creating common MVVG is an ideal way to effectively use data, build a collaborative team, and develop sustainable leadership capacity (see Principles 4, 3, and 6, respectively).

CHALLENGES

Challenge: "This has nothing to do with me and my classroom."

Getting faculty engaged in and supportive of the process can be difficult if they don't perceive it as directly meaningful to them.

Solution: Broad stakeholder involvement at the drafting stage. A top-down dictate will have little effect on the commitment of those on the front lines. The notion of assigning a purpose and a vision for others without obtaining their input is counterproductive. Every stakeholder group needs the opportunity to engage in thinking about a preferred future, to consider what the school stands for and what needs to be done. It is through ownership in the process and the creation of the guiding statements that the plan will become truly meaningful.

Challenge: "I think we used to have a mission . . . or a vision . . . or something like that."

Too often, the excitement that is generated by a new MVVG statement is short lived. School staffs become energized during the drafting and unveiling process but sometimes lose interest in the face of the challenges and pressures that are part of their daily routine.

Solution: Constant reinforcement. Keep your MVVG at the forefront of everyone's mind by constant reiteration and references to them in staff meetings, professional development days, and celebrations. Discuss them in orientations with new staff and in introducing the school to new stakeholders. Refer to them during group decision-making sessions. Create posters and hang them on the school walls. Use every opportunity to clarify and reinforce what the school stands for and where it is headed. Most important is confronting behaviors that are inconsistent with these agreed upon statements of purpose.

Challenge: "I don't have time for more meetings. I have real work to do!"

Time is always at a premium—and it can be a real stumbling block for faculty and staff who are already overworked and exhausted.

Solution: Make the time, and uncover other reasons for resistance. This statement is, on its face, completely legitimate. There is simply no way of getting around it—the process of creating MVVG will require an investment of time. More important, schools will need to make time in the daily schedule for continual professional development. The issue of time is covered in more detail in Chapter 2 and in Resource 7.

CONCLUSION

In this chapter, you have learned the specific processes involved in building the foundation of a professional learning community. Creating, or at least revisiting, MVVG is fundamental to all that follows. Chapter 6 poses and helps resolve one of the greatest challenges schools face: "What happens when children *don't* learn?"

Chapter 5 Resources

Resource 10. Running River Elementary School Mission Statement

Resource 11. Development Process for Mission, Vision, Values, and Goals

These Resources for *Failure Is Not an Option*, Second Edition can be found

1. At the HOPE Foundation Web site at www.hopefoundation.org.

2. In the *Facilitator's Guide* to *Failure Is Not an Option*, Second Edition (ISBN 978-1-4129-8174-3) available for order at www.corwinpress.com.

CHAPTER 6

Principle 2

Ensuring Achievement for
All Students—Systems for
Prevention and Intervention

Not all of us are a mess, you know. . . . People often associate anyone
who's been abused with "There's no hope for that child." . . . Tell people we
can do it. That you can survive all that and be a fully functioning member
of the community. Don't give up on that kid at age 7 and say, "Oh, he's
been through so much; he's never going to amount to anything." . . . The
abused are labeled. But you can change somebody around.

—G. Higgins, *Resilient Adults: Overcoming a Cruel Past*

If we individually make the effort to ensure that each child is known in
our system, our organization will be a caring learning community that
knows and lifts each child.

—Les Ometani, Community School District Superintendent,
West Des Moines, Iowa (quoted in LaFee, 2003, p. 7)

Consider this exchange between two teachers.

Ella: How are things going with your class, Jim?

Jim: Not well. I just gave my first test, and over half the class failed. I don't
know how I'm supposed to teach these kids. They're all reading

below grade level. They appear to have learned nothing in middle school. What am I supposed to do with them?

How do we ensure successful learning for all students? Most educators are trying very hard and come to their work with a genuine desire to succeed with each of their students. However, there are undeniably numerous significant obstacles to learning. These include, but are not limited to, differing learning styles, need for additional time and repetition, low socioeconomic status, a language other than English spoken in the home, and parent or family situations that interfere with the learning process.

In high-performing schools, these variables are addressed in a proactive manner so they do not become barriers to the successful achievement of all students. Teachers are engaged in continuous study of educational research to learn how to prevent failure and how to provide effective interventions for each student in need. They actively seek alternatives to failure, and the concept of "throw-away" students is itself discarded.

Even the most abused and troubled children *self*-correct as they mature in age (Anthony, 1982, 1987; Comer, Joyner, & Ben-Avie, 2004; Garmezy, 1983, 1994; Kaiser & Rasminsky, 2004; Werner & Smith, 1977). Werner and Smith (1977) summarized one part of their 30-year longitudinal study on high-risk youth this way: "We could not help being deeply impressed by the resiliency of the overwhelming majority of children and by their potential for positive change and personal growth" (p. 210).

Teachers are among the most likely mentors and positive influences for underachieving students. And schools can often be the only bastion of stability in a student's life. A committed school faculty, therefore, can do a great deal to enhance the life of every child. When acting in concert to create a reclaiming *environment* and to build *systems* to prevent failure, school communities dramatically enhance the likelihood for student success (Schorr, 1988).

The challenge is getting all staff members to believe in schools' ability to intervene positively in a student's life and to act on this information in a sustained, concerted, systematic manner. That is the focus of this chapter. Here, we look at the research, the "end products" of successful schools, and the processes that high-performing schools undertake to succeed with even the toughest students.

Specifically, we look at three major aspects of ensuring success for all students through comprehensive systems for prevention and intervention:

1. The school community's belief system regarding low-performing students

2. The overarching philosophy that unifies staff behavior

3. Comprehensive systems for assuring success

WHAT DOES THE SCHOOL COMMUNITY BELIEVE?

In most schools, the answer to this question is, "It depends." Beliefs about low-performing students often vary among teachers. A small number of classroom teachers often account for the majority of those students who are referred to the principal's office. At the same time, other teachers are able to succeed with those same students. This is generally not a case of the student's becoming more intelligent or a better person once he or she reaches the classroom of the successful teacher. It has more to do with the varying belief systems in operation within the school.

Consider how two different belief systems resulted in widely varying solutions to the same challenge faced by these two schools. In the first school, student lateness is met with a new policy of locking the school doors after the 8:00 a.m. late bell rings. A few more students wound up coming on time, while many others became truant. In the Case Example below, this school community chose a different path:

CASE EXAMPLE

Creative Scheduling

D.R. Hill Middle School in Duncan, South Carolina, has found an effective way to both reduce tardiness and provide students with a "decompression" period between home and school. Every day at D.R. Hill starts with Tiger Advisory Program (TAP) Time. During TAP Time, faculty advisors work with small groups of students to teach life skills, such as cooperation and collaboration, through hands-on activities and exercises. Every student is involved, including those in special education, and students are grouped heterogeneously, with no segregation of any sort.

Principal Steve Gambrell says that the program has become an invaluable part of the day for both students and teachers. "We feel like it's almost a sacred time," Gambrell says. "It's a time when those kids who bring baggage to school are able to get rid of that baggage so that when they go to their academic classes, they're ready to learn—and teachers are able to teach." A side benefit of TAP Time is that it has virtually eliminated tardiness to academic classes. Because of the experimental and active nature of TAP, students come early to ensure they can participate.

Source: Used with permission from Steve Gambrell.

The underlying assumptions and beliefs of these two school communities led to very different policies and structures as well as student outcomes.

As we stated in Chapter 2, the link between student success or failure and teachers' and principals' expectations for those students is well documented (Bandura, 1986; Edmonds, 1979; Gardner, 1988; Goleman, 1995; Sternberg, 1996). Moreover, the research in Chapter 3 indicates that one of the keys to success for highly reliable organizations (HROs) is both believing in and acting on this information. The difficulty lies in the challenge of getting the entire school community to understand this connection and take appropriate action. Simply reading the research—absent belief and action—is not sufficient to bring about change.

Changing the belief systems of people is an extremely difficult and complex process. Most texts don't address this issue, focusing instead on changing behavior. In the previous chapter, we endorsed this approach as a practical way of addressing behaviors that are inconsistent with organizational values.

It is imperative that a school's entire staff holds high expectations for students, and this chapter addresses some of the practical complexities in this effort. Gaining staff *compliance* alone is not enough. It takes total staff *commitment* to succeed in the thorny work of reaching low-achieving and underserved students.

Addressing the core *beliefs* of the entire school community is a lengthy process. Along the way, it is essential to be sure to hold the line on *behaviors* and *language* that may conflict with organizational values and mission. Doing otherwise creates an environment in which "anything goes." Without at *least* commitment to *behavior* that supports the school's values and mission, the fundamental aspect of almost any school's mission— that "*all* students will learn"—will become invalid. It is essential that the mission really means that *all* students—not *some* students—will learn.

CASE EXAMPLE

Confronting Behaviors

After numerous discussions with Bob, the science teacher, regarding the poor grades his students consistently receive, the school principal meets with Bob:

Principal: Hi, Bob. Did you get those grade distributions I sent you?

Bob: Yes, I did.

(Continued)

(Continued)

Principal: Great, let's just go over them. It's obvious from these numbers, Bob, that students in your class consistently underperform, semester after semester. Something is clearly happening in your class to cause this discrepancy, and I'd welcome any explanations you might have.

Bob: This is the way I teach, Mr. Martin. It's the way I've always taught. I teach responsibility. I'm very tough on them. I'm not going to enable them like these other teachers do.

Principal: It's not our mission to make courses difficult for students, Bob. It's our mission to help them succeed. We need assessments that accurately reflect what they know, and we need approaches that are consistent with our value statement—which you helped create. I'm going to ask you to work with the two other teachers in your division, and with your director, to develop some new assessments that are more in keeping with what we're trying to accomplish. If, at the end of the next grading period, your students' scores aren't in line with those of the other classes, I'll work with you directly to ensure the necessary improvements.

Think It Through . . .

In the case example above, does it seem as if the teacher is being asked to lower his standards? How can we reconcile maintaining high standards and still ensuring success for all students? How do leaders respond to behaviors that conflict with vision, mission, and values?

High-performing schools realize that (1) what they do matters to the learning of each of their students, and (2) all children can indeed perform at high levels. Many school communities do not take direct responsibility for the learning of each of their students. Here are three common reasons why this might be the case, and some suggestions for addressing each:

1. The Teachers May Not Believe That a School Can Succeed With All Students

Some members of the school community have had experiences that, to them, confirm the worst: Not all children can learn! Based on their own predispositions, initial bad experiences, or inabilities to reach all children themselves, some may understandably hold this view. In fact, it wasn't until relatively recently that schools were even considered a possible part of the solution to students' nonacademic life challenges.

Most educators have had minimal experience and training in dealing with the kinds of problems that today's children present. Dealing with students' problems ineffectively or misinterpreting a student's inability to learn is common. The teachers described in the following Case Example, for example, mistook Sidiki's personal problems for an inability to learn.

CASE EXAMPLE

Sidiki's Story

I was called to school for an appointment with the teachers of a 10-year-old boy, Sidiki, to whom I had become "big brother." When I inquired into the purpose of our meeting, one teacher's analysis of Sidiki's performance was, "Sidiki is not performing at the skill level of his classmates. He has difficulty paying attention and refuses to participate in class. His reading comprehension is well below grade level and his scores on our standardized tests indicate that his math skills are only at third-grade level."

The team leader provided a more succinct analysis: "He just doesn't get it! I think he may be learning disabled."

I shared with Sidiki's teachers that he was an African immigrant who already spoke four languages, the last of which was English. I shared how enthusiastic and excited Sidiki could become once he was engaged in our evening tutoring sessions, remaining exclusively focused on his homework for hours at a time—often longer than I could! I also explained the tremendous tumult in his family life, and the pressure and abuse he received from his father.

As I spoke, it was clear that neither teacher had been aware of Sidiki's impressive multilingual abilities, his enthusiasm for learning and capacity for intense concentration, his father's status as an international scholar, or the abuse—physical and otherwise—which Sidiki received from him. As I revealed these facts, a look of empathy began to play on one of the teachers' faces.

Source: Adapted from Blankstein, 1997, pp. 2–3.

When Sidiki's teachers understood the situation, they redoubled their efforts and changed their approach, and Sidiki succeeded. If the challenge is one of school personnel truly questioning whether or not all students can learn at high levels, then this is more easily dealt with than the other challenges on this list. Teachers with a strong sense of self-efficacy can generally change their behaviors readily when faced with new information that calls for such a change. Similarly, professionals in a culture that focuses on continuous learning will be hungry to learn that there is a better way, and they will soon adopt that better approach.

If this is the situation, it is often possible to change behaviors (leading to changed beliefs) by introducing conclusions drawn from research. This will generally create cognitive dissonance for those questioning the possibility of creating a school in which low-performers can turn around. The dissonance, for those with strong self-efficacy, will be resolved in favor of a pilot project testing the new theory, or wholesale change, depending on the school's culture.

Leaders can also create this dissonance, as well as pathways to change. Modeling alternative behaviors, demonstrating success, and forcefully challenging assumptions are all part of good leadership.

It would be helpful, however, to check to see if "lack of information" is the only barrier to change. One could ask, "Do you really believe that you cannot educate all of your students to high levels of achievement? Does this mean that if you found out otherwise, you would try some new approaches and work with me and the team to assure all students' success?" If the answer to either of these questions is no, the real hesitation may be something else mentioned below.

Options for addressing a true information gap include reading and sharing research and best practices. Countless studies point out best practices and school successes in virtually any setting. (See the next chapter on maximizing research through collaboration.) You can also take a field trip to another school that succeeds or bring a speaker/practitioner from a school similar to your own. Most powerfully, discovering who within your own school succeeds with "low performers" opens up great possibilities for others to do the same. The network approach cited in Chapter 1 expedites the "see-feel-do" process for change within schools and across the entire district (Fullan, 2005).

2. The Teachers May Not Feel Personally Competent to Succeed With All Students

This will be harder to uncover than the first reason listed above. The idea here is that the student's failure is actually the teacher's failure once the teacher admits that all students *could* in fact succeed. The response to this becomes one of support, on one hand, and "creative tension" (Senge, 1990) on the other. The idea is to build a sense of self-efficacy among staff members by challenging them to do things they *can* do, while making inertia uncomfortable.

One principal in an urban high school explains,

> When I first got there it was bad—attendance, behavior, academics. . . . [We] decided we'd tackle them in that order, but that we would organize our efforts under one simple heading: "You Can Make a Difference."
>
> I worked to convince the faculty that they would succeed with these kids and that we had to convince the kids that they, too, could succeed. We began with attendance. Our message was "We want you in school." We called parents, sent them postcards about attendance, and had individual teachers follow up with each kid or parent after each absence. Attendance improved. The second year we started on behavior—just some basics about courtesy, language, some more consistency about how we handled discipline and so on. Now we're ready to start on achievement. (Evans, 1996, p. 214)

By collectively generating the motto "You Can Make a Difference" and providing definition with some clear and specific goals, this principal and his staff created an inherent tension, then addressed a means of resolving that tension through small steps and successes. These baby steps in turn built a sense of efficacy among the staff, which enabled them to take on more difficult tasks, which in turn led to enhanced student achievement.

Another way to build creative tension is to bring staff members into closer contact and affinity with the students whom they feel are unlikely to succeed. As affinity increases, it becomes more difficult to dismiss an individual's academic potential.

In her 12-year study of 120 organizations in 35 cities, Milbrey McLaughlin (in Lewis, 2000) found that building relationships with young people as well as holding relation-building events that "allow youth and adults to see each other in new ways" were two of six guiding principles for success (p. 643). Creating opportunities for shared experiences in the form of social events, field trips, or experiential learning activities deepens the affinity and the communication among participants. Figure 6.1 demonstrates the interaction among the elements.

Any time one of the three sides of the triangle is enhanced, the other two sides are strengthened as well. This can also be applied to building support for students within the larger community. Having community

Figure 6.1   Building Affinity

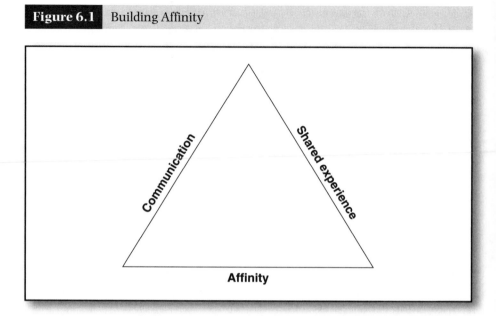

members become mentors for students, for example, builds the communication, shared experience, and affinity for students and the school. Assigning students to research the history of community members has a similar effect while also providing an intellectual experience for the student.

This section presented a handful of ways to help educators overcome their fears of competency associated with committing to success for all students. The general principle is to provide both support and encouragement for the staff member while creating a cognitive dissonance or creative tension to spur movement.

3. Finally, It's Not Worth It!

Most veteran teachers have experienced disappointments at one time or another due to past waves of school reform. The idea of quickly embracing the next new reform seems foolish to some. Past failures may have been due to (1) a premature change of leadership; (2) lack of political, financial, or other capital necessary to ride out the storms involved with the change effort; or (3) a superficial attempt to get teachers to simply "buy in" when committed engagement is actually required. Whatever the past experience may have been, many teachers are understandably reluctant to jump into the waters of reform with both feet.

Understanding is required in such cases. It is also important to bring people's underlying assumptions to the surface so that they may be addressed: "Why do you feel this way? I'm interested in knowing what you have experienced in the past."

Shutting down people's inner concerns will lead only to increased outside conversations or gossip. It is better to hear legitimate concerns firsthand in order to deal directly with the situation, for example, "I see, you have been burned in the past and don't want to dive in again before you know this is 'for real.' That's understandable, and I accept and respect that. Moreover, I will make sure that your concerns are addressed, as you will see over time. However, in the meantime, I would like to ask a favor. Could you withhold any negative commentary or judgment of this initiative until you have watched it unfold for a while? Then if you have any suggestions, can you see me directly?"

Another increasingly common reason for the "Why bother?" mentality, especially among new personnel, is the time and effort involved. The idea of succeeding with every student may indeed seem overwhelming. The latter part of this chapter discusses relieving *individuals* of this task, and instead instituting a collaboratively created, systemwide approach. The following section is a necessary precursor to that approach.

WHAT IS THE SCHOOL COMMUNITY'S UNIFYING PHILOSOPHY?

One of the biggest challenges school leaders face is the tendency toward fragmentation of efforts and focus. Many demands are placed on educators, and those demands come from all directions. Often, the demands from the state, district, parents, staff, unions, and students are at odds with one another. Good leaders, therefore, are called on to make organizational meaning out of apparent chaos. In this section, we provide a framework and philosophy for how the entire school community can deal with one of the most difficult challenges: student failure to meet high academic standards.

Traditionally, when a student did not comply with school policies, he or she was punished. If this punishment didn't work, the student was suspended or expelled. Whether or not the student succeeded academically or grew from the experience was not generally thought to be the school's concern.

Although there may be a place for this cut-and-dried approach to student "misbehavior," there have been many advances in the behavioral sciences. This new information has the power to lead us to different understandings of the complex *interactions* between students and teachers, students and the school environment, and students and their home. We now know that there is more that the school community can do to positively influence behaviors and the development of young people.

Most of the traditional approaches to dealing with student behavior were based on the Skinnerian philosophy of reward and punishment. But students are more complex than rats, and the fact that these traditional approaches often lead to more misbehavior attests to that complexity.

The traditional philosophy regarding student behavior has led to a mismatch between how some schools deal with students who don't comply and what those students actually need in order to improve their behaviors. The behaviors worsen in such cases. This leads to frustration on the part of many teachers and administrators as they sense that "what we are doing isn't working!" Without an alternative to traditional approaches, there is a tendency to see the inefficacy of the "treatment" as the fault of the "patient."

Banishment becomes a popular response to the problem. Some schools in which we work have literally hundreds of suspensions each year. The line to the principal's office looks like one for a rock concert! Labeling, then referring students to remedial programs, special education, and even alternative schools, seem to be the only answer for some beleaguered teachers. This has become so widespread that entire mini-industries, as well as billion-dollar pharmaceutical treatments, have sprung up to treat the latest "disorders." So many of these diagnoses for children happen to begin with the letter D that the 10 Ds of Deviance were created to depict the label used and actions prescribed for each (Figure 6.2).

| **Figure 6.2** | The 10 Ds of Deviance in Approaches to "Difficult" Youth |

Perspective	Problem Label	Typical Responses
Primitive	Deviant	Blame, attack, ostracize
Folk Religion	Demonic	Chastise, exorcise, banish
Biophysical	Diseased	Diagnose, drug, hospitalize
Psychoanalytical	Disturbed	Analyze, treat, seclude
Behavioral	Disordered	Assess, condition, time out
Correctional	Delinquent	Adjudicate, punish, incarcerate
Sociological	Deprived	Study, resocialize, assimilate
Social Work	Dysfunctional	Intake, case manage, discharge
Educational	Disobedient	Reprimand, correct, expel
Special Education	Disabled	Label, remediate, segregate

Once there is a diagnosis for the disorder, the treatment becomes clear. Unfortunately, far less time has been spent creating diagnoses for young people's strengths.

A BETTER WAY

What we want to achieve in our work with young people is to find and strengthen the positive and healthy elements, no matter how deeply they are hidden.

—Karl Wilker, *The Lindenhof*

Over the past 100 years, a relatively small but growing number of leading child psychologists and youth professionals have developed a strengths-based approach to viewing and "treating" young people. They have been surprisingly consistent, in fact, in defining the basic needs that drive behavior (see Figure 6.3).

Figure 6.3 The Basic Needs That Drive Behavior

Source	Basic Needs
William Glasser, MD *Control Theory in the Classroom* (1986)	1. Survival and reproduction 2. Belonging and love 3. Power 4. Freedom 5. Fun
Stanley Coopersmith *The Antecedents of Self-Esteem* (1967)	1. Significance to others 2. Competence 3. Power to control one's own behavior and gain respect 4. Virtue of worthiness in the eyes of others
Martin Brokenleg *Circle of Courage* (1990) Based on Sioux tradition	1. Belonging 2. Mastery 3. Independence 4. Generosity

(Continued)

Figure 6.3   (Continued)

Source	Basic Needs
Boys and Girls Clubs of America *Youth Development Strategy*	1. Belonging 2. Usefulness 3. Competence 4. Influence
Allen N. Mendler *What Do I Do When . . . ?* (1992)	1. Success and being capable 2. Acceptance, belonging 3. Influence over people, events 4. Generosity and helping others 5. Stimulation and fun
Alan M. Blankstein *Failure Is Not an Option* (2004)	1. Contribution 2. Connection 3. Competence 4. Self-control

The Community Circle of Caring synthesizes this body of research to provide a common framework and core philosophy (as shown in Figure 6.4) of action (Blankstein, 2004; Blankstein, DuFour, & Little, 1997).

Figure 6.4   Community Circle of Caring

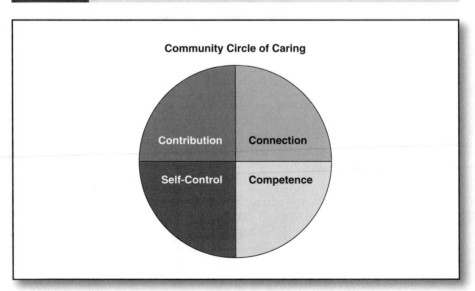

Young people will naturally attempt to meet each of these four basic needs in either a prosocial or antisocial manner. One of the gangs we studied, the Latin Kings, uses a very similar framework, for example, to recruit and retain youth whose needs for connection are not being met prosocially. Young people whose need for competence is not being met in a positive manner may turn to auto theft, for example, to gain a sense of competence. The ultimate goal of the school, then, becomes one of creating an environment and culture that meets students' basic needs. Figure 6.5 shows examples of practices in such an environment, as well as contrary practices.

CASE EXAMPLE

 Building on Students' Strengths

The Bulldog Club was started to provide leadership opportunities to some of our students. We chose the students who had a difficult time making positive choices but had leadership potential. We figured that other children in fifth grade were going to follow the "Bulldogs" no matter if it was in a positive or negative direction, so we decided to make them a part of our "management team." By giving the Bulldogs responsibility and direction, they could make following the rules the cool thing to do at our school. In addition, through mentoring younger students and setting an example, the Bulldogs' personal behavior would change for the better as well.

Through the implementation of the Bulldog program, we have seen a distinct change in our students. The Bulldogs are well respected at Barth and have made a noticeable difference in student behavior at Barth.

Source: Used with permission of Mike DiDonato.

The following chart provides examples of school practices that either enhance or impede development of each of the four Cs.

Figure 6.5	Four Cs: Practices That Promote Connection Versus Disconnection

Connection	Disconnection
Welcoming students even when they are late	Sending students to the principal's office, regardless of circumstances of late arrival
Greeting students warmly at classroom door	Working on paper at desk until all students are seated and the start bell rings
Systematically assuring every student is positively connected to an adult	Leaving personal connections to chance
Using extracurricular engagement data of all students as a measure of school success	Assuming most students are involved in extracurricular activities
Developing Competence	*Building Incompetence*
Allowing make-up work	Having "one chance" policies
Demanding mastery of material	Averaging zeros into semester grades
Testing what is taught	"Surprise" tests and pop quizzes
Finding and emphasizing strengths	Focusing on weaknesses
Self-Control	*Compliance and Obedience*
Allowing students to help create class rules	Telling students what the rules are
Eliciting input on class projects and readings	Recycling prior year's projects
Teaching empathy, self-awareness, and other emotional intelligences	Keeping emotional learning apart from academics
Contribution	*Self-Centeredness*
Allowing older students to teach younger ones	No student-led mentoring
Creating community service and learning opportunities	Holding learning within the school
Encouraging cooperative learning	Teacher directs all learning

It is often the case that several of these Cs can be addressed at once. Consider how the following Case Example simultaneously addresses the needs for connection, competence, and contribution.

 Enriching Activities for Students

Icenhower Intermediate School in Mansfield, Texas, has implemented over 25 extracurricular clubs and activities. "Most of the teachers involved in these clubs do so on a volunteer basis. These clubs may be athletic (basketball, volleyball, hockey), academic (Whiz Quiz, Academic UIL), or "real world" (cooking, green team). We believe that making connections outside of the four walls of the classroom is essential to ensuring success for our students. One particularly successful venture has been our Spanish Club, where some of our ELL students actually become the teachers of this club and help other students learn Spanish. This provides an opportunity for students who do not have a second language to acquire skills in another language and also promotes leadership and ownership by our English language learner (ELL) students as they become integral to the learning process. The Spanish Club along with the Cooking Club team up for a Cinco de Mayo fiesta at the end of the year for parents, where traditional music, the Spanish language, and a meal of Mexican food provide a vehicle to celebrate the success of our students and to engage parents in the entire school program" (see Chapter 9 on engaging family).

Source: Used with permission from Duane Thurston and Reggie Rhines.

The four Cs of the Community Circle of Caring provide a framework for rethinking and coordinating the actions of the entire school community. Once the beliefs and philosophy are agreed upon, it is far easier to create a unifying system for action. The next section gives very specific examples of how two schools have done just that, as well as guidelines and steps to proceed on your own.

WHAT IS THE COMPREHENSIVE SYSTEM FOR ENSURING SUCCESS?

Ensuring achievement for *all* students means having an overarching strategy that encompasses the majority of learners—and then having specific strategies aimed at those who need extra support. Essential components of a plan for all students' success include

- Having an improvement plan for all students;
- Having systems for quickly identifying those in need;
- Providing a continuum of support and targeted strategies for low achievers;
- Publishing results on closing the achievement gap; and
- Using data-based decision making for continuous improvement.

The following sections will discuss each of these components in detail. In addition, this section provides examples of intervention systems from two very different schools.

HAVING AN IMPROVEMENT PLAN FOR ALL STUDENTS

The most effective schools provide a ladder of opportunities for struggling students, ranging from identification of students needing extra support before the school year begins to mandatory enrollment in remedial and/or skills classes. The effect of this range of interventions is to make clear to students that they may *not* fail. It tells students that the only choice is to learn and succeed.

As prescribed in Response to Intervention (RtI), an effective improvement plan for all students includes components of both prevention and intervention. Some prevention strategies are targeted; others apply to the entire student population. The latter include

- Building relationships with students;
- Systematically identifying and building on students' strengths;
- Meeting with students each day;
- Having staff be visible and available;
- Involving students in the decision-making process (*Failure Is Not an Option* video series, HOPE Foundation, 2002); and
- Matching school structures to the real needs of students.

Often, school policies, schedule, or structure simply don't accommodate the young people they're supposed to serve. Consider the following Case Example. Changing the overall structure or policies across the board can often provide the necessary support for preventing potential problems.

CASE EXAMPLE

Aligning Structure With Philosophy to Reduce Suspensions

At Shambaugh Elementary, principal Shawn Smiley emphasizes two methods for decreasing suspensions: (1) building and maintaining relationships and (2) putting in place procedures that reduce behavior issues.

The first thing I did when I got here was to look for patterns of behavior that were keeping students out of the classroom. I found, first, that students were going to lunch and then to recess, and second, that we lacked procedures to keep adults focused on the true task at hand, which was to ensure every minute of the day was devoted to learning.

I changed the schedule for more than one reason. The referral rate was much higher in the afternoon. Students were being brought in from outside in an unruly manner. The teachers were not always there when the kids were returned, forcing the classroom assistants to maintain the "civility" of the beginning of the structured time.

When the schedule changed to have recess precede lunch, the teachers then picked up the students from the cafeteria. Teachers were then on time from lunch and ready for their students to be returned to the rooms in an organized manner. Going from recess to the classroom doesn't make sense regardless of the behaviors that are shown by students. It is hard to believe we can get students from a high-energy, less-structured change of environment to the learning environment and expect them to be successful.

A simple change in procedures changes the way people act and react to the same events. We can now go from 45 minutes of lunch and recess to the classroom ready to learn (and not in the principal's office because the students could not transition well).

Source: Used with permission of Shawn Smiley.

TARGETED INTERVENTIONS

Intervention strategies target students who are not demonstrating learning at the level of expected performance. To be most effective, these strategies are graduated in their intensity. These types of graduated prevention and intervention systems take a pyramidal form; the prevention strategies at the bottom apply to all students, and the high-intensity interventions at the top apply to only a few. You will learn about two of these exemplary "pyramid of interventions" (Noer, 1993) systems: one from Adlai Stevenson High School, which is located in a wealthy suburb, and the other from Coyote Ridge Elementary School, located in a middle-class suburb north of Denver in Colorado. They are in the "What Good Looks Like" section of this chapter.

HAVING SYSTEMS FOR QUICKLY IDENTIFYING STUDENTS IN NEED

Effective schools do not follow the sink-or-swim approach. Nor do they wade in to rescue students only when they have proven that they can't swim. Schools that are committed to success for all students systematically identify struggling students. They identify problems as early as possible—well before students have a chance to fail. The timely identification of problems is what distinguishes intervention strategies from remediation strategies.

Think It Through . . .

How does your school identify students who need additional support? How early in those students' academic careers does such identification and intervention take place?

When prevention systems are already in place for all students, it becomes easy to identify those who are at risk for academic difficulties. Mechanisms for identifying struggling students should ideally be built on the programs already in place for supporting all students. For example, a high school that monitors all incoming freshmen by having staff members submit frequent progress reports automatically has a net in place for catching struggling students.

CASE EXAMPLE

Identifying Students in Need

At Pelham Road Elementary, in Greenville, South Carolina, a special kindergarten class comes under the umbrella of the school's Special Education department. The children in the class are completely unaware that they are in a special program. The object of the class is to give children who have been identified as lacking necessary social or academic skills the boost they need before starting first grade without saddling them with the "special ed" label. The school chooses these students based on interviews with Head Start participants and places the identified students in a smaller-than-average class. The program's goal is to prepare participants for immediate mainstreaming into first-grade classrooms. In the great majority of cases, the program accomplishes that goal.

PROVIDING A CONTINUUM OF SUPPORT AND TARGETED STRATEGIES FOR LOW ACHIEVERS

Students who are moving from one level of schooling to another—from elementary to middle school or from middle school into high school—need a continuum of support that sees them smoothly through the transition. Schools provide the resources necessary to ensure that new students can hit the ground running.

Schools use various mechanisms to facilitate a seamless transition for incoming students. One is collaboration between counselors in the feeder schools and in the receiving school. This allows counselors at the receiving school to become familiar with new students' needs and with what approaches have been successful at meeting those needs in the past.

Other projects and programs include

- Programs to prepare for the next school level (e.g., "Survival Skills for High School");
- Reviews of student records before school starts in order to provide extra supports for children in need; and

- Faculty mentor programs, in which every incoming student is closely monitored by an adult who gets to know him or her well.

Think It Through . . .

What systems are in place in your school for providing incoming students with a continuum of support? What systems are in place to align PreK–12 philosophy and practice? To ensure all students' success?

Once high-performing schools have identified those students who are at risk of failure, they find ways to bolster their weak areas to ensure success. The types of strategies used vary depending on the grade levels served by the school and the needs of the students.

PUBLISHING RESULTS

Making the achievement gaps an agenda item and publishing them for the stakeholder community to review adds focus to the staff's efforts. The schools in San Diego, California, used this strategy to help close their achievement gap.

WHAT GOOD LOOKS LIKE

Effective systems of prevention and intervention ensure that no student slips through the cracks. They are designed so that the majority of students benefit from careful, continuous monitoring and low-level support strategies. They have mechanisms in place to ensure the early identification of struggling students. And they follow a prescribed order so that higher-level strategies are implemented only after lower-level ones have failed to produce results.

The first Case Story below highlights the comprehensive pyramid of intervention created over many years in a wealthy suburban high school outside of Chicago.

CASE STORY 4

Pyramid of Interventions in a Wealthy Suburban High School

One highly developed example of such a system is Adlai Stevenson High School's "pyramid of interventions" (Noer, 1993). The pyramid has several levels, beginning with intensive monitoring of all incoming ninth graders and ending with mandatory remediation for those who fail despite intermediate intervention. (See Resource 12.)

Nine Levels of Intervention

Intensive Intervention	9. Student Support Groups
	8. Mentor Program With Parent Support Group
Targeted Intervention	7. Guided Study Hall
	6. Mandatory Tutoring
Systemwide Intervention	5. Progress Reports After Three Weeks
	4. Faculty Advisor and Upper Classmen
Targeted Early Prevention and Strategies	3. Good Friend Program
	2. Summer Classes
	1. Counselor Watch

Source: Failure Is Not an Option video series, HOPE Foundation, 2002.

1. *Counselor Watch.* Counselors begin by meeting each spring with teachers and counselors at the feeder schools to identify incoming students who will require special support. Those students are "red flagged" and assigned to the counselor watch program.

2. *Summer Classes.* These same students are also invited to attend a preparation program held during the Stevenson summer session, in which they are taught such success skills as time management, note taking, and reading in the content areas.

3. *Good Friend Program.* When school starts in the fall, students meet with their counselors weekly. Students needing extra support are also assigned a "good friend." The good friend is a teacher who sees that student daily in class and takes a few extra moments to get to know the student better and encourage him or her to open up about any problems. This program runs "behind the scenes"; the students themselves never realize that it exists or that they have a designated "good friend."

4. *Faculty Advisor and Upper-Class Mentoring.* Every ninth grader is assigned to a faculty advisor, who meets with groups of 25 students four days a week for 25 minutes. The advisor is assisted by five older student mentors, who serve as "big brothers and sisters," helping the new students to transition smoothly. These student mentors are responsible for explaining school rules to the newcomers, encouraging them to join extracurricular activities, answering questions, discussing common problems, and even helping with homework when students face difficulties.

(Continued)

(Continued)

Each ninth grader is also assigned to a counselor, who comes into the advisory group once a week. Although the counselor will meet less frequently with the students, he or she is expected to know each of them by name within the first two to three weeks of school.

5. *Progress Reports After Three Weeks.* The school issues progress reports on its freshmen three weeks into the school year. Teachers quickly consult with students who do poorly, along with the faculty advisor, the counselor, and the student mentor. Each of them encourages the student to work harder, to get extra help, or to attend voluntary tutoring. For example, if at the three-week report, a ninth grader were in danger of failing mathematics, his or her math teacher would point out the problem and ask that student to begin attending voluntary sessions at the math-tutoring center.

When the student attended the advisory, his or her advisor would also have a copy of the progress report. The advisor would again discuss the math problem, ask the student what he or she planned to do about it, and suggest spending some time each day reviewing math homework with an upper-class mentor. The student's counselor would also have a copy of the progress report and would schedule an individual meeting. Finally, parents receive the progress report, too, and will likely ask their children about the situation.

The outcome of this "quadruple teaming" is that most ninth graders realize quickly that they will not be allowed to slide. The typical student recognizes that it will be easier simply to do the work.

6. *Mandatory Tutoring.* If a student continues to do poorly despite the help of staff and student mentors, the school may require the student to attend daily mandatory tutoring during study hall. Students in the mandatory tutoring program are monitored continuously and receive weekly progress reports.

7. *Guided Study Hall.* If students fail to make sufficient progress in the mandatory tutoring program, they will be taken out of the regular study hall—which has approximately 80 students—and put into a guided study hall, with no more than eight students. Students are required to spend 90 minutes a day in the guided study hall, under the close oversight of an adult supervisor who serves as a liaison with their teachers and oversees completion of assigned work. This liaison—typically a parent volunteer—talks with each student's teachers and therefore already knows the exact status of his or her assignments.

If a student claims that he or she has no work to do on a given day, the liaison will know if this is accurate. If not, the liaison will point out the assignments still to be completed. If the student says he or she has left a book at home, the supervisor produces a book from a stock of extras kept on hand in the classroom. Essentially, the supervisor "hovers" over the student, insisting that assignments be completed. For 95% of students, this level of intervention effectively addresses their academic problems.

8. *Mentor Program With Parent Support Group.* The very few students who fail to benefit from previous interventions enroll in a program in which they receive extensive tutoring, close supervision of their work, and study skills practice. They spend two hours a day in this program. The big difference in this intervention is the mentor parents' support group that parents must attend. Designated parents attend monthly meetings designed to teach them how they can encourage their children's progress.

9. *Student Support Groups.* Students whose persistent low academic achievement is grounded in nonacademic problems such as substance abuse, family breakdown, or social problems are offered a support group in which they meet with students having similar problems and share ways to overcome them.

The following Case Story integrates processes described throughout this book in the creation of a highly effective "pyramid of support" and response to interventions, leading this middle-class elementary school to Accreditation With Distinction in Colorado. The actual pyramid is in Resource 13.

CASE STORY 5

RtI and Pyramid of Support at a Middle-Class Suburban Elementary School

Coyote Ridge Elementary is a suburban school north of Denver, Colorado. For the past six years, the staff has been integrally involved in the implementation of successful RtI. What is it that has caused the high level of achievement for all students? If asked, the staff would clearly articulate the following.

1. The common mission and vision for the school is "all students can and will learn." There are no excuses.

(Continued)

(Continued)

2. All staff members are responsible for every student's success, both academically and behaviorally.

3. There is a clear, articulated pyramid of support for students needing additional assistance or for those already exceeding the standards. (This answers the question "What strategies should we use to support our learners?")

4. There is a comprehensive plan for the implementation of strategies, tracking of data, and design for whole-staff discussion and involvement in supporting students through vertical teams. (This answers the question "How do we ensure that we are meeting the specific needs of individual students based on data?")

5. The focus is on students' needs, not on curriculum, although best practices and strategies for high-quality instruction are integrated into the discussion.

6. Staff unfailingly revisits the pyramid and process for implementation two times per year in order to refine and improve strategies and teamwork. This is focused on data and results of student achievement, as well as on the keys to effective teaming.

Common Mission and Vision

Creating and implementing the comprehensive plan of action was not easy, as the staff was embarking upon unchartered territory in designing a schoolwide process for supporting all students. RtI was not a national or state expectation at the time Coyote Ridge began to discuss and initiate the model it currently utilizes. In fact, the original plan started in 2000 at Skyview Elementary, another suburban school in the same district. The principal, Kari Cocozzella, began the process at this school, and then transferred to Coyote Ridge in 2003. Both schools experienced a high level of growth using the model, even though the demographics of the two schools are vastly different. The initial idea for the model can be traced back to attendance at a HOPE Institute in Denver in the fall of 2000. The concepts of a professional learning community at the high school level and Failure Is Not an Option was the crux of the conference. However, the staff quickly realized that the ideas presented could just as easily apply at the elementary level.

At both schools, it became apparent that the mission and vision of Failure Is Not an Option, "all students are all our responsibility," and "all students can and will learn" must be clearly articulated and adhered to on a daily basis. Staff spent many hours creating clear language that would guide all decision making and programming at school. Leadership from the administration was and is crucial to the continued focus on the mission and vision. Because it is so important to have shared leadership and responsibilities, teacher leaders are identified and given a comprehensible job description, which includes required skills and required classes. These teacher leaders are critical to the success of the implementation of the model currently used. (See Resource 13.)

Pyramid of Support: The Strategies

> *Purpose:* "To identify additional support systems at varying levels of intensity in *order for students to perform at their academic and/or behavioral potential.*"

Teacher leaders met to determine how to create a pyramid of support. They decided to have each grade level brainstorm every intervention or enrichment provided in individual classrooms, in the entire grade level, and included schoolwide programs. After numerous lists were created, the entire staff met to discuss all of the interventions and support systems in place. They then put them in order of most intensive (individual) to least intensive (differentiated grouping within the classroom) to create the three-tiered, color-coded pyramid. Because it is essential to include all students needing additional support, even if they are identified as gifted and talented students, the title *Pyramid of Support* is much more inclusive than *Pyramid of Intervention*.

Vertical Teaming: The Structure and System

> *Purpose:* "Vertical Teams are established to assist children who are not successful in the classroom due to issues of academics, attendance, behavior, family dynamics, and family financial issues. If a child is not showing academic growth or success in the classroom, the team will identify potential interventions/enrichment and monitor progress."

Many schools have created the tiered system of strategies for providing early intervention. They even have a focus on student outcomes rather than student deficits. The problem haunting most schools is not the issue of what to do; it is related to *how* to do it in a systematic, comprehensible, and manageable method. Coyote Ridge created vertical teams, which are facilitated by the teacher leaders. These teams are made up of representatives from grade levels, specials teachers (such as art, music, PE, and technology), special education staff, English language learner specialists, and

(Continued)

(Continued)

gifted and talented coordinators. All staff members are expected to be an integral and active part of the identified team. The group makeup, process for meetings, timelines and purpose of each meeting, and tracking of information is all identified and clearly articulated. This eliminates fragmentation of efforts and creates a laser-like focus. Statements as to how vertical teams will assist staff in becoming more cohesive and collaborative and why the teams will help students to succeed are presented in writing at the beginning of the year (see Resource 13). In addition to supporting students, the teams end up contributing to a "pyramid of support" for teachers. Those new to the building or in their first years of teaching consistently hear of strategies and approaches veteran teachers have utilized in working with struggling or low-achieving students. Veteran teachers also learn from those just starting out. Ideas for how to support parents, instructional best practices, and strategies for creating affective behavior plans for students are provided during discussions. The entire process becomes a highly effective support system for students and teachers. No one feels as though he or she is "in it alone" or "the child is only my responsibility." The opposite is in place: We are all here to help and encourage you and provide additional strategies for the child in need of support. Consequently, the entire culture and climate of the building is enhanced, due to the increased efficacy of its staff.

Constant Improvement Through Revision

Because of constant change, whether it is student population, teacher expertise, or state and federal mandates, it is imperative to revisit the Pyramid of Support and vertical team process at least once, if not two times, per year. New initiatives or legal mandates must be shared, understood, and implemented, and suggestions for more efficient approaches for teamwork serve to increase the effectiveness of the model. The initial team meeting scheduled at the start of the school is focused on the process and system in place, making sure all understand how to implement and utilize the pyramid. Team norms and expectations for participation are also reviewed. In January, the process is discussed again, just to ensure consistency and discuss any issues that may have occurred during the first semester of the year. Three times per year, each grade level meets with the principal to discuss the overall performance of all students based on required district performance assessments. Special attention is given to those students identified on the pyramid and discussed during vertical team meetings.

Student Success

Coyote Ridge has been recognized as a high-performing and high-growth school, acquiring the title of Accredited With Distinction in Colorado. In order to achieve this status, scores for all students (including English language learners and special education students) on state assessments were utilized to determine the level of student growth over time and a decrease in achievement gaps. Coyote Ridge earned 93.75% of the possible points. During the past five years, student achievement in reading, writing, math, and science has consistently increased even though the school has doubled in population and increased its English language learners by 300%. These numbers continue to rise. Conversely, the number of identified special education students has decreased. The school attributes this to the focus on early intervention, the focus on excellent first instruction, and the philosophy that "all students are all our responsibility." This belief permeates the entire building and creates a positive energy focused on the success for all students.

Source: Used with permission of Kari Cocozzella.

IMPLEMENTATION GUIDELINES

Developing a system of prevention and intervention is a major task. The approach you take will depend on both the culture of your school or district and the extent to which such strategies are already in place. Consider this approach as an example:

1. *Get verbal commitment from faculty members and define* success. Schools that have undertaken the development of mission, vision, values, and goals have already gone a long way toward accomplishing this first step. In order for a system of prevention and intervention to work, every member of the school must accept responsibility and commit to ensuring that all students learn. Part of that commitment is a continual assessment so that students who are not learning can be helped immediately.

2. *Provide examples of exemplary programs.* Share with the staff successful programs that have been implemented at other schools (including those in this book). Ask them to thoughtfully review these examples with an eye toward how they could be adapted for use in your own school.

3. *Jointly evaluate and develop a plan of action to be used when students don't learn.* Ask the staff to begin detailing a system of interventions. Aspects of the system that will need to be addressed include

- Optional support opportunities for identified underachievers (e.g., tutoring, mentoring, intensive or review classes in core academic areas, and support groups);
- Mandatory interventions for persistent low achievers (e.g., required study hall or tutoring sessions);
- High-level interventions for students who do not improve in lower-key programs (e.g., counseling and mentoring sessions with parents, support groups led by counselors, and daily check-ins with advisors).

Be sure that your staff uses any existing programs as a starting point. Ask them to consider which existing programs need to be eliminated, modified, or retained in order to fit into the newly developed system.

4. *Agree on criteria for identifying students in need of assistance and ensuring they enter the appropriate programs.* The referral of any student to a prevention or intervention program should be dependent on data that provide good evidence of his or her strengths, weaknesses, and root causes of learning difficulties. (Guidelines for the use of data are in Chapter 8.) In addition, make decisions in advance regarding what will be used as criteria for inclusion in each support program. Questions to ask include

- What criteria, data, or information will be used to identify students who are eligible for each intervention program?
- Who will help provide the information?
- Who will be responsible for gathering and evaluating the data?

5. *Surface objections and address resistance.* Techniques for doing so are covered in detail in Chapter 2 and earlier in this chapter.

6. *Pilot aspects of the new program.* Start slowly, and implement just one easily implemented aspect of the pyramid. This will allow more complete monitoring of the effectiveness of the programs, allow schools to work out any kinks, and allow for an early success to motivate further reform.

7. *Build a culture of success.* As soon as any strategy is implemented, a system for regularly monitoring its effectiveness should be established. As data come in that indicate a positive outcome, celebrate your success. In addition, be alert to any positive actions by staff or students that lead to better performance and an improved school climate. Be sure to acknowledge and praise these efforts publicly. Such public celebrations and "pats on the back" help to build a culture that believes in, values, and expects success.

8. *Refine and add to interventions.* As you receive data on the results of your programs, use the information to refine existing strategies and to better develop new ones. Continue to phase in more intervention programs and strategies as outcome and disciplinary data suggest a need.

CASE EXAMPLE

Developing a Districtwide Plan

One school district, in Pixley, California, used the Pyramid of Interventions as a jumping-off point for developing its own student improvement plan. The district used the following process.

1. Participants were introduced to the Pyramid of Interventions.

2. Participants formed small groups and began to evaluate how their existing strategies and programs could be organized in such a pyramid so that the broadest level of strategies (the base) applied to the largest number of students.

3. Using color coding, participants identified some current strategies that were philosophically sound and didn't need to change, strategies currently in place that needed to be changed to better fit the pyramid structure, and strategies that would have to be added to make the pyramid complete. (See Resources 12 and 13.)

Getting Started

Work with your colleagues to sketch plans or procedures on separate sheets of paper for (1) identifying students in need of extra support and attention; (2) monitoring these students intensively; (3) providing mentors, "good friends," or other adult support to these students; and (4) establishing intervention programs. List programs that already exist; note whether they need to be modified or expanded and, if so, in what ways. For new programs, state the specific goal and then address questions that arise.

See Resource 14 for more specific guiding questions for getting started.

In this chapter, you have seen best practices in meeting the great challenge of providing for students who *don't* initially learn to standards. This has included gaining staff commitment to the task, developing a unifying philosophy, and creating systems of prevention and intervention. These are among the greatest challenges a school will face. How schools respond to the question "What do we do when students *don't* learn?" tells more about the values and collective commitment of that school than anything else. Although this chapter has provided a clear picture of and direction for how high-performing schools tackle this challenge, the subsequent chapters will help you develop the *capacity* to use these practices to address success for *all* students in your school.

Chapter 6 Resources

Resource 12. Worksheet for Developing a School Improvement Plan

Resource 13. Pyramid of Support at Coyote Ridge Elementary School

Resource 14. Developing a System of Prevention and Intervention

These Resources for *Failure Is Not an Option,* Second Edition can be found

1. At the HOPE Foundation Web site at www.hopefoundation.org.

2. In the *Facilitator's Guide* to *Failure Is Not an Option,* Second Edition (ISBN 978-1-4129-8174-3) available for order at www.corwinpress.com.

CHAPTER 7

Principle 3

Collaborative Teaming Focused
on Teaching for Learning

I wonder how many children's lives might be saved if we educators
disclosed what we know to each other.

—Roland Barth, *Learning by Heart*

Central to the success of high-achieving schools is a collaborative culture focused on teaching and learning (Barth, 2001; Hargreaves & Fullan, 1998; Hord, 1997a, 1997b; Kruse, Louis, & Bryk, 1994; Newmann & Wehlage, 1995). This culture supports regular meetings of teachers who share responsibility for assessing needs and developing solutions that address all students' learning. Collaboration of the leadership team is the engine for shaping highly productive school cultures. Likewise, unless collaboration among teachers at all levels is the norm of that school culture, any effort to create a true learning community will fail. In our Beacon of Hope districts, this principle is the fulcrum of change for the entire district as increasingly innovative and productive approaches to collaboration occur between schools and across entire districts.

FOUR TYPES OF SCHOOL CULTURES

According to Hargreaves and Fullan (1998), when it comes to collaboration, there are four main types of school cultures.

1. Individualistic

In this type of learning environment, teachers are accustomed to developing their own practices and techniques for classroom management and may not consider the relevant experience of colleagues. In fact, in traditional school cultures, teachers often regard the intrusion of other adults into their classrooms as an invasion of privacy. In these cultures, one might hear, "Why do I have to collaborate? I'm a good teacher, and my students are doing fine!"

2. Balkanized

This culture is characterized by the presence of deep-rooted cliques within the staff. In a balkanized school environment, small groups of people align themselves with a particular technique or ideology, pitting themselves against other groups that hold opposing ideas.

Teachers may be intensely loyal to the members of their cliques and hold strongly to their ideologies, but they may have little loyalty for the school as a whole. The problem of exclusive cliques is particularly difficult to address because they can be deeply rooted in opposition to one another.

3. Contrived Collegiality

In this culture, teachers appear to be collaborating. They may spend time on committees and in meetings, but they actually don't focus on deeper issues related to teaching and learning. In these cases, the structure of the school may have changed (e.g., meetings now occur), yet the deeper culture (represented by what happens in those meetings) has not. In this instance, teachers collaborate only on the surface without challenging one another's beliefs or approaches to teaching and learning. In this culture, one might hear, "How was your weekend?" or, "Ronnie has presented some behavioral challenges for me. How about you?" or, "Overall, our test scores are improving and that's good. What's next on the agenda?"

Inside a Balkanized Culture

In balkanized cultures, team members often spend their time taking sides and vying to achieve dominance, as in the following example.

Mr. Jones:	Yesterday in my mailbox, I received the final state scores. Looking at them, it's easy to see which members of our team accomplished certain skills and which kids are lacking in certain areas. As a team, we should start talking about how to use these scores.
Ms. Rodriguez:	Well, I was thinking of not necessarily putting students in small groups, because there's not enough time to do that in one class period. They need to be divided according to their ability and placed in a classroom with all similar abilities.
Mr. Hamilton:	I agree—I think we should put them in separate classes.
Mr. Jones:	Sounds like tracking to me.
Ms. Rodriguez:	I don't think that's tracking, because they can always go into other classes depending on their level in that subject. We're not talking about every subject—we're only talking about instances in which students are struggling.
Mr. Hamilton:	I agree. I think we should put them in different classrooms.
Mr. Jones:	Sounds like another name for tracking to me.

4. Collaborative

In a collaborative school culture, professionals are fully committed to and focused on helping students learn by becoming active learners themselves. They work continuously with their colleagues to improve their teaching strategies and better manage their classrooms. They recognize their crucial role in the educational process and know that they can meet the challenges confronting them only by solving problems in concert with their professional colleagues. Teachers in a collaborative culture make specific analyses of the data—by student, by area of challenge, and by teacher—to dig for areas of improvement and change teaching practices accordingly. For example, one might hear, "I noticed your students are scoring higher on problems that test for reading comprehension. Can I watch you teach a class? Would you watch me teach too and provide feedback?" Collaboration, in other words, extends beyond the meeting; it goes into the classroom.

In sum, the collaboration in these schools is based on four elements:

1. Specific data regarding performance by individual students, individual teachers, and specific areas of instruction (e.g., decimals or syntax).

2. Trusting, structured, yet intensive conversations around these data.

3. Commitment to action (example: structured and frequent learning walks—see Resource 15).

CASE EXAMPLE

 Collaborative Teaming in Action

In order to demonstrate the power of a team, a principal in Fort Wayne, Indiana, used an activity called "Consultation" with the staff. The principal recruited a staff member who had a unique student issue that needed a solution. At the next staff meeting, this teacher sat at a table with six other volunteers from the teaching staff. The teacher shared her problem, and then the team asked clarifying questions for 10 minutes.

The teacher then had to remain quiet while the team discussed the situation with each other but not directly with the teacher herself. The teacher then was asked to respond to the discussion she had heard. As this process unfolded, everyone's engagement was very strong. At the end of the session, the staff was asked to comment. One member said, "If this is the power of collaboration and it could help me this way, I'm all for it."

Taking the above example to the next level, teams would then commit to specific actions. There should always be a "now what?" as part of concluding any meeting. As a matter of regular course, future meetings would include these agenda items:

1. What new techniques were tried?

2. What were the outcomes, and what is your evidence for them?

3. What worked? What did not work? What are your recommendations?

4. Evaluation of outcomes from actions decided in number 3 above, continuous improvement of practice, and refinement of goals based on that evaluation.

Schools with a successful culture of collaboration are aware that not all collaboration is necessarily good. Collaboration must take place with the overall success of the students in mind. The type of collaboration these schools foster is an open-ended inquiry that incorporates new ideas from both inside and outside the team. The team itself becomes a mini–learning community, actively seeking best practices from other members, as well as other schools and literature on best practice.

THE AIM OF COLLABORATION

Collaboration among colleagues is a means to an end: enhancing teaching for learning. To accomplish this, team members work *interdependently* toward a common goal (see SMART goals in Chapter 5). This goal, in turn, supports the larger school vision and is aligned with the school's mission and values. As a result, the school's mission, vision, values, and goals provide context and direction for all team members.

Teams will invariably look at data (see Chapter 8) to assess how they are doing relative to their SMART goals. Members collectively brainstorm ways to improve, and they celebrate successes. Being committed to constant improvement, these teams will always find ways to raise the bar once their current goals have been accomplished. The high school that consistently graduates 99% of its students can, for example, determine to gauge their success by readiness of those graduates for success in and after college.

CASE EXAMPLE

Interest-Based Bargaining (IBB) With Teacher Unions: Looking for Common Interests Builds Sustainable Partnership

In looking for examples of districts that were making gains both in assuring teacher quality and in reducing gaps in student achievement, we continually came to two districts, one being Hamilton County, Tennessee.

(Continued)

(Continued)

Success can be directly linked to the collaboration of the local teachers' union and the school district. Their single-minded focus on improving student achievement and a willingness to be flexible allowed these two, potentially adversarial, groups to work together with outstanding results. Their story is proof that unions and districts can collaborate successfully to improve student achievement. Hamilton County also provide guidance to other districts as they seek support in teaching and learning for all. Hamilton County reached a turning point in their reform efforts when union and district leaders began to successfully collaborate on a sustained basis that attracted the interest and support of a critical group of community partners and funders. A major factor in the reform success of Hamilton County was the districts and the teachers' unions utilizing Interest Based Bargaining (IBB), a powerful tool that enables those negotiating to become joint problem solvers. IBB is a negotiation strategy in which parties collaborate to find a "win-win" solution to their dispute. This strategy focuses on developing mutually beneficial agreements based on the interests of all parties.

This is additional background on Hamilton County and recommendations from the report.

Hamilton County, Tennessee: Background

In 1998, City and County school systems merged, bringing together two very different districts:

- 4.1% of students in Hamilton County were African American compared to 62.9% in Chattanooga.
- 6.5% of Hamilton County schools participated in the Title I program compared to 30.8% in Chattanooga. Of these, 92.3% of Hamilton County Title I schools were meeting expectations compared to 20% of those in Chattanooga.
- 19.9% of students in Hamilton County were eligible for free and reduced lunch compared to 59% in Chattanooga.
- Nine of the lowest performing schools in the State of Tennessee were located within the borders of the City of Chattanooga.
- Teachers in the lowest performing schools were extremely dissatisfied, often transferring out of these schools in the fall and leaving them without a full teaching staff for several weeks of a new school year. Hamilton County's challenge was gaining teacher buy-in and leadership support for K–12 systemic change that closes achievement gaps.

The Results and Outcomes of Collaboration

The Hamilton County School District has made impressive improvements in teacher quality and significant gains in student achievement since implementing a collaborative reform effort.

Hamilton County has achieved great success in shrinking the achievement gaps and improving student achievement at all levels. In 1999, 12% of third-grade students in the Benwood schools (schools ranked worst in the city and part of a major reform effort funded by the Benwood Foundation) were reading at proficient or advanced levels. By 2003, more than half (53%) achieved this level—and by 2006, almost three-quarters (73%) had reached the proficient or advanced levels. Additionally, in 2002, the first year in which the union agreed to the "reconstitution" of struggling schools and to the bonuses to attract and retain teachers at these schools, the number of teachers new to their schools reached an all-time high of 31.4%. By 2005, that number had dropped to 17.9%.

Hamilton County has achieved districtwide reforms that improved teaching and learning. These gains were a direct result of the collaboration between the union and the school district and the communitywide partnership that developed to support their work.

- Teacher transfers became more efficient and more supportive of staffing all schools with good teachers, particularly those with a history of low levels of student achievement.
- Pay incentives were implemented to award high-performing teachers and schools.
- Site-based school planning was implemented to support systemic goals, with school leadership teams throughout the district.
- Waivers were granted to allow flexibility at the school level to meet the needs of students.
- Central office positions were eliminated and funds were used to create school-based positions to support teaching and learning.
- Change Coaches were put into place in all middle and high schools.
- Teams were developed across grade levels and within role-alike groups to support teaching and learning.
- Principal networks have been established at each educational level within the district, elementary, middle, and high school.
- Family support specialists serve as a liaison between middle schools and families.
- Small learning communities were developed in all high schools.

(Continued)

(Continued)

- High school curricular and graduation requirements were increased for all students.
- A "vertical team," which includes a high school and all of the elementary and middle schools that feed into it, has been established in one feeder alignment to ensure every kindergarten student graduates from high school with his or her classmates.
- Analysis and use of data to support instruction is a norm throughout the district and is supported by analysts whose job it is to support administrators, teachers and families as they seek to understand and effectively use data.
- Evaluation was built into reform, with feedback from all stakeholders collected and valued.

Since reform efforts began in 2003, the percentage of middle school students scoring advanced and proficient in reading/language arts has risen across Hamilton County, but particularly in high needs schools. A 25.9 percentage point achievement gap in 2003 was reduced to a 19.9% gap in 2006. In those three years, the achievement gap in middle school math dropped from 25.8% to 17.4%. Finally, Hamilton County high schools are also making gains in promotion rates, on-time graduation rates, and numbers of graduates enrolled in college. The percentage of ninth-grade students receiving a "proficient" or "advanced" rating on the Algebra Gateway exam rose, as did performance of tenth graders on the English Gateway exams.

Lessons

Every district will come to reform on different paths, and the reforms they implemented will be unique, yet the lessons drawn from the Hamilton County story will resonate with other districts seeking to improve education for all students. The following points will help guide school districts and teachers' unions as they seek to collaborate and achieve systemic school reform.

1. *Systemic reform cannot take place without the active formal and informal involvement of the district administration and the education association (union).* That point cannot be stressed enough; every other lesson flows from it. These two groups are the core of the reform effort, and their cooperation forms the foundation upon which other partners and funders are willing to invest the time and resources in working with the district.

2. *All stakeholders must have a comprehensive, common vision that focuses on student learning and is guided by instructional improvement.* This common vision must be the focus of the reform plan, implementation

design, investment of resources, professional development, monitoring, and assessments. It must be revisited regularly and modified as necessary throughout the process. The core of this vision for change must be the shared belief that all children—whatever their ethnic, socioeconomic, cultural background or prior academic success—can attain high levels of academic achievement.

3. *It is extremely useful to create a dedicated time and retreat space where the key stakeholders can initially meet to work out the details of the reform plan.* In the case of Hamilton County, the National Education Association's Challenge of Change Conference provided a place away from normal day-to-day operations where the key parties were able to get to know and trust one another.

4. *Interest-Based Bargaining creates a sound structure for working through issues and goals.* IBB shifts the focus of negotiations to the shared goal of student achievement. It is critical that all key stakeholders participate in the IBB training program. Those who find they cannot support the process should withdraw from the process. If a person who must withdraw has a key leadership position (i.e., superintendent, assistant superintendent of instruction, association president or UniServ Director), the capacity to collaborate may be in question and must be reconsidered.

5. *All stakeholders must recognize and respect the fragile, critical, and essential nature of trust relationships and must actively work to protect and nurture this trust, especially at the beginning of the process.* They must be willing to share needed information. If it is not possible to share certain kinds information, the reasons must be given with honesty. This also means that key stakeholders must be willing to work with their constituents to ensure that they understand the basis for and structure of the collaborative process.

6. *All parties must keep their constituencies informed of the reform goals and progress.* Other representatives of stakeholder groups who are not operationally involved in the day-to-day working of the initiative (e.g., board members, other members of the superintendent's cabinet, foundation leadership, teachers, parents) should also be kept informed of the reform processes and progress, to ensure continuing support and later sustainability.

7. *The stakeholder leaders should be ready to approach foundations and outside funders as a team, presenting a common agenda.* When working with funders, leaders should emphasize their common goals, reputation for integrity and cooperation, and history of involvement in quality projects.

(Continued)

(Continued)

In short, building an atmosphere of inclusiveness, trust, and cooperation from the start is essential to the success of the partnership.

Concluding Comments

At the heart of this report is the challenge of change. School districts must constantly evolve if they are to meet the needs of their changing student body. Change can be chaotic, disruptive, and destructive, or it can be harnessed to become a coherent, engaging and constructive process. Hamilton County took the latter path, rising to the occasion with creativity and determination to build better schools, ensuring that improved student achievement would be the ultimate outcome of their reform efforts. Their story stands as evidence that, with strong collaboration among key partners, dedicated education leaders can improve learning opportunities for every child in their community. For more on how Hamilton County made dramatic gains in student achievement through union and school district collaboration, NCTAF's full report *Reducing the Achievement Gap Through District/Union Collaboration: The Tale of Two School Districts* may be found at http://www.nctaf.org/resources/research_ and_reports/nctaf_ research_reports/index.htm

Source: National Commission on Teaching and America's Future and National Education Association, *Reducing The Achievement Gap Through District/Union Collaboration: The Tale of Two School Districts,* http://www.nctaf.org/resources/research_and_reports /nctaf_research_reports/index.htm

Note: The National Commission on Teaching and America's Future is grateful to the NEA Foundation, under the leadership of President and CEO Harriet Sanford, for the generous financial support and assistance in all aspects of producing this report. As a key partner in the Hamilton County reform efforts, the NEA Foundation recognized how important it is to share the story of closing achievement gaps through district/union collaboration. They encouraged the National Commission on Teaching and America's Future (NCTAF) to bring the story to a wider audience, and to add a second district's story to the report. http://www.neafoundation .org; 202-822-7840 (phone) ; 202-822-7779 (fax).

AREAS OF COLLABORATION

In setting up collaborative teams, it is important to choose the appropriate members. Team members should share common students or common problems, and the issues they deal with should be of concern to all members. Following are some areas that may lend themselves to collaboration.

Note how each of these teams' work connects to the other five principles in Failure Is Not an Option.

- *Professional Practice Forums.* Teachers who work with similar grade levels, or who teach related areas, should work together. They present colleagues with accounts of strategies that work for them, share concerns, describe challenges, research best practices, and plan new strategies.

- *Classroom Observation.* Teachers observe classes of colleagues who are experimenting with new strategies or techniques. Through observation, they learn about new strategies and can help evaluate how well the innovation is working. Similarly, teachers can regularly observe classes of teachers having specific problems to provide constructive suggestions and support.

- *Curriculum Planning.* Relevant groups or committees frequently meet to plan and monitor curriculum sequence and coordination. They may determine who teaches what subject area, what content will be covered, what skills they teach, which students they teach, and in what order. They synchronize knowledge and skills that students should have acquired at specific times and when they are supposed to have acquired them. They may also determine which assessments to use in order to gauge whether all students have successfully mastered core knowledge and skills in each academic area.

- *Vertical Teams.* Vertical teams differ from grade-level teams by gathering representatives from different grade levels for collaboration (e.g., reading teachers from Grades 2–5 work together with English language learner specialists and library/media specialists). This eliminates fragmentation of efforts. (See Case Story 5 in Chapter 6.)

- *Professional Study Groups.* Teachers research and report to colleagues on articles and books containing matters of professional interest, or they share the information gained at workshops or conferences. They may occasionally invite speakers or guests from outside the school with expertise on matters of interest to them.

- *Grade-Level or Subject-Area Teams.* These teams can identify curricular outcomes, determine methods of assessing student progress, select instructional materials, plan and present professional development programs in support of team-identified issues, and participate in observation and monitoring programs for mutual support.

- *Interdisciplinary Teams.* Such teams deal with the same groups of students (e.g., all teachers of ninth graders) to focus on the curriculum and the needs of students. Case Story 1 in Chapter 1 provides an example of such a team focused on common reading strategies used in areas as diverse as PE and math.

- *Task Forces.* These teams are drawn from all areas of the school to study and develop recommendations for dealing with a specific problem affecting the entire building, such as the best way to handle tardy students. Task forces dissolve when their task is completed.

- *Teaching Strategy or Professional Interest Teams.* Staff members who are interested in a specific approach or innovation (e.g., cooperative learning) form groups to research the approach; receive training; develop implementation strategies; and provide reciprocal observation, review, and evaluation. As with task forces, these teams are relatively short lived.

WHAT GOOD LOOKS LIKE

Think It Through . . .

Which of the four types of collaboration are most prevalent in your school? How is team effectiveness measured in your school? How frequently and in what ways do staff members in your school work together to solve problems or plan improvements? How are conflicts handled?

Schools where collaboration is the norm share some very distinct characteristics. They include the following.

- The staff members are committed to a shared mission, vision, values, and goals, and they recognize their responsibility to work together to accomplish them.
- Strong leaders engage teachers in meaningful collaboration and support their activities and decisions.
- The school is characterized by a culture of trust and respect that permits open and willing sharing of ideas and respect for different approaches and teaching styles.
- Decisions are data based and depersonalized.
- The staff has real authority to make decisions about teaching and learning.
- Meetings are well managed and truly democratic, following established protocols for setting the agenda and making decisions.
- The functioning of teams is frequently discussed and reassessed.
- A plan is developed to provide meaningful time for teams to meet. (See Chapter 3 and Resource 7 for strategies on making time to collaborate.)
- Each team has clear purposes and goals.
- Educators acquire and share training in effective teamwork strategies.

CASE EXAMPLE

Cross-Departmental Teaming

At the seventh-grade teachers' weekly meeting, one of the science teachers proposes a problem with science and social studies teachers. She explains that although science and social studies are tested on the state tests this year, the class schedule allows much less time for those subjects than for math and language arts. She presents her concern with getting her students ready for the tests, given the limited teaching time.

The team leader acknowledges the legitimacy of the problem and opens the floor for other teachers to propose solutions. Soon, a collaborative strategy is formed:

Language Arts Teacher 1:   I realize that you have a lot of reading material in Science and Social Studies that is difficult. And Mr. Evans and I would be glad to take some of that material and use it for our self-selected reading periods.

Language Arts Teacher 2:   And maybe if you could get us information about what you were going to do during the following week, Ms. Shaw and I could collaborate to make sure that the questions we propose are similar to the kinds of questions asked on the state test. That way, you're not only reinforcing your science and social studies skills but also working on how to answer the questions.

Math Teacher: Regarding the mathematics aspect, Mrs. Atterman and I could help to teach measuring skills. I know that in science one does a lot of measuring—and I know from my student-teaching experience last year that a lot of students really need help with that. Also, if you had a set of data, we could use graphing calculators—especially with the gifted class—and let them do a presentation on that data.

(Continued)

(Continued)

| **Science Teacher:** | Okay . . . well, let's sit down and bounce these ideas off some other people in our department and see what we can come up with in the way of a schedule. We'll also want to determine what a "success" will look like in terms of student learning and how we'll know if this effort is successful. Let's get input on these questions and discuss this again next Friday. |

Think It Through . . .

The first Case Example in Chapter 1 demonstrates how cross-departmental teams addressed the development of writing across subject areas. How are teaching strategies like those shared and continuously improved by teachers throughout your school?

The preceding scenario shows one aspect of true collaboration. The teachers jointly accept responsibility for student learning—*across* subjects, not just in their own classrooms—and work together to overcome an obstacle. They also commit to defining *success* before trying this new approach and assessing their efforts toward that success. While in this meeting, they are addressing structural—and not pedagogical—issues; the spirit of collaboration and jointly solving the problem is clear.

IMPLEMENTATION GUIDELINES

After forming teams to work on different aspects of teaching and learning in your school, teams will establish protocols. Ideally, decisions should be written down and signed by each team member. Some of the questions may appear to impose an unnatural formality on friends and colleagues who have long worked casually together, but deciding these issues in advance will help to avoid future problems. (Note: See the implementation guidelines in Chapter 5 before proceeding. This section assumes an understanding of the material presented there.)

1. Team Organization

- What should the team organization be?
- Will there be a chair? If so, who? What responsibilities will he or she have?
- If there is no chair, how will operational decisions be made? Consider such details as time and place of successive meetings, responsibility for minutes or other team records, and so on.
- Who will be responsible for acting as spokesperson for the team?

2. Decision Making

- Will the team's decisions be made by democratic vote? By consensus? How will conflicts be resolved?
- What commitment can be made to team members who may end up on the losing side of a debate or in a minority position?

3. Managing Meetings

- How will discussions and debates be managed or led?
- In what way can the team ensure that each member will have a turn to speak but that no one will be permitted to dominate or divert the members from the task at hand?

4. Sharing the Workload

- How can the team ensure that all members will share the workload equally, so that no member is overburdened in comparison to the rest?

5. Commitment of Team Members

- Develop an agreement (preferably written, but at least a clearly articulated verbal statement) in which each member commits to (1) attending all team meetings, (2) working toward consensus on each matter of difference, (3) speaking openly and candidly with each other while respecting different opinions, (4) ensuring that each team member's input and views are sought and heard, and (5) supporting the team's decisions when a consensus is reached.

6. Communication Protocols

- As team members work on different tasks, how should they alert other members of problems, situations, events, results, or other matters?
- If a developing problem requires discussion by the entire team, what is the protocol for calling a meeting?
- Who will be responsible for keeping and disseminating minutes of each meeting, copies of information gathered, reports of task forces, survey or focus group results, worksheets and planning forms completed jointly, and any other pertinent documents? These are the basis for the team's communications with the rest of the learning community, and they must be accurately maintained.

7. Monitoring Team Progress

- At what point and in what way will you, as a team, evaluate your effectiveness in carrying out your mandate?
- What steps will you contemplate if it appears you are not working very effectively?

When the previous issues are settled, begin to address your assigned task:

a. Establish Goals

- Articulate short-term or intermediate goals within the larger purpose assigned to you.

b. Prioritize and Assign Tasks

- Decide whether you will work on the short-term goals in sequence or simultaneously.
- If the latter, who will work on each?

c. Decide on a Sequence and Timetable of Tasks

- What are the first steps to take toward achieving the first goals?
- What is the timeline for taking these steps?
- How soon should the team (or a subgroup of the team) meet again to discuss progress, findings, or results?
- What task will each member complete before the next meeting?

8. Implement and Institutionalize the Successes

- How will successes be spread and then institutionalized beyond the team?
- How will you systematically close the "implementation gap"?
- There are high-performing teams and individuals in every school and district. How will one person's successes with low-performing students, for example, become the *norm*, even long after that person has retired?

Other agreements around the eight items just mentioned should also be regularly reviewed and easily accessible. Some 80% to 90% of the challenges in meetings are structural or procedural (sidebar conversations, people coming unprepared, etc.) and are not about content. To eliminate these issues, it helps to standardize meeting formats, posting the "desired outcomes (dos) for the meeting at the top of the agenda, and listing the agenda and protocols for all to see and refer to during the meeting.

CHALLENGES

Collaboration is not natural or common in the traditional school environment. For generations, teachers characteristically closed the classroom door behind them and acted as independent monarchs of their own domains, expecting neither oversight nor support from colleagues. One principal commented that he had to use a crowbar to get one of his teachers out for knee surgery. Teachers with problems may frequently feel ashamed to ask for help, believing that their plea will be interpreted as confusion or a confession of failure. Such feelings and the traditional school culture have given rise to several identified challenges to collaboration.

CASE EXAMPLE

Phasing in Collaboration

When Linda Jonaitis, former principal of Clifford Pierce Middle School, moved to Highland High School, in Highland, Indiana, she knew she would be starting all over again in terms of collaborative teaming. While the

(Continued)

(Continued)

the teachers at her former school had become comfortable with constant collaboration, it was still a new concept to those at Highland. "They didn't know how to do it, and they didn't feel safe or comfortable," she said. "They still felt territorial."

Linda realized that she would have to move slowly and carefully in order to avoid scaring off her new staff. Her solution was to seek out those teachers who were most likely to try something new and draw them into teaming first.

> I identified teachers who felt safe, who appeared as though they might be willing to take risks. I did that by talking with people in the district and by forming relationships with the teachers either through committee work or one on one.

She explains, "I'm working with them first, and then will use them as role models to encourage risk-taking and build that climate of safety."

Source: Used with permission from Linda Jonaitis.

Challenge: "Sure, I'll collaborate . . . whatever."

Collaboration is an ideal that is often articulated by the administration and staff of a school but, in fact, is not optimized. When teamwork is undertaken, the goal is often not seen as serious or as drawing on the pooled experience and knowledge of team members. Without a shared commitment to work together to address a common concern, and real responsibility for developing a solution, collaboration becomes an empty gesture.

Solution: This requires changes in the school culture. Making a structural change is not enough to truly foster collaboration among teachers. The culture will need to shift to one in which collaborative teaming is valued as the most effective way to help students learn. Information about making culture shifts is found in Chapter 3.

Challenge: "I'll go to the meetings, but I really can't take on any responsibilities beyond that."

Members who assume that their presence at meetings suffices as a gesture toward collaboration can undermine the improvement process. Meetings are actually only the visible part of collaboration; every successful team requires members to think, read, discuss, write, phone, or do any of a number of other tasks between meetings. If nothing of this sort is done, successive meetings simply retread old ground.

Solution: Clarify expectations at the outset. Make sure team members understand what collaborative teaming is really all about—and what role they will be expected to play in it. Don't sugarcoat the process or lead them to believe that it will consist only of meetings that take place from 9:00 to 9:50 a.m. Also, be sure that each team has enough members, so that assigned tasks, when shared equitably, are not too burdensome for any one member.

Challenge: "I'll go to the meetings, but I'm not going to get sucked into the discussion."

Silent resistance is a common challenge among teams, with certain members simply refusing to become engaged in the group's conversations or efforts.

Solution: Break into smaller groups. Break the larger team into several subteams, so each member will have the responsibility for collecting information or ideas and then reporting back to the larger group. It may also be possible to ward off fatigue or complacency with groups by encouraging physical activity in a meeting. These moments can prevent disaffected members from retreating into passivity. Consider also a regular and well-facilitated book study to develop a common knowledge base and group cohesion. If there are holdouts to participation after using these and other such techniques, there may be other concerns that need to be addressed. See Chapter 3 and Resource 9 on dealing with resistance.

Challenge: "I'm willing to collaborate . . . but exactly what are we trying to accomplish?"

Collaboration must have the goal of improving student achievement if it is to pay off. Team members can lack focus and direction, ultimately accomplishing little.

Solution: Set and clarify the desired outcome of the meeting in keeping with the larger context or purpose of the team's overall work. When teachers understand that the end goal of their collaborative efforts—and of every meeting—is to boost student success, they tend to be much more focused and productive. Providing feedback and data on "quick wins" and short-term goals is also motivating.

Challenge: "Why are we always tinkering with the way things work? I'm happy with the way my classes are run, and my students are doing just fine."

In Chapter 3, we stated that people may like a given change, but often don't like changing. Ironic as this may sound, it is a common problem—people often resist change, especially when it means that *they* have to change.

Solution: Let people see the possible outcomes. Before launching the change process, make sure faculty members understand what the change is designed to accomplish. If you have developed a compelling vision statement and clear measurable goals, use these tools to paint a picture of where you are headed, and why. (Additional strategies are in Chapter 3 and Resource 11.)

Challenge: "There's no way I'm doing this. I'm completely opposed to it."

Occasionally, a team member will resist a team decision, no matter how much consensus building may have taken place within the team.

Solution: Confront dissenters in a respectful and positive way. Confront team members who seem to be holding back, listen to their reservations or negative response to a team decision, and then insist that the team's consensus decision must be enacted in spite of the individual member's opposition. Then lay out a plan that combines support for the teacher who must change as well as oversight to make sure the change occurs.

Often, as pointed out in Chapter 3, real challenges to collaboration, such as lack of time, become reasons for abandoning the effort altogether. The story below provides an example of how a district addressed multiple issues related to collaboration.

CASE EXAMPLE

Making Time for Teaming

The Newport News elementary schools, in Newport News, Virginia, solved the problem of collaboration years ago—and though it wasn't an easy change at first, it has paid off. The school system extended its school day by 15 minutes on Monday, Tuesday, Thursday, and Friday, gaining an extra hour of instructional time. On Wednesdays, the students are released early—and the entire staff has collaborative planning time. The time is dedicated exclusively to collaboration and cannot be used for anything else.

Convincing the community to accept the new schedule was difficult; parents and other caregivers were unprepared for the Wednesday early dismissal. The school system had to work hard to build support for it, meeting with community agencies, parks and recreation representatives, and other leaders. Ultimately, however, the community not only accepted the new schedule but actively embraced it, developing new programs and opportunities for kids to take advantage of on Wednesdays. (See Resource 7 for strategies for making time.)

CONCLUSION

Building truly collaborative teams is a difficult but necessary component of school success. This chapter illuminated four types of cultures relative to collaboration. Brief examples of productive collaboration in schools throughout North America were also provided.

The next chapter addresses gathering and using the essential fuel for productive collaboration: meaningful data tied to results for all students. Chapter 8 will go into detail on how to collect, analyze, discuss, and put such data into action on behalf of student achievement.

Chapter 7 Resource

Resource 15. Instructional Learning Walks

This Resource for *Failure Is Not an Option,* Second Edition can be found

1. At the HOPE Foundation Web site at www.hopefoundation.org.

2. In the *Facilitator's Guide* to *Failure Is Not an Option,* Second Edition (ISBN 978-1-4129-8174-3) available for order at www.corwinpress.com.

CHAPTER 8

Principle 4

*Data-Based Decision Making
for Continuous Improvement*

Effective assessment procedures and use of the resulting data are fundamental to a school's improvement. Since the first edition of this book, there have been many advances in the tools for collecting and dissecting data, as well as use of that information for meaningful assessments. In the beginning of this chapter, we provide well-established frameworks for determining which data to collect and how to best use it. The latter part of this chapter is dedicated primarily to some advanced work recently completed with Jay McTighe, based on his and Ken O'Connor's seven assessment and grading practices to enhance learning and teaching (McTighe & O'Connor, 2005; HOPE Foundation, 2009b).

POSSIBLE USES OF DATA

Good data used appropriately offer a multitude of benefits for schools and their stakeholders:

- To provide feedback to students on academic progress
- To screen students for special programs
- To inform parents of student performance and inform the larger community of school and district gains
- To inform teacher judgments about improving classroom instruction
- To organize schoolwide learning support programs to assure no student falls through the cracks

- To validate student and teacher efforts to improve
- To guide professional development activities
- To gauge program strengths and identify opportunities for program improvements
- To promote public accountability
- To monitor continuous progress (Fullan & St. Germain, 2006).

To successfully use data to drive continuous improvement, schools need to answer three important questions:

- What data should be collected?
- How should data be used?
- Who should be involved?

Each of these points will be discussed in the sections that follow.

WHAT DATA SHOULD BE COLLECTED?

Many schools rely on state or provincial and national standardized test scores as the primary indicator of student learning. These scores can provide evidence of systemwide and schoolwide achievement and, when properly disaggregated, can help identify students in need of additional support and intervention (as outlined in Chapter 6). Increasingly, schools are tracking a broader set of data types to more fully assess their progress. Data sources include the following:

Academic Outcomes

- Outcomes on nationally normed tests
- Student performance on district or school-level common assessments
- Grade spread on unit tests or semester exams, compared with previous results
- Course and curriculum analysis to measure alignment with state and national standards
- Graduation rates for high schools
- Continuing education levels, such as the percentages of graduating students pursuing higher education or the percentage of students entering regular or honors high school classes (after junior high or middle school)
- Outcomes on state or provincial achievement tests compared with previous years and with other schools of similar demographics

Correlates to Student Achievement

- Engagement levels of students in extracurricular activities
- Attendance numbers, including enrollments and dropouts during the course of a year and hour-by-hour or class-by-class attendance figures
- Discipline actions, such as the number of in- or out-of-school suspensions, the number of repeat cases, and times and places of their occurrence

Descriptive Data

- Census, enrollment, and lunch subsidy applications, to profile the demographics of the whole school
- Observations of daily activities, occurrences, and situations that would not appear in any type of formal record keeping
- Surveys of students, staff, and parents to gauge satisfaction and attitudes toward the school

Data overload is common, and narrowing what is needed and how to best use it is a challenge. The Case Example below demonstrates how one Beacon of Hope District school is grappling with it.

Think It Through . . .

In your school or district, what data besides test scores have guided recent decisions and planning? Can you think of other data sources that would have provided you with helpful information to make better decisions? How do you present and share data to get a comprehensive picture of each student?

CASE EXAMPLE

A Hard Approach to Soft Data

At Icenhower Intermediate School in Mansfield, Texas, grade-level Student Success Teams (SSTs) piece together a comprehensive picture of each student using shared spreadsheets to track student behavior, office referrals, academics, engagement, attendance, and other data. "You may think a student is excelling in your classroom," commented one teacher, but when you look at the data on the spreadsheet, you realize there are extreme deficits somewhere else. And even though you see those kids all day long, you may not know to what extent they are struggling in another class.

Sixth-grade counselor Reggie Rhines notes that SST members consider themselves to be facilitators:

We track what they're doing and what they've done in the past at their different schools. So, if they come to us already struggling and at risk, we refer to a rich array of data to diagnose the situation. We look to and talk with the parents, we try to put in modifications to help them be more successful, whether it be adding constant mastery to their day or reducing the amount of work they have to get done because they struggle so much. And then, of course, we place them into tutoring groups and other realms where they can get extra help as well.

Combining hard demographic and formal assessments with soft data about engagement and behavior—while protecting student confidentiality— is a complex task. Principal Duane Thurston comments, "You can't boil it all down to get one answer; it is much more complex than that. Yet, having a group of professionals looking at the same expansive set of data helps."

Source: Used with permission from Duane Thurston and Reggie Rhines.

HOW SHOULD DATA BE USED?

What has been discovered is that first, people will not voluntarily share information–especially if it is unflattering—unless they feel some moral commitment to do so and trust that the data will not be used against them. . . . Data without relationships merely causes more information glut. Put another way, turning information into knowledge is a social process and for that you need good relationships.

—Michael Fullan , *Leading in a Culture of Change*, p. 6

In addition to collecting and formatting data for good decision making, the analysis of data itself is a skill that requires development. There are many conclusions that can be derived from a given set of data. The following Case Example provides one example of how a school team sorted through test scores to determine the root cause of some student-performance issues.

CASE EXAMPLE

Using Data to Identify Root Causes

One Illinois school district used data analysis to pinpoint an easily resolved problem area. The approach of DuPage District 88 to analyzing test scores involved looking at individual test items to discover areas of weakness. Nancy Sindelar, former assistant superintendent for curriculum, instruction, and development, explained,

> When you get the assessment results, there are a number of things that you can change: curriculum, instruction, or assessment. In the course of one of our analyses, we discovered that our high-scoring students were struggling with measurement—so we researched the issue further to see why.

> In that particular case, the school opted to change the curriculum. "It turned out that when our students were in sixth grade, they learned both standard and metric measurements simultaneously, and they were confused," Nancy said. "We changed the curriculum so that it had more material on measurement, and we purchased rulers that had both kinds of measurements. After that, we saw an improvement in measurement-related assessment items."

Source: Used with permission from Nancy Sindelar.

Ideally, achievement data are at the foundation of constructive, collective decisions regarding instructional goals, curricular emphases, prevention and intervention systems, and overall programs and policies. One of the most powerful and effective ways of working with data is for vertical or grade-level teams to analyze student work together based on common assessments or assignments. This process encourages all faculty members to share in the responsibility for success of *all* students.

Results-oriented data analysis should include such questions as

- What criteria will be used to determine proficiency?
- Does this piece of work show proficiency?
- In what areas are students doing particularly well?
- What are patterns of weakness?
- What can be done to address the weak areas?

Teachers who are accustomed to using data strictly as an evaluative or summative device—to determine whether students did or did not learn what was required—may need training and encouragement to add formative assessment to their instructional practice. As trust among teachers grows (see Chapter 4) and as team-meeting protocols become well established (see Chapter 7), data sharing among teachers becomes easier. This is always done with the intent of collegial sharing of internal best practices. It is never used to rank or blame individual teachers for poor performance.

CASE EXAMPLE

Overcoming Fear of Data

Principal John E. McKenna (2009b) of Mullen Elementary School in Tonawanda, New York, reports that his school relies on "data, data, and more data . . . to ensure that we maintain an absolute focus on student achievement." Grade-level teams and vertical teams in language arts, math, science, social studies, and technology integration use running records, Qualitative Reading Inventories (QRIs), and daily anecdotal notes from guided reading sessions. Teams meet for data reviews at frequent intervals:

- *Quarterly.* To assess data from the prior quarter and to set benchmarks and action plans for the quarter to come
- *Monthly.* To discuss instructional goals and data
- *Weekly.* To assess progress against benchmarks
- *Daily.* For a 30-minute common planning period before school. (McKenna, 2009b)

An essential first step to implementing the new protocol was McKenna's realization that he had to build relational trust to help teachers move past their fear that data might show they weren't good teachers or that data might be used against them by school administrators. "I had to stop using top down, judgmental methods and move to a nonjudgmental, bottom up approach where we worked together and assumed mutual responsibility for our students' success," says McKenna.

Specific methods and strategies recommended by McKenna for principals who want to help teachers learn to trust data include

- *Direct Involvement.* Principals who administer assessments to students and correct them with teachers are "getting in the trenches." This changes data dialogue from top-down and directive to affiliating and collaborative.
- *Be Proactive.* Developing an assessment map or schedule outlining all of the year's formative and summative assessments helps teachers know what to expect and how to prepare with no surprises.

(Continued)

(Continued)

- *Periodic Review.* Align team meetings to analyze and discuss data with the year's assessment schedule. The more dialogue about data, the more comfortable teachers feel about it.
- *Set Specific and Realistic Goals.* Measure goals in small, incremental steps, building on success.
- *Develop a Long-Range Plan.* Identify data goals for three to five years in advance. Each time teachers achieve incremental goals, principals can remind them that they are one step closer to the long-range goal.
- *Shift Responsibility of Analysis to Teachers.* Principals who begin with direct involvement—modeling data analysis and leading conversations in data review meetings—can scaffold the transfer of responsibility to staff as competencies increase.
- *Empower Teacher Leaders.* Some teachers will grasp the data better than others. In fact, many will surpass the principal's knowledge because they apply it daily. It is important to empower these teachers to lead data meetings and present at faculty meetings. They can serve as turnkey trainers and mentors for other teachers and new staff.

"I know I've been successful in working with teachers when I say very little in a meeting," says McKenna. "The teachers know where their strengths and weaknesses are. They feel comfortable with the data and feel proud of their accomplishments. That's when data actually become the teachers' friend."

Source: Used with permission from John McKenna.

WHO SHOULD BE INVOLVED?

Often, data are collected too far from the source to be useful to those who need the information. To be most effective, the use of data is best determined at least in part by those most responsible for learning. For example, teachers should be involved in determining which data most closely measure the current level of achievement and which data will be used to gauge and monitor improvement.

Think It Through . . .

Who, in your experience, usually collects the data for your school or district? Who controls access to the data that are available? Does everyone "own" the data pertaining to their students?

GUIDELINES FOR DATA QUALITY

A school's ability to make improvement plans is directly tied to the quality of its data. Without clear, quantifiable information about the school's current status, leaders will find it very difficult to create focused improvement plans. Data from diverse sources guide each step of planning and implementing initiatives for academic improvement. At a minimum, useful data should be multisourced, relevant, timely, consistent, and disaggregated.

Multisourced Data

The data collected should be drawn from a variety of sources in order to give a complete picture of a school's progress. Many of those sources are discussed in the first section of this chapter, titled "What Data Should Be Collected?" Data should include demographic and socioeconomic information, absentee rates, dropout rates, suspension and disciplinary rates, report card grades, and, of course, scores on state and nationally normed tests.

A school is more than a set of numbers, however, and student, teacher, and parent perceptions of their learning community are an essential part of its achievement. Uncovering and recording these perceptions is a fundamental part of the improvement process. Doing so requires a variety of "soft" data and the use of information-gathering strategies such as surveys, questionnaires, interviews, focus groups, brainstorming, or round table discussions. (See the first Case Example in this chapter.)

CASE EXAMPLE

Gathering and Using Anecdotal Data

Linda Jonaitis, principal of Highland High School in Highland, Indiana, believes that a wealth of valuable data is available in the perspectives and opinions of students and families. Jonaitis instituted a Student Issues Committee, whose members were responsible for gathering information from peers and bringing it back to the administration in monthly meetings. This information was then incorporated into the school improvement planning process as data.

"It's really important in the framework of school improvement that we have a means of communication, a way to share information," Jonaitis says. "If I had not been in a position to listen to the students, I might have drawn some wrong conclusions about where their heads

(Continued)

(Continued)

were." Ultimately, these soft data will be systematically collected and tabulated to eliminate biases and provide a more complete picture of the school.

Source: Used with permission from Linda Jonaitis.

Relevant Data

Think It Through . . .

What data are most relevant to achieving your SMART goals? How often and by whom are these data reviewed? How does this change *your* instructional practice?

To be useful, data must be relevant to the school's goals. Schools revamping their curriculum to align more closely with new standards, for example, will want to look closely at the results on related tests. Schools that have adopted a goal of improving writing skills through a program of writing across the curriculum may find that samples of current student work provide the best indicators of progress.

CASE EXAMPLE

Data Collection at the Source

Sometimes data collected by teachers can provide unexpected insights into what's going on in the classroom. This was the case recently at Edison Middle School in Milwaukee, Wisconsin, when the eighth-grade math teachers began analyzing results from a special assessment they'd designed. As part of the assessment, they had included questions that tested both pure content knowledge and the application of that knowledge. In reviewing assessment data, the teachers were surprised to discover that students were not struggling with the math concepts being taught, as they had suspected. They *were* struggling, however, with how to apply those concepts to solving problems. With this finding, the teachers were able to respond quickly, changing their instructional focus to emphasize problem solving.

Relevant assessment data

- Align with the curriculum and the overarching SMART goals of the school;

- Are sufficiently specific to show achievement and progress of all groups of students and to drive targeted interventions; and
- Reveal problem areas, and areas of strength to build on.

Timely Data

Since large proportions of student populations turn over annually, outcomes of last year's tests may not reflect the strengths and weaknesses of this year's enrollment. Curricular goals and emphases also change, and they do not always correspond to state test standards. The most useful data for teachers and students, therefore, are the more immediate feedback from formative assessments.

In many schools, the timeliest data are generated by internal assessments and measurements. Teachers cannot rely solely test results to guide their daily decision making. The data on which they base their day-to-day instructional decisions must be more immediately derived from classroom tests, homework, class work, and observations. We'll take a closer look at formative assessment practices.

Another important data source for teachers is administrator feedback. According to Gary Burgess (HOPE Foundation, 2002):

> When people don't get feedback, they begin to think the worst of a situation, of themselves and what they're involved in. When people can say immediately "This is good" or "I like the way you're doing this" or "Have you thought about that," it reinforces what the teacher is doing—or it may suggest an alternative approach.

Consistent Data

In order for assessments to indicate trend lines, outcomes from the same assessment instruments are viewed at different points in time. Data from this year—whether test scores, absentee rates, or average numbers of writing exercises completed per student—need to be compared with similarly collected data from previous years to be meaningful. Only a comparison of results from several years will indicate the trend line of the school.

Disaggregating Data

All data should be analyzed in terms of the identifiable ethnic and socioeconomic groups in the school. Although district-level enrollment information available from the central office may not reveal a child's cultural, ethnic, linguistic, or socioeconomic status, creative improvement teams can develop the information by correlating test results, grades, and other outcomes with subsidized lunch lists, English language learner (ELL) class enrollments, residential addresses, and other recorded information.

They can also require teachers to correlate the children in their classes with pre-established categories (e.g., limited English proficient, newcomer to the community, and living in public housing), then compare the scores of these groups with those of the school as a whole. Such analysis allows schools to set goals and prioritize prevention and intervention strategies for the children who need them most.

CASE EXAMPLE

Disaggregating Data

When Gary Burgess served as principal of Pendleton High School in Pendleton, South Carolina, he and his staff dug deep into the data to look at various groups within the overall population.

> We met with teachers to discuss the data. We asked, Are the males doing better in this area than the females? Are the African American kids doing as well as the white kids? Are kids on free or reduced lunch doing as well as kids who are not?

In the course of the analysis, Burgess and his staff discovered that ninth-grade students appeared to be struggling with the transition into high school. Within that group, ninth-grade African American males were performing especially poorly.

Responding to what the data indicated, the school developed a mentoring program called "Generations." Initially, the program paired African American males with junior and senior male mentors, who were required to keep logs of their contacts with the ninth graders. Reviewing these contact logs, along with disciplinary data, Burgess and his staff saw that the program was working only moderately well. "There seemed to be a tendency for the juniors and seniors to start acting like ninth graders instead of serving as more mature role models," Burgess explained.

To make the program stronger in its second year, he added a new layer of mentors: adult males in the community. While the upperclassmen continued to mentor the incoming ninth graders, the adult males mentored the mentors themselves. The program was also expanded to include Caucasian males.

Since it began incorporating adult mentors, the program has been successful at reducing dropout rates among ninth-grade boys. Its success has also led to the creation of a parallel program for ninth-grade girls called "No Limitations."

Source: Used with permission from Gary Burgess.

GUIDELINES FOR USING DATA

Once data have been collected and analyzed, teachers and administrators can find ways to apply the results of their data explorations to their day-to-day efforts with students. Following are some ways in which data can be effectively used.

Using Data to Drive Decisions and Set Goals

The selection of goals, instructional practices, materials, programs, and policies in a school should be directed by good information. If a school's data reveal a strong correlation between discipline problems and a particular time of day or place in the school, for example, staff schedules and assignments can be adjusted accordingly.

Data can be used first to determine where the needs are, what kinds of goals need to be established, and whether a goal is achieved. A measurement (or rubric) must be chosen to indicate whether progress has occurred. For example, a school that is determined to raise students' math performance needs to decide how to measure improved performance: What test or observable performance demonstrates how well students are doing? How will the school know when the goal is attained? The selection of the measure and a target score are best established at the outset and articulated as part of the goal.

Using Data to Target Interventions

The more current the data are, the better they can be used to create on-the-spot interventions for struggling groups of students. Teachers can

CASE EXAMPLE

 The Data Wall for All

To emphasize data-based instructional practice, principal Shawn Smiley set up a data wall in the faculty lounge at Shambaugh Elementary School. "It's a ginormous piece of butcher paper about 10 feet tall and about 15 feet wide," says Smiley. Set up as a grid, the data wall shows Grades K–5 as column headings and achievement levels down the rows: *Above Grade Level* is the top row, followed by *At Grade Level, 0–6 Months Below Grade Level,* and *6 Months + Below Grade Level* below.

Each student's first name, last initial, and reading score are then listed on a sticky note and positioned in the appropriate grid on the data wall. "Some teachers didn't like that, I'll be honest with you," says Smiley. "At the beginning of the year, they were offended to see students' names showing that they were reading below grade level. But we wanted everyone to know the data, including the students."

Smiley reports that students understand the data too:

If you ask students in the hallway what their reading levels are, they're going to know it. They also know where they're supposed to be. So if a student is at 450 and supposed to be at 480, they know where they are, the goals they're supposed to have, and how we're going to get there.

The data wall is paying off with real results. "If I talk to somebody about numbers, it's just numbers," says Smiley,

but if they walk into the lounge and see this giant green butcher paper on the wall with 441 sticky notes on it representing 441 students, that's real. As time passes and students who were reading below grade level begin to shift to the middle or upper part of the grid, that's rewarding for teachers to see.

Source: Used with permission of Shawn Smiley.

now get real-time data on student performance using white boards and other monitoring devices (see Formative Assessments, Figure 8.2 for more strategies). It is no longer necessary to wait until the grading period to identify and assist struggling students. Interventions can be immediate.

Using Data Continuously in Collaborative Teams

Classroom assessments offer some of the best inputs for creating new interventions. The information from state or provincial testing is less usable than what is learned from district testing—which is less usable than what comes from classroom testing. Teachers use data from classroom assessments for instructional planning and also for evaluating whether they should reteach or revisit a concept or skill.

Using Data to Support Change Initiatives

Change is hard (see Chapter 3). It is in the interest of school leaders to use relevant and credible data to support their calls for change to teachers and other stakeholders. A bar graph showing declining student success over time, for example, can be a powerful motivator for action.

Using Data to Guide Continuous Improvement and Redefine Success

Although it may seem that data can most effectively be used to identify problem areas within a school, it can also be used to discover areas of strength that could be made even stronger (see Figure 8.1).

Continuous improvement can play out at the school level in various ways. One way to improve is through periodic evaluation of teaching plans, lessons, unit designs, and assessments by using a set of design standards. Such an approach compels administrators and teachers to apply these same standards to their own work:

> If we critically look at our curriculum designs, against design standards, often we see ways in which they can be improved. What this implies, however, is a collegial model that has teachers sharing lessons, units, and assessments with each other, looking at them as critical friends against a set of design standards and giving each other feedback upon which we can make our work better. (Jay McTighe, quoted in HOPE Foundation, 2002)

Using Data to Monitor Progress

The value of any instructional practice should be judged according to its results. When implementing a new instructional strategy such as differentiated instruction or response to intervention (RtI), teachers must use data to monitor outcomes regularly and frequently to determine how well the new practices work.

Figure 8.1   Collecting and Examining Data in Your School

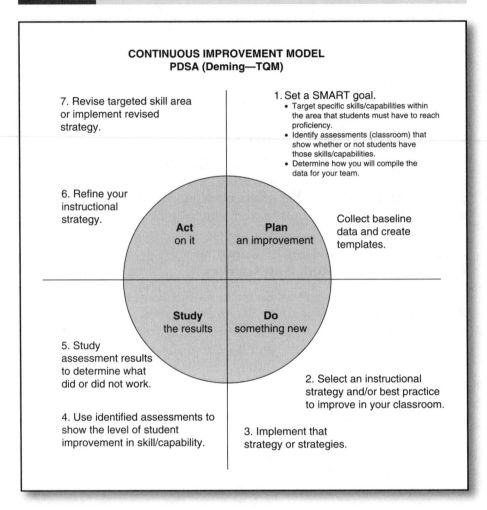

Source: Used with permission from Linda D'Acquisto, Pat King, and the HOPE Foundation.

Using Data to Guide Professional Development

In Grand Island, Nebraska, the school district has developed a curriculum-based assessment system that includes various performance assessments, common rubrics, and high school exams based on district and state standards. In addition to providing assessment results to teacher teams, the district uses the results to target staff development efforts.

"Rather than having the flavor of the year, the programs are much more data-driven," says Jay McTighe (quoted in HOPE Foundation, 2009b), an author and consultant who has worked with the district. "If the scores indicate that students are better at creative writing than persuasive writing, then that suggests the need for a professional development focus on strategies for teaching persuasive writing." Such a curriculum-based system provides several assessment points throughout the year, enabling schools and teachers to monitor ongoing progress and make necessary adjustments along the way.

McTighe goes on to note that this approach is compatible with a sports coaching model. "We don't wait until the game to see how we're doing," he says. "We run scrimmages and look for the problem areas, and that's what we work on in our practices" (HOPE Foundation, 2009b).

WHAT GOOD LOOKS LIKE

Teachers in high-performing schools don't view "data" as abstract, out-of-context information that shows whether they're meeting their goals; they interact with data in a much more personal way, using data of various kinds to make daily decisions about teaching.

Consider the following exchanges. Each one illustrates either an effective or ineffective use of data. Can you identify which ones are effective and why? Place an E for effective or an I for ineffective on the line beside each example, and note why you made that choice.

Exchange 1 _____

Principal: I received our state test results earlier this week, and I've got nothing but good news to share. Our average score is in the 88th percentile—that's the highest it's been in the last 10 years. Congratulations to all you, and keep up the good work.

Exchange 2 _____

Principal: We're here to talk about what we can do to ensure learning for all our students.

Teacher 1: It seems as if we're *already* doing it . . . our test scores are great.

Teacher 2:   It's true that our overall scores are good. But when we look more closely at the scores, it appears that we have a population—about 10% of the student body—that isn't doing well. This correlates highly with poor attendance, which makes a lot of sense. A lot of these same children also receive subsidized lunch. We should evaluate how well our pyramid of support interventions are being applied to *these* students and whether the supports themselves need reevaluation.

Exchange 3 _____

Department Head: Okay, if you'll look at page 2, you'll see that our science scores as a whole took a rather sharp drop this year.

Teacher: I actually have a question about that. I think all the science teachers would agree that we've seen no marked improvement in our students' daily work this year as compared to past years—and I wonder if the drop in numbers might be attributed to the redesign of the test rather than to an actual decline in what students really understand.

Principal: That might be. Let's see how our curriculum and teaching strategies align with the new test.

What's your analysis? We think Exchange 1 illustrates ineffective use of data, whereas Exchanges 2—and possibly 3—show effective use.

In Exchange 1, we see a principal and staff taking test data "at face value" without digging deeper for opportunities to improve. Their *average* score is high, but that doesn't tell what's happening with those students who scored on the low end of the scale. Nor does it provide insights into which grades or which subject areas are performing especially well or poorly. This approach to the data reveals very little that could help guide improvement plans and decisions.

In Exchange 3, the problem is data inconsistency. Because the science test has been redesigned, the data it collects can't be reasonably compared to data collected in previous years. Therefore, the fact that the test scores have dropped *may or may not* mean that student learning has declined. For data to be useful, they must be consistent over time. Reevaluating alignment of curriculum, instruction, and assessment may be in order.

Exchange 2 also illustrates an effective use of data. In it, we see a school really digging into its test scores to see what's hidden beneath the surface. Although this school's overall scores are good, Teacher 2 realized that they do not show the whole picture. Moreover, this professional learning culture makes it possible for her to freely dispute the less complete data analysis of Teacher 1. In a growing number of schools, the performance of Teacher 2's students would already have been addressed by his peers in team meetings. Finally, the use and evaluation of their supports for students comes into question versus the students' abilities to succeed.

A CLOSER LOOK AT STUDENT ASSESSMENT

Jay McTighe and Ken O'Connor recommend that teachers focus on seven assessment and grading practices to enhance learning and teaching (McTighe & O'Connor, 2005; HOPE Foundation, 2009b):

1. Use summative assessments to frame meaningful performance goals.
2. Show criteria and models in advance.
3. Assess before teaching.
4. Offer appropriate choices.
5. Provide feedback early and often.
6. Encourage self-assessment and goal setting.
7. Allow new evidence of achievement to replace old evidence.

Applying these practices before (diagnostic assessment), during (formative assessment), and after (summative assessment) instruction ensures a continuous flow of timely, relevant, and multisourced data that empowers learners and teachers throughout the school year (see Figure 8.2).

Diagnostic Assessment

Diagnostic assessment tools are used before teaching to plan appropriate instruction (McTighe & O'Connor, 2005; HOPE Foundation, 2009b). They allow teachers to

- Find out what students know and what they don't know;
- Learn about student misconceptions;
- Understand student interests, learning styles, learning preferences, and multiple intelligences; and
- Inform students of learning goals and performance assessment criteria.

Figure 8.2	Summary: Diagnostic, Formative, and Summative Assessment

Diagnostic Assessment (Preassessment)	Formative Assessment (Feedback)	Summative Assessment
"Diagnostic assessment is as important to teaching as a physical exam is to prescribing an appropriate medical regimen." (Jay McTighe & Ken O'Connor)	"Formative assessment is probably the most important assessment . . . assessment that happens while the learning is going on. . . . It provides information that enables teachers and students to make adjustments in their learning." (Ken O'Connor)	"Educators should frame the standards and benchmarks in terms of desired performances and ensure that the performances are as authentic as possible. . . . Then present the summative performance assessment tasks to students at the beginning of a new unit or course." (Jay McTighe & Ken O'Connor)
Characteristics • Used *before* teaching • Based on short, nongraded instruments • Helps to find out what students know, what they don't know • May reveal misconceptions • May inform about student interests and learning styles **Cautions** • Inform students of learning goals, performance assessment criteria (offer models) • Preassessment strategies should not diminish students in the eyes of their peers	**Characteristics** • Ongoing and continuous • Uses formal and informal, nongraded techniques • Provides teachers with information about students' learning progress • Guides teachers in modifying lesson plans • Helps students see progress and improve work • Teaches students to self-assess work **Guidelines: Good Feedback Must Be . . .** • Timely • Specific • Understandable • Allowing for self-adjustment	**Characteristics** • Aligned with learning goals • Authentic (knowledge and skills can be transferred) • Offers options to students to display learning • Evaluated against clear criteria **Cautions** • Options should address and demonstrate students' mastery of learning goals • Tasks should be worth students' time and energy—no busy work! • Be realistic about your own time and energy—no need to offer a great variety of options

Diagnostic Assessment (Preassessment)	Formative Assessment (Feedback)	Summative Assessment
A Few Strategies • Concept maps • Know-Want to learn-Learned (K-W-L) charts • True-False quizzes • Drawings • Surveys • Brain drains	**A Few Strategies** • Quizzes • Observation • Skills checklists • Oral questioning • Individual white boards • Personal communication • Hand signals • Exit cards • Graphic organizers **Prompts for Self-Assessment** • What part of your work was most effective? What is the evidence? • What part of your work was least effective? Why? • What actions will improve your product or performance? • What will you do differently?	

Source: Reprinted with permission from *Failure Is Not an Option 3: Effective Assessment for Effective Learning* [Video series]. Bloomington, IN: HOPE Foundation, 2009.

Ideally, diagnostic assessments are short and nongraded. Students can enjoy them and they should not diminish students in the eyes of their peers. Preassessment strategies could include concept maps, Know-Want to learn-Learned (K-W-L) charts, true-false quizzes, drawings, surveys, brain drains, and so forth (HOPE Foundation, 2009b).

Resource 16 offers a checklist for using diagnostic assessments.

Formative Assessment

Formative assessments provide continuous feedback to teachers and learners about progress. They focus on assessment *for* learning (Black, Harrison, Lee, Marshall, & Wiliam, 2003, 2004; Stiggins, 2004; Stiggins

Arter, Chappuis, & Chappuis, 2007) rather than assessment *of* learning (summative assessment). Formative assessment strategies may be formal or informal, graded or nongraded, daily, weekly, or as needed. Tools may include quizzes, skills checklists, individual white boards, personal communication/conferences, oral questioning, observation, hand signals, clickers, exit cards, graphic organizers, rubrics, and so forth (HOPE Foundation, 2009b).

CASE EXAMPLE

Rubrics for Learning

Jay McTighe recommends the use of rubrics throughout the learning process. In the HOPE Foundation video series *Failure Is Not an Option 3: Effective Assessment for Effective Learning* (2009b), he comments,

> Rubrics are valuable in helping students to see their levels of performance across several criteria so that they can make appropriate decisions about what they need to work on to achieve greater success. When students can set personal learning goals, they're more likely to set forth the effort to achieve them. (See Resource 5 for a sample rubric.)

McTighe also emphasizes that rubrics allow students to understand what is most important for them to learn and how teachers will evaluate their work. "They need to know in advance the characteristics of a quality performance and the criteria that will be used to judge their work," says McTighe. "A scoring rubric identifies the key elements of the product or performance being evaluated and the criteria that describe varied levels of quality for each of those key elements."

Teachers can use the data from formative assessments to differentiate instruction, modify lesson plans, and choose appropriate interventions. Carol Tomlinson (in HOPE Foundation, 2009b) comments, "The formative assessment allows me to see where students are in relation to what really matters. And then, the most important piece is to say, what do I do tomorrow? What adjustments do I need to make?"

Jay McTighe (in HOPE Foundation, 2009b) emphasizes the benefits for learners: "Formative assessments help students to see their learning progress and to see the importance of taking an active role as learners by monitoring their own growth. Effective learners use habits of mind that include goal setting and self-assessment." Good feedback for students must be timely, specific, understandable, and allow for self-adjustment by the learner (Wiggins, 1998; McTighe & O'Connor, 2005). Effective self-assessment prompts for learners could be

- What part of your work was most effective? What is the evidence?
- What part of your work was least effective? Why?
- What specific action or actions will improve your product or performance?
- What will you do differently next time?

Resource 17 offers a checklist for using formative assessments.

Summative Assessment

Jay McTighe and Ken O'Connor (2005) advise educators to use summative assessments to frame meaningful performance goals and to allow new evidence of achievement to replace old evidence. When teachers have successfully used diagnostic assessments before teaching and formative assessments during teaching, the results of summative assessments should be evidence of student mastery and cause for celebration.

Effective summative assessment should be aligned with learning goals and evaluated against clear criteria. Ideally, it will be authentic—meaning that students can demonstrate transfer of knowledge and skills to real-world problems—and it should offer students options to display their learning not only through tests but also with portfolios, essays, videos, performance, and so forth. "Effective summative assessment," says Ken O'Connor (in HOPE Foundation, 2009b), "provides opportunities for students to demonstrate that they know, understand, and can do whatever are the learning goals. . . . Ideally, it involves some transfer from general knowledge, understanding, and skill concepts to specific, authentic tasks."

Resource 18 offers a checklist for using summative assessments.

CHALLENGES AND SOLUTIONS

Challenge: "Our test scores are great. Why mess with success?"

In high-performing schools, the staff can be challenged to "add value" to the student learning experience.

Solution: Develop more authentic performance tasks that assess for understanding and transfer. Such contextualized assessments are often more challenging, but also more relevant to students than typical state and national standardized tests. Their development and use can help a school or district move from good to great. Consider adding new goals for social-emotional growth, wellness and whole-child initiatives, and career success as new benchmarks for measuring student success.

Challenge: "Testing data are great for periodically making sure you're on track, but I don't use them to make day-to-day decisions."

Solution: Help teachers understand how to analyze relevant and timely classroom data by providing appropriate staff development to team leaders. Once teams are established, they can watch and learn from one another by visiting other team meetings. (See Case Story 1, Chapter 1.)

Challenge: "Data analysis is just a fancy name for a witch hunt. What the administrators really want is to find out which teachers aren't getting their kids ready for the state tests."
    The idea of slicing data by classroom puts some teachers on the defensive. They may feel that if their students' scores are low, they will be unfairly blamed.

Solution: Use one of the following approaches:

1. Have teachers collaborate to look at data that have been "depersonalized" in such a fashion that teachers aren't able to focus on students' specific classroom, level, or teachers. For example, an administrator might draw a team together to look at students' tests or assignments, using codes in order to avoid connecting the work under evaluation to a specific teacher. Teachers can score anonymous student results, then spend the rest of the meeting looking for patterns and designing appropriate intervention strategies.

2. Get teachers together in vertical (cross-grade-level) teams to discuss what students are expected to know and be able to do, how to know if they have achieved proficiency, and what must be done to ensure success for all students.

3. Build general trust among teachers, and back it with specific actions. It is critical that teachers know that administrators will never use student achievement data to rank teachers against one another. Nor should this information be used in any public forum until a high degree of trust allows for that. (In several schools in which we work, the staff has decided to use data walls to publicly share both student and teacher performance—all to the end of the entire community working on behalf of success for 100% of the students.) Without making this commitment, it is very difficult to collect accurate data.

Challenge: "I don't have time for this. It's overwhelming!"

According to Linda Jonaitis (HOPE Foundation, 2002), one of the greatest obstacles to the effective use of data is finding the time to both collect and analyze the information needed.

Solution: Methods for creatively structuring time can be found in Chapter 3 and Resource 7.

In a study of data use at six Milwaukee public schools, researcher Susan Mason (2002) identified six challenges faced by schools building capacity for data-based decision making:

1. Cultivating the desire to transform data into knowledge;

2. Focusing on a process for planned data use;

3. Committing to the acquisition and creation of data;

4. Organizing data management;

5. Developing analytical capacity; and

6. Strategically applying information and results. (p. 6)

Acknowledging Teacher Frustration With Data

When principal Donna Welty moved to Payne Elementary School in 2007, the school had the lowest test scores in the district in reading and math according to the Kansas State Assessment. So, it was with a sense of urgency that the staff began studying data both from the state and DIBELS (Dynamic Indicator of Basic Early Literacy Skills). Using the data, they grouped students by skill need for 30 minutes of small-group, intensive intervention each day and monitored progress weekly or biweekly to get immediate data on whether or not the strategies they were using were working and to change instruction as needed.

Welty reports that teachers found the process time consuming and frustrating:

> Because of this frustration, we decided to focus our energy into going deeper with reading instruction and diagnosing holes in student learning. The intermediate teachers realized that there were many students who couldn't comprehend what they were reading due to missing basic phonics skills. The data gave them specifics about what the students needed and they were able to immediately intervene with very targeted instruction. As those students improved those basic skills, their comprehension also improved.
>
> Once teachers began to see the benefit of these frequent assessments and the conversations about results, they were much more accepting of the work involved. They talk about students needs and ways to more effectively meet those needs. Due to the work we did with data in reading, teachers began to apply those same ideas with math. Teachers now automatically look for specific error patterns when formally and informally assessing students in both reading and math and adjust instruction accordingly.
>
> As a result of digging deeper into the data, Payne saw a gain of 10.8 points in reading and 14.3-point gain in math for the first year. Preliminary data for the second year show an 8.5-point gain in reading and a 17.6-point gain in math.

Source: Used with permission from Donna Welty.

GETTING STARTED

Table 8.1 (Reeves, 2002a) presents a simplified method of collecting and examining data in your own school. You might want to start by looking at a fairly narrow subset of data to make the exercise manageable (Table 8.1).

Table 8.1	Collecting and Examining Data in Your School

Find the Data

1. Develop a list of the types of data you want to examine (e.g., reading scores, math scores, writing scores, and free or reduced-cost lunch, Title 1, special ed, attendance, and extracurricular engagement). Note that to show trends, you will need to collect data from more than just one school year.

2. Determine how you want to categorize and disaggregate the data (e.g., by grade level, by classroom, or by gender).

3. Design a graphic organizer that will help you get the best picture of your school's overall data (e.g., a simple table or graph, with types of data across the top and disaggregation categories down the side).

4. Search for and record the data on your chart.

Analyze the Data

1. Use the data to answer the following questions:
   - In which content areas has improvement been made?
   - Which content areas still need improvement?
   - Which are the areas of greatest potential growth?
   - Which student groups need the most assistance?
   - Where are the same students alternately weak and strong?

2. Draw conclusions. Record your findings and observations. Note that general statements like "Math scores are low" or "Fifth- and sixth-grade reading scores are the lowest" may not be specific enough. Better statements might be "Math achievement of students taking the bus is disproportionately low" or "Reading achievement of high-mobility students is low."

Reflect

Review your findings. Did you learn something new by charting the data? Below, list three facts that are new to you or that stand out more clearly than before.

1. _____

2. _____

3. _____

(Continued)

Table 8.1   (Continued)

Based on the data you collected, what are your school's three greatest causes for celebration? Its three greatest areas of concern?

Celebration

   1. _____

   2. _____

   3. _____

Concern

   1. _____

   2. _____

   3. _____

Source: Adapted from Reeves, D. B. (2002). *Making Standards Work* (3rd ed.). Denver, Co: Advanced Learning Press. Used with permission.

CONCLUSION

This chapter featured guidelines for the productive use of data by instructional teams focused on ensuring student success. Additional tools and strategies centered around diagnostic, formative, and summative assessments. The next chapter shows how successful schools grapple with bringing about meaningful student, family, and community engagement.

Chapter 8 Resources

Resource 16. Checklist for Using Diagnostic (Preteaching) Assessments

Resource 17. Checklist for Using Formative Assessments

Resource 18. Checklist for Using Summative Assessments

These Resources for *Failure Is Not an Option,* Second Edition can be found

   1. At the HOPE Foundation Web site at www.hopefoundation.org.

   2. In the *Facilitator's Guide* to *Failure Is Not an Option,* Second Edition (ISBN 978-1-4129-8174-3) available for order at www.corwinpress.com.

CHAPTER 9

Principle 5

*Gaining Active Engagement
From Family and Community*

Alan M. Blankstein and Pedro A. Noguera

There is a major difference between involving parents in schooling and engaging parents in learning. While involving parents in school activities has an important social and community function, it is only the engagement of parents in learning in the home *that is most likely to result in a positive difference to learning outcomes.*

—Alma Harris and Janet Goodall,
"Do Parents Know They Matter?"

The research is abundantly clear: Nothing motivates a child more than when learning is valued by schools and families/community working together in partnership. . . . These forms of involvement do not happen by accident or even by invitation. They happen by explicit strategic intervention.

—Michael Fullan,
What's Worth Fighting for in the Principalship?

Does the following exchange sound familiar?

Teacher 1:   How's it going?

Teacher 2:   Not good. My kids don't seem to care about learning at all. They're not motivated, they don't study, and some of them don't even seem to care if they fail.

Teacher 1:   It's such a shame, but it all starts in the home you know.

Teacher 2:   What can we do if the parents don't care?

The common corollary to the above scenario is often found in wealthy districts where "helicopter parents" seem to want to run the school. Regardless of the circumstance, it is clear that the proper support and involvement of students' families and the community at large is fundamental to student achievement in schools. Joyce Epstein at Johns Hopkins University, James Comer and Ed Zigler at Yale, and Maurice Elias at Rutgers University all speak eloquently on the topic of parental/guardian involvement in schools. Their research concludes that greater parental involvement leads to higher levels of student achievement and improved student behavior, irrespective of such factors as socioeconomic status or ethnic background. That same research shows that the most accurate predictor of student academic achievement is the ability of the student's family to create a home environment that encourages learning; to communicate high, yet reasonable, expectations for achievement; and to stay involved in the student's education in meaningful ways (Comer, Joyner, & Ben-Avie, 2004; Elias & Arnold, 2006; Epstein et al., 2009).

These findings and others like them (Hill & Tyson, 2009) have captured the attention of U.S. policy makers. In 1994, Congress added a goal focusing on parental involvement to the National Educational Goals. Goal 8 states, "By the year 2000, every school will promote partnerships that will increase parental involvement and participation in promoting the social, emotional, and academic growth of children" (National Education Goals Panel, 1995). A similar emphasis is expressed by the new administration, as the grant guidelines for the American Recovery and Reinvestment Act of 2009 make clear (see www.ed.gov).

In some schools, these goals present a significant set of challenges. In communities where student achievement is consistently low or where wide disparities exist in patterns of student achievement, relations between school, family, and community can often be strained—a recipe for misunderstandings, misinterpretations, and disagreements. (Note that 10 years after the initial goal was to have been achieved, we're still a long way from reaching it.)

In schools where parental involvement is minimal, educators may assume that parents simply don't care about their children's education. However, a vast body of research shows that most parents want to see their children succeed academically, and many have a genuine interest in being involved in the schools their children attend (Marx, 1996). This raises an important paradox: If both parents and teachers want the same thing—student success, why is it that strong partnerships between parents and schools can be so hard to create?

Partnerships must be based upon common interests and an understanding that there is a common goal: student success. However, creating strong relationships sometimes takes a lot of understanding, a bit of work to make time for the partnership, and a willingness on the part of educators to communicate effectively with the parents they serve.

Unfortunately, in some schools, it is common to blame parents for low student achievement and to complain that parents are not doing their part. As in the opening vignette, it is common to hear that parents send children to school late, unfed, and unprepared for their classes, and that they are not doing enough to address behavior problems when they occur at school. Even when these complaints are accurate, it is a mistake to conclude that parents don't care or that they don't want their children to succeed. Many parents are struggling to make ends meet and are overwhelmed in their efforts to raise their children. After a long day of work, some parents are too tired to supervise homework, much less attend a meeting at their child's school. Furthermore, parents who lack college degrees and formal education may simply not know what to do to support their child's education. Empathy, rooted in an understanding of the challenges that parents face, while not making excuses for those who may be negligent, is essential if we are going to create partnerships that reinforce the importance of learning.

There is no consensus on where the responsibility rests for ensuring parental involvement in schools (Harris & Goodall, 2008). According to a 1994 survey (Center on Families, Communities, Schools, and Children's Learning), 90% of teachers surveyed felt that parental involvement was needed in schools and supported the idea of parent volunteers. However, only 32% felt that it was their responsibility to initiate such involvement, and 50% indicated that they did not have enough time to do so. Given those statistics, it is perhaps unsurprising that 70% of parents surveyed said they had never been invited to volunteer in their children's schools.

The trends shown in these studies, many more than a decade old, are still evident today, leaving much for all of us still to think through. In fact, the pressure on parents is greater than ever, and nowhere is this more likely to be true than for children in so-called failing schools. Parents of children in such schools often develop distrust and even hostility toward educators they may believe are not serving their children well. Disaffection often results in low levels of parental involvement and hostile relations between parents and teachers.

Schools that are not performing need strong partnerships with parents, and they must find ways to overcome distrust and suspicion to develop positive relationships with the families they serve. All of the research we've cited shows that parental support at home is an essential ingredient in producing higher levels of student achievement.

Successful schools devise a variety of plans and activities throughout the academic year for involving families, and they must make sure that the first communication between parent and school is not a call about bad behavior or poor academic performance. Relationships with parents are too important to school and student performance to be treated as a low priority.

Think It Through . . .

How would you characterize your school's relationships with parents and guardians? Which parents are least likely to be involved? Do they feel welcome at your school? Do staff members know how to communicate effectively with parents of different racial, socioeconomic, and linguistic backgrounds?

Some schools surmount the many obstacles in their way and succeed in forging close and productive relationships with parents and community members alike. In this chapter, we'll look at some of the approaches and principles these schools have in common.

BUILDING POSITIVE FAMILY AND COMMUNITY RELATIONSHIPS

Schools that have become true professional learning communities have addressed the gap between parents and schools by employing three key principles to build positive family relationships:

1. Mutual understanding based upon empathy and recognition of shared interests

2. Meaningful involvement of family and community in a variety of school activities

3. Regular outreach and communication to family and community

Mutual Understanding and Empathy

The first step toward building or repairing home-school relationships is to gain a common understanding, with empathy for students' families. This means that the school staff becomes aware of the specific challenges that affect many families and make it difficult for them to support their children's learning. This includes recognizing that many parents have had negative experiences with school and are afraid to become involved. They may be intimidated by feelings of ignorance and uncertainty, and they may assume that their children will experience the same kinds of difficulties that they encountered while in school. Additionally, many parents are struggling to make ends meet. Some are working more than one job and have little time to supervise homework. Others are grappling with layoffs, housing foreclosures and lack of health benefits. Instead of penalizing children and criticizing their parents for lapses and failures in attendance or preparation, teachers in high-performing schools work with families to help them overcome problems and barriers.

Schools that are committed to student success devise creative ways to respond to the difficulties that students face. Some areas in which schools can extend understanding and support include

- Creating afterschool homework centers so that children who don't have someone at home to help them are not penalized because they have not completed assignments;
- Creating schedules, policies, and programs that take into account students' home-life challenges;
- Providing translators who can communicate with non-English-speaking families and producing versions of important school announcements and communications in the languages spoken by the families that are served;

CASE EXAMPLE

Empathetic Decision Making

Nancy Brantley, principal of Pelham Road Elementary School in Greenville, South Carolina, tells a story that illustrates how the challenges of a child's home life can spill over into life at school. On the first day of state testing at Pelham Road, school buses were late arriving from an outlying neighborhood. When the buses finally arrived, the students on them were visibly upset and agitated. There had been a shooting in the neighborhood the night before.

One little girl, in particular, was extremely upset, so Brantley took her aside for a private talk. The student explained that the shooting had occurred in her apartment building. Without a phone to call the police, she and her family were powerless to do anything other than "hide and cry."

The little girl wanted to know if she had to take the test that day. Recognizing that the student faced personal issues that far superseded academic ones, Brantley readily excused her from the testing. "While testing is important, on that particular day, that child was lucky to even get to school," Brantley said. "Children should never ever have to live in situations like that—something that we hope we'll never have to experience."

Brantley's decision in this case was very much in keeping with other Pelham Road policies, such as its policy on tardiness. When a student arrives late to school, he or she is not penalized. In most cases, the child simply receives a pass and is sent on to class. Even with a chronically tardy student, the school does not seek to punish or reprimand. Rather, it looks for ways to help parents resolve the problem even as it also stresses the importance of punctuality. Brantley says,

> If it's a real big problem, although it rarely is, we call the parents in to see if we can help. Because sometimes they simply cannot get an old car started, they don't have a way to school, they've missed the bus—so that's where we step in as a community school to help.

Source: Used with permission from Nancy Brantley.

- Creating waiting areas (with coffee and tea) at school for parents and other visitors so that they don't have to stand at the counter while waiting to speak to a member of the staff;

- Arranging for transportation of students to afterschool activities, and for families to school events;
- Setting up alternatives to telephone communication for families who lack telephones; and
- Holding meetings for parents at public libraries and community centers when transportation to school is a problem.

Effective Involvement of Families in the School

According to Barbara Eason-Watkins (quoted in HOPE Foundation, 2002), the best way to ensure parental and community involvement in a school is to welcome people into the school. Although this may seem obvious, it is actually a common stumbling block in community-school relationships. Eason-Watkins says, "In many conversations I've had with parents and members of the community, they felt that most schools didn't want them to participate, didn't want them to be part of the school" (HOPE Foundation, 2002). This feeling of being unwanted and shut out sometimes stems from parents' own experiences in school. Those parents who struggled in their own academic careers may feel resentment, distaste, or even anxiety about interacting with school authorities.

In other cases, language and cultural differences create a barrier to parental involvement in schools. In some districts, many parents speak and read English imperfectly or not at all, making meaningful involvement in the school difficult, if not impossible. Parents who don't speak English may be hesitant to contact schools and unsure of how best to communicate with school personnel about their student's needs. In many cultures, educators are treated with an authority and status that makes families less willing to ask questions or voice complaints.

Barriers like these make it obvious that family involvement in the schools is not something that occurs naturally or easily when cultural, economic, or racial barriers are not addressed. Partnerships with parents must be purposely cultivated and planned for. Professional learning communities can cultivate such

Think It Through . . .

How do you want parents to be involved this year? Develop a plan for activities and a timeline that will involve parents throughout the school year. What will you do to get them to come to your school? What would make up a good outreach strategy? What will you do to insure they will return? Think of explicit advice and strategies that you can provide to parents so that they leave your school each time they visit with clarity around what they can do to help their children.

involvement by bringing parents and other adults in to share their expertise and talents in meaningful ways and by creating parent-to-parent support networks. These schools recognize the value of the contributions that family members can make to the achievement of the school's educational mission.

Ways of encouraging meaningful parent involvement include

- Establishing a parent-to-parent outreach that contacts all parents to see what they can contribute to student learning;

- Inviting parents and community members to provide lessons in the language and/or culture of ethnic groups that are represented in the school community;

- Inviting parents and community members to provide leadership for extracurricular clubs based on special interests; and

- Training teachers and the school receptionist in how to greet parents and conduct productive parent-teacher conferences.

Think It Through . . .

Which parents are least involved at your school? What might you do to make them feel welcome and get them more involved? What barriers might be limiting their involvement? What are some of the contributions parents or community members could make that would be especially useful?

CASE EXAMPLE

Engaging Parents in Their Child's Curriculum

One way to involve parents in the school is to keep them informed about what their children are learning—even to the point of offering parent workshops. Many schools tackle this objective by sending home a syllabus and posting it weekly online so parents can track exactly what students are learning each week. A middle school in Boston uses the quarterly report card as a time to celebrate student achievement by inviting parents to come in and meet teachers while the band plays music in the auditorium, food is served in the cafeteria, and friendly basketball games between teachers and students take place in the gymnasium.

Other school districts are taking similar approaches:

- Icenhower Intermediate School in Mansfield, Texas, offers "Culture Night" for families. Academic teams select geographic regions of the world and invite parents and families to sample the music, food, art, clothing, and geography of each region.

- Thornton Township High School in Illinois District 205 has a "Parent Academy" in each of its buildings to offer adult classes on topics ranging from word processing to Spanish language to swimming. Not only are the courses *attended* by parents and community members, but many courses are also *taught* by parent volunteers.
- Eagle Academy, an all-male public school in Bronx, New York, offers weekend Parent Academies, with workshops on helping students in applying to college, talking to teens about sex and drugs, and maintaining strong positive relationships. The workshops are consistently well attended because parents value the information that is made available to them.
- Fort Wayne Community Schools has a "Real Men Read Program" with Thursday story hours. Adults read a book to students and the children get to keep the book. This volunteer effort is so successful that summer sessions have been added.

Parents or community members can serve as translators to facilitate communication between the school and non-English-speaking families. They can also make presentations—talks, slide shows, or videotapes relevant to current events, areas, or subjects being studied. Principals and teachers who lack the language skills can also develop partnerships with local churches and community-based organizations to help in doing outreach and providing translation to immigrant parents.

CASE EXAMPLE

Using Parents' Unique Abilities

At Pelham Road Elementary School in Greenville, South Carolina, parents use their abilities and experiences to enrich the lives of students through special-interest groups and clubs. Two bilingual parents volunteer their time twice a week to meet with the afterschool Spanish Club. Other parents, who have literary interests, work with the school's Authors' Club, to guide students through the process of writing and publishing a book. To meet the needs of Eritrean immigrants, one Oakland middle school hired a parent who had been a teacher in Eritrea to work at the school as an instructional assistant.

Getting parents into the school on a more formal basis can be an opportunity to provide a positive experience, expand the relationship, and encourage meaningful and helpful interactions between parents and their children. Teacher wisdom for maximizing parent-teacher collaboration includes asking parents to

- Mentor and tutor students who need extra help;
- Assist with classroom writing projects, science experiments, and so forth;
- Direct or assist with dramatic productions;
- Present performances of puppet shows, musicals, dramas, or dramatic readings; and
- Play Oprah-for-a-Day, and lots more. (Shubitz, 2008)

Reaching out to parents and inviting them into the school—and especially into the classroom—can inspire a cultural change for teachers. Parents must be given clear guidance on what to do in the classroom so that they do not interfere with teachers. Changing the school's culture to embrace and value in-class volunteers is a prerequisite for an effective parent volunteer program. If the teachers don't accept the idea of having parents in the classroom, it won't work.

Reaching Out to Family and Community

In effective schools, teachers and administrators go the extra mile to reach those children and families whose problems stand in the way of their full involvement in schooling. Part of reaching out is simply making staff members visible in the neighborhood fast-food restaurants, malls, and other places students and families are likely to visit.

Gary Burgess (in HOPE Foundation, 2002) says that *wherever* you meet parents—whether at the barbershop, the gym, the church, or the community center—becomes the locus of your campaign to get them into the school. In other words, recruiting parents is not an activity restricted to specific hours at specific places: It is a constant, ongoing process that is central to the operation of the school. Burgess recommends a "bring the mountain to Mohammed" approach for providing information about school activities and efforts to the community. In his district, school principals hold periodic informational meetings at local churches and other public meeting places. He notes that these meetings are sometimes better attended than those held at the school because parents and community members perceive them as less threatening and more convenient. Burgess also uses a teacher log to record all parent contacts and then evaluates the information with teachers. By formalizing, valuing, and monitoring these contacts, he has been able to change teachers' behavior.

SCHOOL AS COMMUNITY HUB

A growing number of school leaders here and abroad are becoming more outward looking (Southworth, 2009). Some are returning to "wrap-around" approaches from the 1980s as developed by James Comer, Ed Zigler, and others (e.g., Head Start and Co-Zi Schools).

These schools are in effect providing children a web of support to compensate for overstressed families. Since community services are often disjointed, these school leaders coordinate law enforcement and community agencies for the social, emotional, and academic success of their students. For example, programs might be devised to ensure that homeless children do not have to transfer to new schools throughout the year. As another example, at PS 28 in Brooklyn, the local YMCA runs the afterschool programs based at the school, and youth on work release from Rikers Island have been trained to make repairs on the school as part of their rehabilitation.

CASE EXAMPLE

Working With Local Agencies

Newport News School District in Newport News, Virginia, has worked with local agencies to create "Homework Clubs" for latchkey children. In 12 different locations throughout the city—including housing projects, shelters, and other community centers—the district has established quiet, safe places for studying after school. Each Homework Club is equipped with computers and classroom materials and staffed by a teacher and a parent who has been trained as a teacher's assistant.

The district has also worked with housing projects in disadvantaged neighborhoods to create four computer labs for both parent and student use. In the evenings, the computers are available for student use. During the day, while students are at school, the labs are used to train adults in computer skills, with paid trainers teaching everything from computer maintenance to software design. These community resources, funded in part by a federal grant, serve both to prepare parents for the workforce and to help them become better teachers for their children.

(Continued)

(Continued)

Similarly, PS 28 in the Bedford Stuyvesant section of Brooklyn, New York, has developed an array of partnerships with local agencies to provide job training and ESL classes for parents and extended learning opportunities for students after school. These partnerships have made it possible for the school to provide its students with an enriched education that includes art, music, dance, and swimming lessons. Despite the fact that over 40% of the students served at PS 28 are homeless, it is also a high-performing school that has received numerous awards from the district and the state of New York. In explaining how the school has accomplished so much despite the odds it faces, school principal Sadie Silver says proudly, "Our parents are our partners. We can't do it without them."

Schools acting as a community hub can also benefit when they reach out to the local business community. Local businesses have a considerable stake in the quality of graduates that the schools produce—and they are often quite willing to contribute time, expertise, guidance, and funding. One middle school in Atlanta receives donations of blue jeans, backpacks and sneakers each fall so that children have new gear at the start of school. David Douglas High School in Portland, Oregon, has an extensive array of partnerships with local businesses that provide internships and job training opportunities to students, some of whom go on to become future employees. In the San Francisco Bay Area, seven high schools, two community colleges, and one four-year college have formed a partnership with several leading biotech firms that is now in its 15th year. The partnership has produced good paying entry jobs and a pathway to college for the hundreds of students it has served.

What Good Looks Like

Each of the following scenarios offers an example of how schools can interact with parents and community members. Can you think of ways in which the interactions could be improved so that both parties come away with a more constructive approach to addressing the problem?

Scenario 1

Teacher: Marissa, this is the third time this week that you haven't had your homework done. The last two times, I gave you second chances—but you just don't seem to be trying.

Marissa: I'm sorry. I didn't have time again last night because I have to help take care of my brother on the nights my mom works.

Teacher: I understand that you have a responsibility, but I can't continue to overlook the fact that you aren't completing your work. From now on, if you don't turn in homework when it's due, I'm going to have to give you a zero for it.

Scenario 2

Parent: I am sorry to be registering my daughter a few days late for school but we just moved here and I had trouble figuring out what I needed to do. I understand that my daughter will be attending this school in the fall. I wondered if you'd mind giving us a tour?

Principal: We gave tours before school started. Now your daughter is already behind. That's not a great way to start the school year.

Parent: Well, it wasn't my intention for her to start late, but I didn't know what to do. I'm concerned that she may have a hard time adjusting now because she's new.

Principal: Well, this is a great school and we've got good kids and wonderful staff. The main thing is to get her caught up on her work. I hope we can count on you this year to do your part so that she doesn't fall behind.

Scenario 3

Teacher: Miguel, I've noticed that your mother has not been signing your weekly assignment sheets. Have you been showing them to her and asking her to help you check your work, as I asked?

Miguel: I did ask her, Mrs. Torphy, but she says her English isn't good enough to check my work. She says she doesn't understand most of my homework at all.

Teacher: I'm sorry, Miguel. Maybe you can translate it for her. Unfortunately, no one on our staff can speak Spanish.

What are your thoughts about each of these scenarios? We've provided our analysis in past chapters; now we're taking off the "training wheels." Have fun with this!

IMPLEMENTATION GUIDELINES

The National PTA lists six national standards for family involvement programs, along with associated practices (National Parent Teacher Association, 1998). These standards and practices can be found at http://www.pta.org/documents/National_Standards.pdf.

CHALLENGES AND SOLUTIONS

Teachers and administrators face numerous challenges as they work to strengthen school and community ties. Below are some of those challenges—and some of our suggestions for resolving them.

Challenge: "I've *tried* to reach out to the parents of my students . . . but most of them, especially the parents of the kids who are struggling, don't seem to care, and some are downright hostile. The ones who do care are generally parents of kids who are doing well and some are so overly involved that they second-guess my every move."

In many schools, the parents of students who do least well academically are also least likely to be involved. All of the research shows that reaching out to these parents can serve as an important step in improving the performance of these students.

Solution: Parents and administrators, and designated parent coordinators, need to actively reach out to parents and families not connected to the school. It is very important that the first communication not be a call home about bad behavior or poor academic performance. Make contact before problems occur. Demonstrate empathy and understanding to parents who may be struggling to make ends meet. Let them know that you value their support and that you truly believe their children can succeed if you work together. Meeting them places where *they* feel comfortable will facilitate the communication *and* the school professionals' empathy.

Challenge: "Our school has no problem communicating with parents! In addition to the full binder of material we send home with every student at the beginning of the year, we send weekly newsletters and calendars of upcoming events. Every teacher maintains a current 'homework hotline,' so parents can call in and check their children's assignments. And we post everything on our Web site and update it every two weeks."

Many schools mistakenly believe that communication flows in only one direction—that as long as they're getting information to parents, they're doing their part. Meaningful communication, however, must be two way, constantly alternating between informing and listening.

Solution: Look into interactive modes of communication—including, but not limited to, voice mailboxes, suggestion boxes located both in the school office and in key locations around the community, parent surveys, and direct phone calls to ask for parent feedback and input.

Challenge: "We have some great parents, and I know they want to be involved in their kids' education—but they just don't seem to have a clue how to go about it."

Clearly, achievement is enhanced when students receive help with schoolwork at home. However, not all parents know how to help, and they may not feel qualified to offer guidance on subject matter they themselves are unfamiliar with.

Solution: Set up community-based homework support. Use students in the National Honor Society, students earning community service credit, and other peer tutors. Set up tutoring after school and during the weekends at the school, community center, or local library. Invite parents in and show them how best to help their children with homework. Remember that the children who most need the help often have parents who are not well prepared to provide the needed assistance.

GETTING STARTED

As you begin preparing to open the lines of communication with parents and other community members, first take a moment to evaluate where your school currently stands with regard to community and parental involvement.

- How many community members participate as members of teams for various improvement activities in your school?
- How many parent volunteers does your school have?

- In what capacities are those volunteers used?
- Of the ethnic and cultural groups forming significant parts of the school population, how many are represented on school teams? As parent volunteers?
- What outreach initiatives have been undertaken to recruit community members?
- What forums or meetings have been organized to explain school-related issues and answer families' questions?

Consider these strategies for engaging parents in genuine partnerships:

- Change middle and high school handbooks so that they emphasize the positive, identity-building opportunities awaiting students. Feature interviews and stories with graduates. Place less emphasis on disciplinary infractions, but do present school rules that contribute to the positive identity of the school.
- Develop positive feedback systems to show appreciation of social-emotional intelligence, small amounts of progress, and academic success. Create progress reports about progress of all kinds, and change report cards to include indicators of life skills that parents will understand and appreciate.
- Provide parents with multimedia-formatted guidance with regard to how parents should support, at home, the work of the school.
- Create forums for dialogue about cultural and ethnic differences; create networks of parent liaisons composed of educators, parents, and community residents who can help new families of different ethnic groups adapt to the neighborhood.
- Create opportunities for community service and more meaningful, widely participatory student government. Publicize what happens in these contexts so parents can see what the school is doing and gain a better understanding of the interests and competencies of their teenagers.
- Provide forums for parent discussions and mutual support around the various developmental issues, familial stressors, and parent-child communication concerns that can be expected during the adolescent years. (Elias, Bryan, Patrikakou, & Weissberg, 2003)

CONCLUSION

This chapter has provided scores of strategies and a framework for productively engaging family and community in the school. We have included many examples of what successful schools are doing to engender broad-based support and to strengthen their entire school community in the process.

The next and final chapter addresses an issue that is crucial to sustaining the successes that arise from following the practices described in this and preceding chapters. Building sustainable leadership capacity at all levels has enabled school communities to maintain focus and continue to improve even while withstanding massive changes. Chapter 10 explains how this can be accomplished.

CHAPTER 10

Principle 6

Building Sustainable Leadership Capacity

Alan M. Blankstein with
Andy Hargreaves and Dean Fink

It took about five years before I felt we had really turned a corner. . . . But the process never ends. There is no single mountain to climb. At the top of one peak is another just beyond.

—Richard DeLorenzo, Superintendent, Chugach
School District, Anchorage, Alaska (quoted in LaFee, 2003)

This final chapter focuses on three key words for long-term school success: *leadership, capacity,* and *sustainability.* Taken together, these words emphasize the importance of continually developing the human resources of the school community so that success lasts well beyond the initial implementation of school improvement efforts.

This implies a steadfast depth of commitment to change—a depth that comes from the commitment of the entire school community to a compelling *long-term* vision that impacts the school culture. When

Authors' Note: This chapter includes text that has been adapted, with permission, from "Sustaining Leadership" by Andy Hargreaves and Dean Fink, *Phi Delta Kappan, 84*(9), May 2003, pp. 693–700.

developed with care and forethought, sustainable leadership capacity enables school cultures to thrive despite challenges, including transition of the leadership.

The following section addresses the *why* question—specifically, why should we build leadership capacity in our teaching staff? The current realities for principals and teachers are included here, as are obstacles to change and the means of addressing each.

This is followed by a definition of *leadership.* The summary of research leads us to propose a form of leadership that is enduring and outlasts any single *leader.*

Next, we address the issue of capacity. Although building leadership capacity at all levels—including students, family, and the community—is the ideal, here we focus on teachers as leaders. What does this mean? What roles would a teacher leader play? What examples exist? How can teacher leadership be instituted systematically? All of these questions are addressed in this section.

Finally, Hargreaves and Fink address sustainability using Case Studies from their multiyear projects in Finland; Ontario, Canada; and the United Kingdom, with attention given to "leadership of learning," "distributed leadership," and "leadership succession." In-depth Case Studies are provided to exemplify these critical components of sustaining leadership capacity.

WHY BUILD LEADERSHIP CAPACITY

The Job Is Too Big

Our proposed purpose of education—*sustaining high-achieving schools because failure is not an option for any student*—is a big job. Making the statement that all children will succeed (or learn to high levels) can be energizing. Trying to operationalize it as the sole leader of the school can be depleting. The distance between the ideal and the reality for building leaders is often great, as evidenced in this National Association of Secondary School Principals survey (*Priorities and Barriers in High School Leadership: A Survey of Principals,* 2001, discussed in Schiff, 2002): "Principals feel the most important aspects of their job are establishing a learning climate, dealing with personnel issues like hiring and evaluations, and providing curricular leadership. Yet of the average 62 hours a week they work, only about 23 are spent on these activities. The rest are spent on parent issues, discipline, community relations, and school management."

Regarding the chasm between the demands on educational leaders and what they are actually able to do, Richard Elmore (1999–2000) writes,

Instructional leadership is the equivalent of the Holy Grail in educational administration. Most programs that prepare superintendents and principals claim to be in the business of training the next generation of instructional leaders. . . . This is mainly just talk. In fact few administrators of any kind or at any level are directly involved with instruction. (p. 9)

The principal's job is too big and too complex to be done alone. Moreover, principals who try to "fly solo" often feel isolated and tend to burn out. It can be lonely at the top!

Yet, giving up control and the traditional roles and views of authority is difficult and not often accomplished (Elmore, 1999–2000). This task requires the courage, described in Chapter 2, to take the risk of letting go of some control, trusting staff members, as described in Chapter 4, to lead in major areas of decision making, admitting that you don't know everything, and becoming a learner alongside your staff, as did Principal Nancy Duden (see Chapter 3).

According to Principal Gary Burgess (HOPE Foundation, 2002), this is the most effective way to be a strong leader. "When you keep power, people will not work with you," he says. "When you invest power in other people, it always, inevitably comes back to you." Redefining *strong leadership* in terms of being a developer and facilitator of other leaders requires courage within oneself, and the *en*couragement of others.

SHARED LEADERSHIP DEVELOPS COMMITMENT AND YIELDS HIGHER STUDENT ACHIEVEMENT

As indicated in Chapter 1, distributed leadership across a network of schools can exponentially build staff capacity, something that would be exceedingly difficult to do in a traditional hierarchy.

Other benefits of teacher leadership include teacher efficacy, retention of good teachers, commitment to change efforts (Fullan, 1993), and increased accountability for results (Darling-Hammond, 1997). Merideth (2007) uses the acronym REACH to capture the values of teacher leadership: risk-taking, effectiveness, autonomy, collegiality, and honor. As articulated by teacher leader Mike Pringle (personal communication, 2009) of Brooks Wester Middle School in Mansfield, Texas,

The decisions at our school are driven, first of all, by our kids and secondly by the teachers. Our administration allows us to be a big part of what we do and have say in the process, which gives us the ownership that we need to make it work.

Although experience and the research clearly support the notion of teachers as leaders, the reality is that many teachers are reluctant to play that role. Their hesitancy arises from three areas: First, they may not feel *able* to be a "leader." Their training has not been in this arena, and they have never considered themselves in that role. The legitimate question these teachers may ask is, "What *exactly* do you want me to do, and how am I supposed to do *that?*" The request for very specific information on what to do and how to do it puts the teacher again in a role of follower and seems to minimize the risk of failure. This teacher may feel unable to meet the challenge.

Teachers feeling unable to rise to the challenge need first to understand the positive impact they will have on student achievement by assuming an active role in the school.

Talking with teachers about the important role they can play *outside* their classroom to affect student achievement is one strategy. Specifically, principals can use the data provided earlier and that which was used to build the organizational mission, vision, and values. Encouraging teachers to witness other teachers playing these roles in similar school settings is another strategy. Seeing is believing.

Second, teachers who feel less than able to lead need encouragement and peer support.

Calling on early adopters within the school to model the leadership role that can be played is perhaps the most powerful strategy for persuading others of its feasibility. A recent study in Mattoon, Illinois (HOPE Foundation, 2009c), identified readiness for change as a key factor in school success. This was brought about in part through structures that supported lateral learning (see Lessons Learned in Chapter 1). The approach has led to teachers designing and leading professional development days and developing ways on their own to learn from one another (see Chapter 7).

According to Huffman and Hipp (2004),

Teachers teach teachers. [We] have our computer liaison and our building computer person who train here on campus, and we have the other elementary schools that come here for training from our teachers. . . . Our teachers are great at what they do. Others see this and say, "I'd like to try that!"

Any one or a combination of the above approaches may be effective in addressing teachers' fears of assuming new roles within their school. (Additional means of overcoming obstacles are listed in Chapter 3.) Most important to success, however, is the issue of relational trust (see Chapter 4). There is a high correlation between the trust and confidence in teachers displayed by the leaders and the amount of risk those teachers will take.

The second challenge facing teachers is in rethinking their traditional role as followers. The new and unaccustomed role of making and being responsible for decisions requires a major shift in thinking.

> Once we had the CLA team at Williamston, everything wasn't coming from the principal anymore. Team members and colleagues were running our staff meetings and our inservices. We were the ones up there running people through the norms, talking about values, and looking at our mission. It had a different feel than your principal or administrator always giving you things from the top-down versus everyone invested in the system as a whole. (Laura Hill, personal communication, 2009)

> Our principal gives us responsibility, so that we feel a valued part of what's happening. Before, I just did what I was told. . . . I just stayed in my classroom . . . but I didn't feel like I had any impact at the school level. Now I feel more involved. (Huffman & Hipp, 2004)

The third challenge is that many teachers don't want to be leaders, at least not as leadership is traditionally defined. The charismatic, dynamic, highly public concept of a leader is much less appealing to many teachers than would be a role of humble yet courageous leader focused on curriculum and instruction. These are areas in which many teachers would pursue the opportunity to play a leadership role and make meaningful decisions. Many professionals with whom we work say, "I would like to be a part of deciding what we teach and how we teach it!" This desire is understandable, and it provides a good entry point for developing leadership and responsibility.

In addition to the strategies mentioned above, a new definition of *leadership* would be helpful for many of these teachers—one in which they could see themselves and thus feel impassioned. Many appealing leadership roles for teachers are listed in the section below on "Building Capacity." First, however, let us provide a brief summary of some recent leadership literature, as well as an operational definition of *leader.*

DEFINING *LEADERSHIP*

Traditionally, the role of the leader has been that of a bold, action-oriented figure who solves most of the problems and draws others to his side in the effort. John Wayne did it in the old West, just as Will Smith, Bruce Willis, and countless others do it in today's movie shoot-em-ups.

Although there may be some call for such a style of leadership today, particularly in life-threatening crises, a growing body of research calls for a more participative approach in our schools (Hord, 1997b; Huffman & Hipp, 2004; King & Newmann, 2000; Newmann & Wehlage, 1995; Spillane, Halverson, & Drummond, 2001). Goleman, Goleman, Boyatzis, and McKee (2002) define six styles of leadership. Two styles most closely associated with the "traditional" model—pacesetting and commanding—are the least effective (Figure 10.1).

| **Figure 10.1** | Leading in a Culture of Change |

Leadership Styles

- Visionary
- Coaching
- Affiliative
- Democratic
- Pacesetting
- Commanding (Goleman et al., 2002)

	Goleman's Leadership Styles		
	How It Builds Resonance	*Impact on Climate*	*When Appropriate*
Visionary	Moves people toward shared dreams	Most strongly positive	When changes require a new vision or when a clear direction is needed
Coaching	Connects what a person wants with the organization's goals	Highly positive	To help an employee improve performance by building long-term capabilities
Affiliative	Creates harmony by connecting people to each other	Positive	To heal rifts in a team, motivate during stressful times or strengthen connections

(Continued)

Figure 10.1   (Continued)

	Goleman's Leadership Styles		
	How It Builds Resonance	Impact on Climate	When Appropriate
Democratic	Values people's input and gets commitment through participation	Positive	To build buy-in or consensus or to get valuable input from employees
Pacesetting	Meets challenging and exciting goals	Because too frequently poorly executed, often highly negative	To get high-quality results from a motivated and competent team
Commanding	Soothes fears by giving clear direction in an emergency	Because so often misused, highly negative	In a crisis, to kick start a turnaround, or with problem employees

Source: Adapted and reprinted by permission of Harvard Business School Press. From *Primal Leadership: Realizing the Power of Emotional Intelligence* by D. Goleman, R. Boyatzis, and A. McKee. Boston, MA: 2002, p. 55. Copyright © 2002 by Daniel Goleman; all rights reserved.

There are other definitions of leadership. Marzano, Waters, and McNulty (2005), for example, cite 21 characteristics of effective leaders. The following section by Hargreaves and Fink addresses distributed leadership.

In the leadership system described by Jim Collins (2001), the highest level attainable is a "Level Five" leader. In addition to being able to create a compelling vision and galvanize people to implement it (Level Four leaders do this also), the Level Five leader has intense professional will and deep humility. This enables submergence of the ego to the greater purpose of the organization. Leaders who "begin with their core" (see Chapters 1 and 2) make a point of clarifying that greater purpose and thus make Level Five leadership possible. Ultimately, this allows the organization to survive and even thrive, even after that leader's departure. Ego-driven "charismatic" leaders, according to Collins, often leave a large hole in their wake, and their organizations falter. (See "Leadership Succession" in the subsequent section by Hargreaves and Fink.)

Thus, the most effective school leaders are able to collaboratively create and sustain changes that *continually* enhance student achievement. They display the following characteristics:

1. They start by building in themselves and others the courageous leadership imperative, focused on sustaining success for *all* students, creating a culture in which failure is not an option.

2. They work collectively with all staff to assure the resources and support necessary to bring about this mission of achievement for all students.

3. They do this with a long-term view of sustainability so that internal capacity will continually thrive and enhance student outcomes, even in the face of external threats and their own departure. Increasingly, "networks" are key to this (see Chapter 1).

The preceding definition of leadership allows for the development of leaders at every level of the organization. The responsibility for success shifts from one or two people to the entire learning community. This does not imply that everyone plays the same role, but that every role is important and that most entail some level of leadership. The next section of this chapter focuses on specific leadership roles played by teachers in high-performing schools.

BUILDING CAPACITY

As mentioned above, we are witnessing a small but growing shift today toward teachers as leaders. Among the obstacles to this much-needed change is the narrow definition of leadership and the minimal number of roles that it comprises. Districts that work with teachers to define various leadership roles have begun to systematically invite new teachers to select one of these roles to pursue once hired. They then provide support throughout the process of new teachers taking on leadership roles. These schools and districts are well on their way to building vital leadership capacity.

Staff development has traditionally been delivered by outside experts. In a growing number of school districts, it is coming into line with the recommendations of the National Staff Development Council that leadership be embedded in the school culture (Darling-Hammond, Wei, Andree,

Richardson, & Orphanos, 2009). This has included teachers taking on the role of teaching other teachers (see Case Story 1 in Chapter 1). This happens through teacher mentors; teachers being recognized as content-area specialists; master teachers; and teachers leading curriculum writing teams, standards development teams, and professional development programs.

The San Francisco school district relies heavily on Teachers on Special Assignment (TSAs). These professionals make a three- to five-year commitment to coordinate and facilitate professional development for the district. They also help schools implement site-based plans. The TSAs work with teacher leaders, who in turn lead instructional content areas and assist individual schools in implementing professional development. These teacher leaders also mentor and do peer training, coaching, and team-building in schools throughout the district.

Beyond this, teachers in high-performing schools may engage in a particular intellectual pursuit. This has included teachers who wrote and received grants for more intensive study on teacher self-efficacy, for example. This fits neatly with schools' interest, so they become a resource to the school while enhancing their own knowledge base. This, in turn, furthers their commitment to the school. One school formalized this process by creating a "Scholar of the Year" program.

This approach can be expanded in many ways. TSAs, for example, may take a year off to do intensive research and/or speaking in a way that builds school capacity.

The school-based leadership teams we work with support team learning so that teachers gain organizational and administrative skills as they simultaneously share and enhance their teaching skills across a district. Teachers back at the school site engage the larger learning community to develop their knowledge and consensus positions and implement and later report on strategies used in between Academy sessions. Among the peer education approaches that these teachers routinely play are speaking at a teacher luncheon, sharing during weekly team meetings, posting summaries on the bulletin board (or school Web site), modeling new practices for peers to see, creating and leading professional development days (see Case Story 1), and calling colleagues on the phone to discuss possible implications for implementation at the school.

It is helpful to institutionalize and systematize capacity-building approaches. Once this is done, they can become both a means of screening and recruiting prospective job applicants. New employees would also be given both the expectation and the support necessary to become a part of a learning team and a project or endeavor that taps both their passions and interests in leadership.

At the Icenhower school, in Mansfield, Texas, for example, principal Duane Thurston expects teachers to participate in the school's hiring decisions:

> When we interview any person for this staff, it's a team effort. We look for someone who has a heart for students and ask if that is someone we want to have as a part of our staff. It they don't have the six principles in their heart, they won't get hired to teach here. (Personal communication)

In Mattoon, Illinois, similar learning community practices have led them to be inundated with applicants well beyond the norm for the region.

In the next section, Andy Hargreaves and Dean Fink define *sustainability* and provide Case Examples that demonstrate how some schools build it into their culture.

SUSTAINABLE LEADERSHIP

Andy Hargreaves and Dean Fink

In this section, we connect the concept of sustainability to the leadership literature in education and outline different interrelated principles that underpin the ideas and practices of "sustainable leadership." We draw on the *Change Over Times* study (Hargreaves & Goodson, 2003), as well as on very recent material on districts and countries that perform above expectations and in which leadership is a key factor, along with preliminary findings from a study of succession management in three countries: Canada, England, and the United States (Fink, in press). We use three positive and negative sets of Case Examples to illustrate our analysis of sustainability in leadership. Specifically, we focus on (1) leadership of learning, (2) "distributed" leadership, (3) leadership succession, and (4) integrating leadership.

Background of Sustainability

For many years, change theorists and change agents have been concerned with the problem of how to move beyond the *implementation* phase of change, in which new ideas and practices are tried for the first time, to the *institutionalization* phase, when new practices are integrated into teachers' repertoires and begin to affect many teachers, not just a few (Stiegelbauer & Anderson, 1992). "Institutionalization means a change is taken as a normal, taken for granted part of organizational life; and has unquestioned resources of time, personnel, and money available" (Miles, 1998, p. 59).

Many longstanding practices—the graded school; the compartmentalized, hierarchical, bureaucratized secondary school; tracking or streaming according to students' abilities; and didactic, teacher-centered teaching—are examples of policies and practices that have been institutionalized over long periods of time and that have become part of the "grammar" of schooling (Tyack & Tobin, 1994). The persistence of this grammar and of everyone's ideas of how schools should really work as institutions have repeatedly made it exceptionally difficult to institutionalize other changes, innovations, and reforms that challenge accepted practice, that imply a different and even deviant institutional appearance and way of operating for schooling (Meyer & Rowan, 1977).

Innovations that challenge the traditional grammar of schooling often arouse intense enthusiasm. They prosper and flourish in well-supported pilot projects, in specially staffed and charismatically led schools, or among an atypical minority of teachers and schools whose teaching careers and identities are characterized by risk and change (Fink, 2000a; Fletcher, Caron, & Williams, 1985; Riley, 1998; Smith, Dwyer, Prunty, & Kleine, 1987). But typically, innovations fade, lighthouse schools lose their luster, and attempts to spread initiatives across a wider, more skeptical system—to scale them up—meet with little success (Elmore, 1995). Even those few innovative settings that survive often serve as outlier exceptions—giving the system a safety valve where all its most critical and questioning educators and their clients can be congregated together in one site (Lortie, 1975; Sarason, 1990).

In the face of the traditional grammar of schooling, and those whose interests are served by its abstract academic orientations, the vast majority of educational change that deepens learning and allows everyone to benefit from it neither spreads nor lasts. Sustainability, in the deeper sense, raises questions about the preoccupation of policy makers with short-term success over long-term improvement, statistical appearances that make them look good over sustained changes that ensure students learn well, and timelines for change that address electoral cycles of popularity rather than change cycles of durability.

Some contemporary discussions of sustainability in educational change repeat these traditional preoccupations with how to keep change going over time. In doing so, however, they often trivialize the idea of sustainability (Barber, 2001), reducing it to *maintainability*—to the question of how to make change last—but adding little to our understanding of change. Now, however, we have learned how to sustain change over time.

The Meaning of *Sustainability*

Sustainability is about more than endurance. It concerns more than the life and death of a change. Lester Brown, founder of the World Watch Institute, first coined the term *sustainability* in the environmental field in the early 1980s (Suzuki, 2003). He defined a sustainable society as one that is able to satisfy its needs without diminishing the opportunities of future generations to meet theirs.

The key and most widely used definition of the slightly different but closely related idea of sustainable development appears in the Brundtland Report of the World Commission on Environment and Development in 1987: "Humankind has the ability to achieve sustainable development—to meet the needs of the present without compromising the ability of future generations to meet their own needs" (World Commission on Environment and Development, 1987). Adapting this definition, we have argued that

> sustainable educational leadership and improvement preserves and develops deep learning for all that spreads and lasts, in ways that do no harm to and indeed create positive benefits for others around us, now and in the future. (Hargreaves & Fink, 2005)

Drawing on the environmental and corporate literature, as well as our Spencer Foundation study of *Change Over Time* in eight U.S. and Canadian secondary schools over 30 years through the eyes of the teachers and leaders who worked there in the 1970s, 80s, and 90s (Hargreaves & Goodson, 2006), we have created an explanatory framework of seven principles of sustainable leadership.

Sustainable leadership is characterized by *depth* of learning and real achievement rather than superficially tested performance; *length* of impact over the long haul, beyond individual leaders, through effectively managed succession; *breadth* of influence, where leadership becomes a distributed responsibility; *justice* in ensuring that leadership actions do no harm to and actively benefit students in other classes and schools; *diversity* that replaces standardization and alignment with networks and cohesion; *resourcefulness* that conserves and renews teachers' and leaders' energy and does not burn them out; and *conservation* that builds on the best of the past to create an even better future.

What contribution can leaders make to sustainable improvement according to the sense of sustainability we have outlined? In our view, leaders develop sustainability by how they approach, commit to, and protect deep learning in their schools; by how they sustain others around them to promote and support that learning; by how they sustain themselves in doing so, so that they can persist with their vision and avoid burning out (see Chapters 1 and 3 also on sustaining your vision and yourself); and by how they try to ensure that the improvements they bring about last over time, especially after they themselves have gone (Fink, 2005; Hargreaves & Fink, 2005). We will now look at three particular aspects of what we call *sustainable leadership* that illustrate most of the different components of sustainability (and nonsustainability) that we have outlined: leading learning, distributed leadership, and leadership succession. Last, we add final material from a district and a country to show how sustainable leadership is also integrating leadership that works beyond the school within and outside the immediate community.

The examples are drawn from our research reported in detail in the *Change Over Time* study (Hargreaves & Goodson, 2003), a special edition of the *Educational Administration Quarterly* (Hargreaves & Goodson, 2006), and experience of working directly with four, then six, secondary schools over five years (1997–2002) to help them implement a major set of legislated changes in secondary school reform in ways that were consistent with principles of successful school improvement and with their own professional values as educators.

All schools were located in a large urban and suburban school district in Ontario, Canada, which funded the project in partnership with the Ontario Ministry of Education and Training. Two very recent examples are then added from the world's highest performing country on many international tests—Finland—as well as *the most improved urban school district in England.*

The Canadian project design generated relationships of trust and candid disclosure among the schools and between the schools and the project team, and it accordingly built an authentic understanding of how teachers and leaders were experiencing and coping with reforms over a relatively long five-year period when other major changes were also affecting their schools.

Examples of Sustainability and Nonsustainability

Let's look now at the three paired examples of sustainability and failed sustainability in our project schools.

Leading Learning

The prime responsibility of all school leaders is to sustain learning. Leaders of learning put learning at the center of everything they do: student learning first, then everyone else's learning in support of it (Glickman, 2002; Stoll, Fink, & Earl, 2002). The leader's role as a leader of learning is put to the strongest test when his or her school faces demanding measures or policies that seem to undermine true learning or distract people's energies and attention away from it.

High-stakes testing can push teachers to deliver improved results but not necessarily to produce better learning. What educators do in this situation depends on their commitment to student learning and on their attitudes to their own learning. In 2001, the Canadian province of Ontario introduced a high-stakes literacy test in Grade 10. It was applied to virtually all students, and they were required to pass in order to graduate. High stakes, high pressure!

CASE EXAMPLE

Two Approaches to High-Stakes Testing

Ivor Megson was the new principal at Talisman Park Secondary School. Promoted from being assistant principal at the school, Megson was dedicated to his work as a leader but did not like to rock the boat too much. Most of his staff had been at the school a long time. They liked being innovative in their own academic subjects but were skeptical and often cynical about larger-scale reform agendas. A coffee circle of embittered staff members met every morning before school to complain about the government's latest (almost daily) initiatives and announcements. Like many principals, Megson saw his responsibility as being to protect his staff from the deluge of reforms that descended on the school. This, he felt, was the best way he could help them.

With his staff, Megson therefore figured out the most minimal and least disruptive school response to the Grade 10 test—one that would produce the best results with the least amount of effort. Quickly, Megson and his staff began identifying a group of students who, on pretests, indicated they would fall just below the pass mark. The school then coached or "prepped" these students intensively in literacy learning so they would perform acceptably when taking the real test. Technically, the strategy worked. The school's results looked good.

But teachers' energies are finite, and as staff concentrated on those students near the cut-off point, the ones who really needed help with literacy, and had little chance of passing the test, were ignored. At Talisman Park, authentic literacy and learning for all—especially for the most needy—were sacrificed to appearances and results.

(Continued)

(Continued)

Charmaine Williams was the principal of Wayvern High School, just up the road from Talisman Park. Wayvern was a culturally and ethnically diverse school and had a high number of students for whom English was their second language. Wayvern had a lot to lose on the literacy test. Yet Williams's school made literacy, not the literacy *test,* one of their key improvement goals.

Williams engaged her staff in inquiry about how to improve literacy so it would benefit all students in the long term instead of focusing on how to manipulate the short-term scores on the test. Working with large staff teams, across disciplines, and with workshop training support, Wayvern undertook an audit of existing literacy practices in classrooms, researched effective literacy strategies that might be helpful, and undertook a gap analysis to see what improvements would be necessary.

Teachers shared their literacy strategies across subjects, then dedicated a whole month to a high-profile focus on literacy learning in the school and with the community. They also continued a successful literacy initiative they had already made where everyone in the school read together for 15 minutes each day. Williams harnessed her staff's learning in support of student learning. The immediate results were not spectacular (as is usual with more sustainable change), but together the staff and parents were confident that long-term improvement mattered the most. Wayvern teachers were convinced that, in future years, scores would increase as genuine reflections of learning and achievement, rather than because of cynical manipulations of the testing process (Nichols & Berliner, 2007).

One reform; two principals; two schools—but different outcomes! Especially in the most adverse circumstances, those principals who are leaders of learning make the most lasting and inclusive improvements for their students in their schools.

Distributed Leadership

CASE EXAMPLE

Different Leadership Styles; Different Outcomes

Outstanding leadership is not just the province of individual icons and heroes (Saul, 1993). In a complex, fast-paced world, leadership cannot rest on the shoulders of the few. The burden is too great. In highly complex, knowledge-based organizations, everyone's intelligence is needed to help the organization to flex, respond, regroup, and retool in the face of unpredictable and sometimes overwhelming demands. Locking intelligence up in the individual leader creates inflexibility and increases the likelihood of mistakes.

But when we use what Brown and Lauder (2001) call "collective intelligence"—intelligence that is infinite rather than fixed, multifaceted rather than singular, and that belongs to everyone, not just a few—the capacity for learning improvement is magnified greatly. For these reasons, more and more efforts are being made to replace individual leaders with more distributed or distributive leadership (Harris, 2008; Institute for Educational Leadership, 2000; Spillane et al., 2001). In a distributed system, leadership becomes a network of relationships among people, structures, and cultures (both within and across organizational boundaries), not just a role-based function assigned to, or acquired by, a person in an organization who then uses his or her power to influence the actions of others. Leadership is viewed as an organic activity, dependent on interrelationships and connections (Riley, 2000).

Mark Warne was the principal of North Ridge High School. Three years from retirement, Warne has a keen intellect and a deep knowledge about imposed change and its effects; he valued and was skilled at seeing the big picture of reform. When legislated reforms were announced, Warne produced detailed, thoughtful written and projected timelines for implementation responses that he circulated to staff members for comment. The response was disappointing, though, and Warne confided that his staff was generally apathetic about getting involved with change. His strength was his great intellectual clarity, but he could not develop the capacity among his staff to share his vision. The big-picture change belonged to Warne alone, not to everyone. His office was packed with policy statements, resources, and materials that might better have been distributed around the school.

Warne controlled the directions of his school through the line management of the department heads. The department heads were quite autonomous in their areas; staff involvement, therefore, depended on the leadership style of each head. One of his assistant principals (also close to retirement) performed traditional discipline and administrative roles. The other was battling with what sadly turned out to be a terminal illness.

Warne delegated to his subordinate department heads and accepted their advice in areas where they were more expert than he. The department heads generally described him as "supportive," "compassionate," and "well-intentioned." Yet, the larger staff was excluded from decisions and ill

(Continued)

(Continued)

informed on important issues. They considered their principal to be "indecisive," "inconsistent," and "lacking a personal vision." At a school improvement workshop we ran with the whole staff, they were the only school of the six to identify themselves as "cruising" (Stoll & Fink, 1996)—their mainly affluent students were getting good results, but the school lacked purpose and direction. The chief problem the staff chose to address at the workshop was "communications with the administration."

Soon after this, the school began to change dramatically, but not through a change of principal. In 1998, two new assistant principals were appointed. Together, they infused the school's administration with renewed enthusiasm, optimism, and focus. Diane Grant's athletic bearing and infectiously energetic style brought her sophisticated knowledge of curriculum and classroom assessment to the problem of reform. Before long, she was skillfully leading the staff in curriculum-gap analysis or having them share successful experiences in classroom assessment by seating them in crossdisciplinary tables at the staff picnic, where they scribbled their ideas as graffiti on paper tablecloths. Meanwhile, Bill Johnson, the other deputy, drew on his counseling skills to develop effective communications and relationships with and among the staff. Grant aroused teachers' passions, and Johnson calmed them; as a team, they were able to set a common vision for the school and a more open style of communication. In this new style, the staff focused on collaborative learning, inquiry, and problem solving. Warne's strength was having the good sense to distribute the leadership of important classroom-related changes to his assistant principals, who in turn redistributed much of the leadership among the staff, who learned to be critical filters for government mandates rather than mere pipelines for implementing them.

Leadership Succession

Sustainable leadership outlives particular individuals. It does not disappear when the leaders leave. There is evidence that the departure of the initiating principal or a critical mass of early leaders from model or beacon schools is the first symptom of decline (Fink, 2000b; Sarason, 1972). MacMillan (1996, 2000) has observed that the practice in some school districts of regularly rotating leaders between schools can harden teachers against change because they come to see the school's principalship as little more than a revolving door in a building where they are the permanent residents. Whether principal rotation is formalized or not, leadership succession always poses a threat to sustainable improvement.

How Two Schools Dealt With Leadership Succession

Bill Matthews was a tall, commanding figure who brought vision, energy, and intellectual rigor to his role. The son of a police officer, he believed strongly that students came first and pursued this belief with a sense of clear expectation and relentless determination. Some staff respected his commitment to children and his willingness to take action and put himself on the line for their sake. Prior experience of principalship buttressed his self-confidence, and in a teacher culture that reveled in argument and debate, his somewhat adversarial style (Blase & Anderson, 1995), which encouraged and entertained well-reasoned and supported opposition to his ideas, suited a sizable number of staff very well. It also stimulated some extremely lively staff meetings. Matthews led Stewart Heights School with firm expectations and clear example, accompanied by lively argument and considerable humor. The most outstanding instance of leading by example was when he personally solved the scheduling problems of 80 students to demonstrate that better service for students was indeed possible.

Matthews was quick to move to action by getting staff members to analyze data consciously and to make action plans on the basis of what they learned. He integrated several improvement teams to permit far greater voice and participation for teachers in the work of the school compared to the previous dominance of the department heads' council. In this culturally diverse school, Matthews encouraged the staff to initiate a range of changes that made students feel more included and parents feel more welcome. Structures, planning, and initiation, backed by his own personal interactions with people and his visibility around the school, were the ways in which Matthews brought about change. Many staff members, including most of those on the School Success team, warmed to his decisiveness and sense of direction. Staff referred to him as a "visionary," "change agent," and "efficient manager." Others, however—especially women—indicated they respected him but questioned his somewhat "authoritarian" style.

The two assistant principals offered complementary, indeed dramatically contrasting, approaches within Matthews's administrative team. One presented a quieter, more restrained, and more procedural version of masculinity in leadership than his more "up-front" principal. The other took a more relationship-centered approach to students, curriculum, and staff development, in which caring coupled with hard work and high expectations played an important role. With their contrasting styles, they too fostered greater teacher participation in the work of the school.

(Continued)

(Continued)

Bill Matthews felt it had been a struggle to change the school culture to provide "a service to kids and the community." Yet, when he presented the staff with survey data showing that 95% of staff members were satisfied with the school, but only 35% of students and 25% of parents were, this created a common problem that the staff had to work together to solve.

With more time to help staff members work through their doubts and difficulties, Matthews and his team may well have been able to convert the temporary success of short-term innovation into sustainable improvement. But by the end of his third year, changing circumstances within the school system resulted in his moving to a superintendency, one of the assistant principals to his first principalship, and the other to her second deputy principalship. Stewart Heights' new principal was new to the school and to the role; he had to feel his way carefully into both of them. Meanwhile, the mandated reform agenda was quickly gathering pace. The result of these converging forces was that the staff and their new principal turned their attention to implementation more than improvement. Observations at the school climate meetings indicated that with the previous principal's departure, student-centered policies now gave way to more conventional behavior-code initiatives. The early achievements of school improvement at Stewart Heights quickly began to fade. If school improvement is to be sustainable, one essential factor is continuity of tenure or at least longer tenure for the initial principal, as well as consistency in philosophy among those who come after.

By comparison, Blue Mountain School, an innovative model school established in 1994, planned its own leadership succession from the outset. The fate of most innovative schools is to fade once their founding principals have left. Blue Mountain's principal anticipated his own departure and worked hard to create a school structure that would survive his departure and "perpetuate what we are doing." He was especially alert to the threats posed by leadership succession (Fink, 2000b; Hargreaves & Fink, 2000; MacMillan, 2000), in which an ensuing principal might import a different philosophy. He therefore "negotiated very strongly [with the district] to have [his] deputy principal appointed principal." After four years, the system moved the principal who founded the school to a large "high profile" school in the system and promoted his deputy in his place. In her words,

> We talked about [this move] and we talked about how we could preserve the direction that the school is moving in, and we were afraid that if a new administrator came in as principal that if he or she had a different philosophy, a different set of beliefs, then it would be quite easy to simply move things in that particular direction and we didn't want that to happen.

Blue Mountain is a rarity. In general, planned succession is one of the most neglected aspects of leadership theory and practice in our schools, and one of the most persistently missing pieces in the efforts to secure sustainability of school improvement.

Sustainable Leadership as Integrating Leadership

An Example From Finland

Finland is the world leader on results in the Program for International Student Assessment tests of sophisticated, applied knowledge in mathematics, science, and literacy, as well as on international ratings of economic competitiveness. It avoids shortsighted and unsustainable standardization along with national standardized tests altogether and reaches high levels of educational achievement and economic success (it ranks number 1 in the world on economic competitiveness according to the International Monetary Fund) by attracting highly qualified teachers with supportive working conditions, strong degrees of professional trust and an inspiring mission of inclusion and creativity.

With a team of colleagues, one of us reviewed the Finnish system for the Organization for Economic Cooperation and Development (Hargreaves, Halász, & Pont 2008). We found that school principals have been able to lead communities of highly qualified teachers who develop their school curriculum together within broad national guidelines.

They work in cultures of trust, cooperation, and responsibility, seeing themselves as one of a society of experts who work with fellow professionals and neighboring schools to achieve compelling and inspiring purposes together that rebuild their communities and their nation around knowledge, society, and principles of inclusiveness and creativity. Indeed, in the city of Tampere, high school principals told us that when they agree together on an important initiative for their community, if one school is short of resources, the principal can call the others and one of them will say, "We have a little bit extra, would you like some of ours?" Finnish teachers think about more than "me and my class." And Finnish principals think and act beyond "me and my school." It is not just teachers who need to stop operating as independent contractors. Principals do too!

An Example From London

If the culturally homogeneous and overwhelmingly "White" example of Finland seems irrelevant to the urban centers of America and elsewhere, the London borough of Tower Hamlets is an equally compelling example of sustainable leadership as integrating leadership. Tower Hamlets is improbably situated directly opposite the office towers of glass and steel that formed the setting for the G20's restructuring of the global economy in 2009.

The borough was originally the residence for the yeomen who guarded the Tower of London. For much of the 20th century, it was a prosperous working class community of dockworkers. After the collapse of London's docking industry in the 1970s when supertankers and container ships could no longer navigate the tight bends of the River Thames, waves of immigrants moved into the newly impoverished area—many from rural areas of Bangladesh, one of the world's poorest countries. Despite the reconstruction of part of the Docklands into the fashionable global finance and media center of Canary Wharf, the white-collar workers who came and went on the new high-tech transit line were barely aware of the immigrant community in their midst.

Tower Hamlets' Bengali community suffered from high unemployment rates and some of the greatest incidences of poverty in the country, with more children on free school meals than almost anywhere else. Educators' aspirations for student achievement were startlingly low, and in 1997, Tower Hamlets was proclaimed the country's worst performing Local Education Authority, with the lowest performing primary school in the nation.

Ten years later, the transformation of the schools in Tower Hamlets is dramatic. The schools perform around and above the national average. On standardized achievement tests, high school examination results, and rates of students going on to university, the borough ranks as the most improved local authority in Britain. It has significantly reduced achievement gaps in relation to children with special educational needs, those from cultural minorities, and those on free school meals. These gains have been achieved with largely the same population and in comparison with the more modest national gains posted in the same time period.

Systemwide Turnaround

What explains this systemwide turnaround? In a research project codirected with Alma Harris, called *Performing Beyond Expectations*, one of us has studied the secrets of Tower Hamlet's success (Hargreaves & Shirley, 2009). At the center of the story are the following components that relate to sustainable and integrating leadership:

- The *visionary leadership* of a new director (superintendent) who was a self-confessed workaholic and who believed that "poverty is not an excuse for poor outcomes," that aspirations should be extremely high, that efforts to meet these aspirations should be relentless, and that everyone should work on this together.

- The *successful succession* of this first driving leader by a more developmentally inclined, yet equally persistent one, with just a short period of instability in between.

- A commitment developed with and by the schools' leaders to set and reach ambitious *shared targets* for improvement in "a culture of target setting" so that "everybody owns them"—these were more ambitious than the targets imposed by government.

- *Active trust and strong respect* where "lots of our schools work very closely together and with the local authority" and where inspectors' reports refer to the "enthusiasm and high level of morale among the workforce."

- *Knowledge of and presence in the school* by all stakeholders to provide support, build trust, and ground intervention in consistent and direct personal knowledge and communication more than in the numerical data that eventually appear on spreadsheets.

- A commitment to *cross-school collaboration* so that when one of the authority's 13 secondary schools fell into the failing schools category after taking in Somali students from refugee families in a neighboring authority, all the other secondary schools rallied round to help.

- *Strengthening of community relations and engagement.* Tower Hamlets schools affect the communities that affect them. They have done this by working with faith-based organizations and forming agreements with imams from this largely Muslim community to counter the effects of children taking extended absence from schools to attend and then stay on after family events such as funerals in Bangladesh, by treating extended unauthorized absences as culpable truancy. Tower Hamlets has also developed some of its schools into wrap-around community centers that keep a school open from 8:00 a.m. until 10:00 p.m.—providing resources and recreation for both students and the community's adults. (See also Chapter 9 on schools as community hubs). Last, the employment of large numbers of classroom assistants and other staff from the community to support teachers builds strong relationships and trust between professionals and community members and enables and encourages some of these community members to go on to become professionally trained teachers themselves.

In Tower Hamlets, as in Finland, leaders with a robust and resilient sense of purpose engage in successful, integrating, and sustainable system leadership that stays close to and is undertaken with schools and that is performed together in an ethic of schools helping schools and the strong supporting the weak. These leaders think and work sustainably beyond their isolated schools—with other schools and also with their surrounding communities.

Discussion and Conclusion

Our definition and dimensions of sustainability in education and our Case Example illustrations carry a number of implications for what it might mean to develop sustainable leadership.

1. *The future of leadership must be embedded in the hearts and minds of the many and not rest on the shoulders of a heroic few.* We want dedicated and committed professionals in school leadership, not martyrs to management— severed heads whose all-consuming devotion to their work comes at the cost of their families, their lives, their health, and themselves.

School leadership is not the sum of its individual leaders, still less its separate principals. School leadership is a system and a culture. Schools are places where principals, teachers, students, and parents all lead. To sustain quality leadership, school systems must apply systems thinking to their mandate of leadership quality, qualifications, and development—not just by setting common standards and criteria but also by applying systems thinking to all initiatives. Leadership must be a culture of integrated qualities rather than merely an aggregate of common characteristics.

As we discussed in Chapter 1, school jurisdictions should see leadership as a horizontal system across space, where leaders can learn from each other within and across their schools through peer support groups, online dialogue, pairing of schools and their principals (Stoll & Fink, 1996), joint research and development projects, and so on. As we experienced in our school improvement project, one of the components most consistently valued by school leaders is the regular opportunity to meet and converse with each other to talk openly about shared professional, and sometimes personal, concerns.

2. *Educational systems should see leadership as a vertical system over time.* The efforts of all leaders are influenced by the impact of their predecessors and have implications for their successors. No leader is an island in time.

Principals and their systems tend to put all their energy into what is called *inbound knowledge*—the knowledge needed to change a school, improve it, make one's mark on it, turn it around. Little or no attention is devoted to outbound knowledge—the knowledge needed to preserve past successes, or keep initiatives going once the originating leader has left. The moment that head teachers and principals get new appointments, they immediately start to focus on their new school, their next challenge, or on how to ensure that their present achievements live on after their departure.

Few things in education are more fragile than leadership succession. Heroic heads do not plan for their own obsolescence. The emphasis on change has obliterated the importance of continuity. In inner-city schools, teachers see their principals come and go constantly; they learn quickly how to resist and ignore each new leader's efforts (MacMillan, 2000). The result is that school improvement becomes like a set of bobbing corks; many schools rise with one set of leaders, only to sink under the next. If we want *sustainable* as well as successful leadership, we must pay serious attention to leadership succession (Fink, 2000b). Leaders must be asked, and must ask themselves, these questions: What will be my legacy? How will my influence live on after my departure? The time for leaders to ask such questions is at the very beginning, not when their tenure is drawing to a close.

3. *The promise of sustainable success in education lies in creating cultures of distributed leadership throughout the school community, not in training and developing a tiny leadership elite.* Amid today's contextual realities—sky-high expectations, rapid change, and a youthful profession in the first decades of the 21st century—teachers cannot be the mere targets of other people's leadership, but must see themselves as being, and *encouraged* to be, leaders of classrooms and of colleagues from the moment they begin their careers.

Distributed leadership means more than delegation. Delegation involves passing on lesser and often unwanted tasks to others. The individual leader decides what will be delegated and to whom. Distributed leadership means creating a culture of initiative and opportunity, in which teachers of all kinds propose new directions, start innovations—perhaps sometimes even challenging and creating difficulties for their leaders in the higher interests of the pupils and the school. In its fullest development, distributed leadership extends beyond the staff to pupils and parents. Distributed leadership gives depth and breadth to the idea and practice of leadership.

4. *Recruiting new leaders means focusing on their potential rather than recycling their existing proficiencies.* At first glance, the challenge of leadership succession that faces most jurisdictions in the Western world can be viewed as strictly a problem of mathematical misalignment as the large baby boom generation slips into retirement to be replaced by a much smaller Generation X (Pont, Nusche, & Moorman, 2008). But the problem has more to do with politics and educational philosophy than with issues of supply and demand. A report for the Wallace Foundation (2003) states that "there is no shortage of qualified candidates for the principalship, it makes little sense to rely on strategies aimed solely at adding more candidates to the pipeline." The real challenge of leadership succession is to find and assign the right warm body to the right place, at the right time, for the right reasons. While timing and location may not always be controllable, hiring for the right reasons is always possible. Educational leaders, regardless of their roles, must see themselves as leaders of learning—their own, their teachers and other staff, and of course their students. They must be "passionately, creatively, and steadfastly committed to enhancing 'deep' learning for all students—learning for understanding, learning for life, learning for a knowledge society" (Fink, 2005, p. xvii). From this perspective, there is a succession challenge of major proportions looming in most Western countries to replace the vanishing leaders with new leaders who have the commitment, values, qualities, and intellect to advance student learning to new heights of genuine achievement and accomplishment.

The Wallace Foundation (2003) report suggests that school jurisdictions need to move beyond a

replacement planning strategy designed to fill up the pipeline with certified people and focus far more attention and resources on reforming policies and practices to

- Adjust incentives and working conditions to enable non competitive schools and districts to attract qualified candidates;
- Bring local hiring practices into line with heightened expectations for principals performance; and
- Redefine the job itself in ways that allow principals to concentrate on student learning above all else. (p. 12)

Gradually, this advice is catching on. We are seeing a subtle but important shift in thinking over the past few years among some educational decision makers. Where once money spent on leadership recruitment and development was considered a cost, it is now viewed as an investment in the future, and as a result, some school authorities and districts have shifted focus from "replacement planning" in which specific people are identified as possessing the proficiencies to fill certain jobs, usually through open competition, to a "succession management" approach which involves "the accelerated development of a select group of high-potential individuals for both current and future roles that may not be identifiable at present" (Busine & Watt, 2005, p. 225). Rather than "hire and hope," these school authorities have adopted a "grow your own" philosophy.

5. *Sustainable leadership requires strategies of integrating development across school systems and networks, not just preparation of individuals.* Sustainable leadership is systemic leadership (Hopkins, 2008). It addresses how leadership spreads out in a school through distributed leadership, including teacher leadership, rather than resting on the shoulders of the principal alone. It pays attention to how leadership is stretched out over time, from one leader to the next, so that a school's success does not end with the exit of its leader. And last, it considers how schools and their leaders affect each other within and across their communities and addresses how to turn that to shared advantage. This positive interconnectedness of sustainable leadership occurs in several ways:

- *In networks of accreditation and evaluation.* In Rhode Island and Illinois, the School Accountability for Learning and Teaching project engages schools in developing self-evaluations, which are then connected to external evaluations administered by teams of peers drawn from other schools—improving capacity not only in the host schools but also in the teams who evaluate them.
- *In networks of learning and improvement.* More than 700 high schools in England's Raising Achievement/Transforming Learning project have improved at double the rate of the national average by networking schools that have experienced a dip in their performance with similar schools and with self-chosen mentor schools that have stronger records of performance with similar students, to exchange and develop short-term and long-term strategies of change related to student achievement (Hargreaves & Fink, 2005). Networks and partnerships like these often begin best at a distance among schools that are not in direct competition for clients.

- *In area-based cross-school collaboration* focused on the greater good of the shared community. Divided by district boundaries that reflect class-based or race-related residential patterns, opposed by the ruthless competition of the market, and isolated by the fear of betraying secrets to the enemy, schools in the same town or city are often the hardest to network of all. But as in Finland and Tower Hamlets, much is to be gained when stronger schools help weaker peers in similar demographic circumstances. Inspiring system leaders can appeal to the common commitment to the future of the community. Funding formulae can encourage and incentivize area-based collaborations within and across local districts. Schools and their leaders can also learn that helping others increases their own confidence and capacity too.

10 Things That Are Sustainable About You

Sustainability sounds fine philosophically, but what does it mean practically? Here are 10 closing, practical ideas for developing sustainable leadership in your system or your school:

1. Refocus your curriculum, use of materials, and school design to include ecological sustainability as a core aspect of teaching and learning for all students. Consult UNESCO or the World Wildlife Fund for curriculum ideas on education for sustainable development. And look at schools that already employ this emphasis to deepen learning, raise achievement, and pay attention to the future of the planet (Senge, in press).

2. Begin all discussions about achievement and how to raise it with conversation and reflection about the learning that underpins the achievement. Put learning first, before testing and even before achievement. Get the learning right and the others will follow.

3. Insist that all school improvement plans should contain leadership succession plans. This does not mean naming successors, but it means having continuing conversations and plans, shared by the community, about the future leadership needs of the school or the district.

4. Make it a condition of professional employment that every teacher and leader is part of a learning team in his or her school district that meets within scheduled school time on a regular

basis as well as outside of it. This focus of the learning teams should be self-guided, not administratively imposed.

5. Write your own professional obituary. It makes you think hard about the legacy you want to leave, and how, deliberately, you can bring that into being.

6. Form a three-sided partnership with a lower- or higher-performing district or school in your own country and with a school or district in a less-developed country, so all are learning and inspired, everyone needs and gives help, and no one is top dog on everything.

7. Establish a collaborative of schools in your town or city, across district boundaries, to commit to community development initiatives beyond the interests of particular schools.

8. Create a system where principals and leadership teams in successfully turned-around schools can take on a second school or even a third (as well as their own), with dramatically improved salary (with resources being provided to maintain and replace capacity in their "home" schools), to develop administrative careers for administrators without having to abandon their close connections to learning, to provide peer assistance (rather than top-down intervention) to struggling schools, and to lighten district administration at the top in favor of more interconnected leadership within and across districts from below (England has already started this).

9. Coach a teacher who looks like they have little capacity for leadership—and not just ones who look like they already have leadership in them. All leadership is learned, even though some will struggle more than others to learn it. There will be little distributed leadership unless the pool of leaders is widened to include those who do not even yet aspire to lead at all.

10. Spend more time in schools (if you work in the district) or classrooms (if you are principal in a school), not just to check up on people as in the overused management walk-through, but as a way to develop genuine interest in, curiosity about, and knowledge of what teachers and students are doing. Know your people first. Check the data and spreadsheets second. Not the other way around.

CONCLUSION

I wrote the first edition of *Failure Is Not an Option* with a dedication recognizing its simple history: a grandmother who was unwilling to give up on her grandson (Blankstein, 2004). This is similar to the untold story of so many of our successes with students in schools. One teacher, one principal, one cafeteria worker, or one janitor is unwilling to give up on a young person, who then succeeds as a result.

Taken independently, each of these courageous acts—these acts of the heart—are extraordinary. They have ripple effects that continue for generations. Creating a collective culture in which such courageousness is the norm—creating places in which the entire school community can realistically expect sustained success for themselves and for all of their students—is what this book is about.

As demonstrated throughout this book, success is at hand! Schools and districts throughout North America are overcoming real and perceived obstacles, using their moral outrage and courageous leadership to tackle both fears and traditions of failure.

Since that first edition was released, many of its more than 200,000 readers have stepped forward to "push the envelope" on what can be accomplished—not only in a school, but across a district, region, state, or province. This edition begins to capture their actions as well as the mentality that success is the only option. Combined with research and practice from Canada, Finland, New Zealand, Australia, the United Kingdom, and the United States, this edition illuminates a more nuanced view of the precious *how to's*, but, even more important, the *who* and the *why* of success. These small islands of possibility have now become oceans of hope, creating communities where failure is no longer an option.

With a clear focus on why we are in this profession, the development of our courageous leadership imperative, and information about how to create sustainable communities of learning, there is little that can stand in the way of our success; the research in this book now demonstrates that. Grandma wouldn't have had it any other way; and now, with the additional motivation of baby Sarah, neither can I. Thank you for making it this far and for all you do for our children.

Bibliography

Ackerman, R. H., & Maslin-Ostrowski, P. (2002). *The wounded leader.* San Francisco: Jossey-Bass.

Anthony, E. J. (1982). The preventive approach to children at high risk for psychopathology and psychosis. *Journal of Children in Contemporary Society, 15*(1), 67–72.

Anthony, E. J. (1987). Risk, vulnerability, and resilience: An overview. In E. J. Anthony & B. J. Cohler (Eds.), *The invulnerable child* (pp. 3–48). New York: Guilford Press.

Anthony, E. J. (1998, Fall). Attachment and belonging. *Journal of Emotional and Behavioral Problems, 7*(3).

Bandura, A. (1986). *Social foundations of thought and action: A social cognitive theory.* Englewood Cliffs, NJ: Prentice-Hall.

Barber, M. (2001). High expectations and standards for all, no matter what: Creating a world class educational service in England. In M. Fielding (Ed.), *Taking education really seriously: Three years of hard labour.* London: Routledge/Falmer.

Bardwick, J. (1996). Peacetime management and wartime leadership. In F. Hesselbein, M. Goldsmith, & R. Beckhard (Eds.), *The leader of the future* (pp. 131–140). San Francisco: Jossey-Bass.

Barth, R. S. (2001). *Learning by heart.* San Francisco: Jossey-Bass.

Barth, R. S. (2003). *Lessons learned: Shaping relationships and the culture of the workplace.* Thousand Oaks, CA: Corwin.

Barth, R., DuFour, R., DuFour, R., & Eaker, R. (Eds.). (2005). *On common ground: The power of professional learning communities.* Bloomington, IN: Solution Tree.

Barty, K., Thomson, P., Blackmore, J., & Sachs, S. (2005). Unpacking the issues: Researching the shortage of school principals in two states in Australia. *Australian Educational Researcher, 32*(3), 1–18.

Bennis, W. G. (1989). *On becoming a leader.* New York: Addison-Wesley.

Black, P., Harrison, C., Lee, C., Marshall, B., & Wiliam, D. (2003). *Assessment for learning: Putting it into practice.* Maidenhead, UK: Open University Press.

Black, P., Harrison, C., Lee, C., Marshall, B., & Wiliam, D. (2004). Working inside the black box: Assessment for learning in the classroom. *Phi Delta Kappan, 86*(1), 9–21.

Blankstein, A. M. (1992). Lessons from enlightened corporations. *Educational Leadership, 49*(6), 71.

Blankstein, A. M. (1997). Fighting for success. *Reaching Today's Youth: The Community Circle of Caring Journal, 1*(2), 2–3.

Blankstein, A. M. (2004). *Failure is not an option: Six principles that guide student achievement in high-performing schools.* Thousand Oaks, CA: Corwin.

Blankstein, A. M. (2007). Terms of engagement: Where failure is not an option. In A. M. Blankstein, P. D. Houston, & R. W. Cole (Eds.), *Engaging every learner.* Thousand Oaks, CA: Corwin.

Blankstein, A. M., DuFour, R., & Little, M. (1997). *Reaching today's students.* Bloomington, IN: National Educational Service.

Blankstein, A. M., Houston, P. D., & Cole, R. W. (Eds.). (2007). *Engaging every learner.* Thousand Oaks, CA: Corwin.

Blankstein, A. M., Houston, P. D., & Cole, R. W. (Eds.). (2008). *Sustaining professional learning communities.* Thousand Oaks, CA: Corwin.

Blankstein, A. M., Houston, P. D., & Cole, R. W. (Eds.). (2009). *Building sustainable leadership capacity.* Thousand Oaks, CA: Corwin.

Blankstein, A. M., & Swain, H. (1994, February). Is TQM right for schools? *The Executive Educator, 16*(2), 51–54.

Blase, J., & Anderson, G. (1995). *The micropolitics of educational leadership: From control to empowerment.* New York: Teachers College Press.

Block, P. (2002). *The answer to how is yes: Acting on what matters.* San Francisco: Barrett-Koehler.

Bolman, L. G., & Deal, T. E. (1991). *Reframing organizations: Artistry, choice, and leadership.* San Francisco: Jossey-Bass.

Bolman, L. G., & Deal, T. E. (2002). *Reframing the path to school leadership.* Thousand Oaks, CA: Corwin.

Bonstingl, J. J. (2001). *Schools of quality* (3rd ed.). Thousand Oaks, CA: Corwin.

Bower, E. M. (1964). The modification, mediation, and utilization of stress during the school years. *American Journal of Orthopsychiatry, 34,* 667–674.

Bowser, B. A. (2001, May 24). Principal shortage. *Online NewsHour.* Public Broadcasting System. Retrieved July 28, 2009, from http://www.pbs.org/newshour/bb/education/jan-june01/principal_05-22.html

Brendtro, L. K., Brokenleg, M., & Bockern S. V. (1990). *Reclaiming youth at risk: Our hope for the future.* Bloomington, IN: National Educational Services.

Brown, P., & Lauder, H. (2001). *Capitalism and social progress: The future of society in a global economy.* New York: Palgrave.

Bryant, A. (2009, May 24). In a word, he wants simplicity (Interview with Eduardo Castro-Wright, vice chairman of Wal-Mart Stores). *New York Times,* Sunday Business Section, p. 2.

Bryk, A., Camburn, E., & Louis, K. S. (1999). Professional community in Chicago elementary schools: Facilitating factors and organizational consequences [Special issue]. *Educational Administration Quarterly, 35,* 751–781.

Bryk, A. S., & Driscoll, M. E. (1998). *The school as community: Theoretical foundation, contextual influences, and consequences for teachers and students.* Madison, WI: National Center for Effective Secondary Schools.

Bryk, A. S., Easton, J. Q., Kerbow, D., Rollow, S. G., & Sebring, P. A. (1994). The state of Chicago school reform. *Phi Delta Kappan, 76*(1), 74–78.

Bryk, A. S., Lee, V. E., & Holland, P. B. (1993). *Catholic schools and the common good.* Cambridge, MA: Harvard University Press.

Bryk, A. S., & Schneider, B. (2002). *Trust in schools: A core resource for improvement.* New York: Russell Sage Foundation.

Bryk, A. S., & Thum, Y. M. (1989). The effects of high school organization on dropping out: An exploratory investigation. *American Educational Research Journal, 26*(3), 353–383.

Buckingham, M., & Coffman, C. (1999). *First, break all the rules: What the world's greatest managers do differently.* New York: Simon & Schuster.

Busine, M., & Watt, B. (2005). Succession management: Trends and current practices. *Asia Pacific Journal of Human Resources, 43*(2), 225–237.

Champy, J. (1995). *Reengineering management.* New York: HarperCollins.

Clarizio, H. F., & McCoy, G. F. (1970). *Behavior disorders in school-aged children.* Scranton, PA: Chandler.

Clark, C. M. (1988). Asking the right questions about teacher preparation: Contributions of research on teaching thinking. *Educational Researcher, 17*(2), 5–12.

Cole, A. L. (1989, April). *Making explicit implicit theories of teaching: Starting points in preservice programs.* Paper presented at the Annual Meeting of the American Educational Research Association, San Francisco.

Collins, J. (1996). Aligning action and values. *Leader to Leader, 1*(1) 19–24.

Collins, J. (2001). *Good to great.* New York: HarperCollins.

Combs, A. W., Miser, A. B., & Whitaker, K. S. (1999). *On becoming a school leader: A person-centered challenge.* Alexandria, VA: Association for Supervision and Curriculum Development.

Comer, J. P., Ben-Avie, M., Haynes, N. M., & Joyner, E. T. (1999). *Child by child: The Comer process for change in education.* New York: Teachers College Press.

Comer, J. P., Haynes, N. M., Joyner, E. T., & Ben-Avie, M. (1996). *Rallying the whole village: The Comer process for reforming education.* New York: Teachers College Press.

Comer, J. P., Joyner, E. T., & Ben-Avie, M. (2004). *Six pathways to healthy child development and academic success.* Thousand Oaks, CA: Corwin.

Connelly, G., & Tirozzi, G. N. (2008, September 10). A new leader, new school leadership support? *Education Week, 28*(3).

Cooper, N. (2007, May 8). How to create meaning in the workplace. *Personnel Today.*

Cooperrider, D. L. (1990). Positive image, positive action: The affirmative basis of organizing. In S. Srivastva, D. L. Cooperrider et al. (Eds.), *Appreciative management and leadership: The power of positive thought and action in organizations.* San Francisco: Jossey-Bass.

Coopersmith, S. (1967). *The antecedents of self-esteem.* San Francisco, W. H. Freeman.

Corbett, D., Wilson, B., & Williams, B. (2002). *Effort and excellence in urban classrooms: Expecting—and getting—success with all students.* New York: Teachers College Press.

Costa, A. L., & Kallick, B. (Eds.). (2000). *Discovering & exploring habits of mind.* Alexandria, VA: Association for Supervision and Curriculum Development.

Covey, S. R. (1989). *The 7 habits of highly effective people.* New York: Simon & Schuster.

Cushman, K. (Ed.). (1995, March). Making the good school better: The essential quesiton of rigor. *Horace: The Journal of the Coalition of Essential Schools, 11*(4), 2.

Darling-Hammond, L. (1996). The quiet revolution: Rethinking teacher development. *Educational Leadership, 53*(6), 4–10.

Darling-Hammond, L. (1997). *The right to learn: A blueprint for creating schools that work.* San Francisco: Jossey-Bass.

Darling-Hammond, L. (1999). Target time toward teachers. *Journal of Staff Development, 20*(2) 31–36.

Darling-Hammond, L., Wei, R. C., Andree, A., Richardson, N., & Orphanos, S. (2009). *Professional learning in the learning profession: A status report on teacher development in the United States and Abroad.* Dallas, TX: National Staff Development Council.

Datnow, A., & Castellano, M. (2000). *An "inside look" at success for all: A qualitative study of implementation and teaching and learning.* Baltimore: Johns Hopkins University, Center for Research on the Education of Students Placed at Risk.

Deal, T. E., & Peterson, K. D. (1999). *Shaping school culture: The heart of leadership.* San Francisco: Jossey-Bass.

Deming, W. E. (1986). *Out of the crisis.* Cambridge, MA: MIT Center for Advanced Engineering Study.

Dewey, J. (1927). *The public and its problems.* New York: Holt.

Dietz, M. E. (2002, Winter). Triangulated student data to inform instruction. *Portfolio Newsletter, NSDC Portfolio Network, 15.*

Donaldson, G., Jr. (2001). *Cultivating leadership in school: Connecting people, purpose, and practice.* New York: Teachers College Press.

Drucker, P. (1992). *Managing for the future: The 1990s and beyond.* New York: Truman Talley Books.

DuFour, R. P. (1991). *The principal as staff developer.* Bloomington, IN: National Educational Service.

DuFour, R. (2003, Winter). Leading edge. *National Staff Development Council, 24*(1).

DuFour, R., & Eaker, R. (1992). *Creating the new American school.* Bloomington, IN: National Educational Service.

DuFour, R., & Eaker, R. (1998). *Professional learning communities at work: Best practices for enhancing student achievement.* Bloomington, IN: National Educational Service.

Duke, D. (1988). Why principals consider quitting. *Phi Delta Kappan, 70*(4), 308–313.

Eaker, R., DuFour, R., & Burnette, R. (2002). *Getting started: Reculturing schools to become professional learning communities.* Bloomington, IN: National Educational Service.

Earley, P., Evans, J., Collarbone, P., Gold, A., & Halpin, D. (2002). *Establishing the current state of leadership in England.* London: Department for Education and Skills.

Eastman, C. (1902). *Indian boyhood.* New York: McClure, Phillips & Co.

Easton, L. B. (2004). Tuning protocols. In National Staff Development Council & L. B. Easton (Ed.), *Powerful designs for professional learning* (2nd ed., pp. pp. 239–240). Dallas, TX: National Staff Development Council.

Easton, L. B. (2009). *Protocols for professional learning.* Alexandria, VA: Association for Supervision and Curriculum Development.

Edmonds, R. R. (1979). Effective schools for the urban poor. *Educational Leadership, 37*(10), 15–24.

Education Trust Fund. (1999). *Dispelling the myth: High poverty schools exceeding expectations.* Washington, DC: Author.

Education Trust Fund. (2002). *Dispelling the myth revisited.* Washington, DC: Author.

Elias, M. J., & Arnold, H. (Eds.). (2006). *The educator's guide to emotional intelligence and academic achievement.* Thousand Oaks, CA: Corwin.

Elias, M. J., Arnold, H., & Hussey, C. S. (Eds.). (2003). *EQ + IQ = Best leadership practices for caring and successful schools.* Thousand Oaks, CA: Corwin.

Elias, M. J., Bryan, K., Patrikakou, E. N., & Weissberg, R. P. (2003). *Challenges in creating effective home-school partnerships in adolescence: Promising paths for collaboration.* Chicago: Collaborative for Academic, Social, and Emotional Learning.

Elias, M. J., Frey, K. S., Greenberg, M. T., Haynes, N. M., Kessler, R., Schwab-Stone, M. E., et al. (1997). *Promoting social and emotional learning: Guidelines for educators.* Alexandria, VA: Association for Supervision and Curriculum Development.

Elias, M. J., Friedlander, B. S., & Tobias, S. E. (1999). *Emotionally intelligent parenting: How to raise a self-disciplined, responsible, socially skilled child.* New York: Three Rivers Press.

Elias, M. J., Kress, J. S., & Novick, B. (2002). *Building learning communities with character: How to integrate academic, social, and emotional learning.* Alexandria, VA: Association for Supervision and Curriculum Development.

Elmore, R. F. (1995). Structural reform in educational practice. *Educational Researcher, 24*(9), 23–26.

Elmore, R. F. (1999–2000, Winter). Building a new structure for school leadership. *American Educator, 23*(4), 6–13.

Elmore, R. F. (2000). *Building a new structure for school leadership.* New York: Albert Shanker Institute.

Elmore, R. F. (2002). Hard questions about practice. *Educational Leadership, 59*(8), 22–25.

Epstein, J. L., Sanders, M. G., Sheldon, S. B., Simon, B. S., Salinas, K. C., Jansorn, N. R., Van Voorhis, F. L., et al. (2009). *School, family, and community partnerships: Your handbook for action* (3rd ed.). Thousand Oaks, CA: Corwin.

Evans, R. (1996). *The human side of school change.* San Francisco: Jossey-Bass.

Ewing Marion Kauffman Foundation. (2002). *Set for success: Building a strong foundation for school readiness based on the social-emotional development of young children.* Kansas City, MO: Author.

Fenstermacher, G. D. (1986). Philosophy of research on teaching: Three aspects. In M. C. Wittrock (Ed.), *Handbook of research on teaching* (3rd ed., pp. 37–49). New York: Macmillan.

Ferguson, R. (2002). *What doesn't meet the eye: Understanding and addressing racial disparities in high-achieving suburban schools.* Oakbrook, IL: North Central Regional Educational Laboratory.

Financial Executive International (FEI). (2001). *Building human capital: The public sector's 21st century challenge.* Retrieved June 19, 2003, from www.fei.org

Fink, D. (2000a). The attrition of educational change over time: The case of an innovative, "model," "lighthouse" school. In N. Bascia & A. Hargreaves (Eds.), *The sharp edge of educational change.* London: Routledge/Falmer.

Fink, D. (2000b). *Good schools/real schools: Why school reform doesn't last.* New York: Teachers College Press.

Fink, D. (2005). *Leadership for Mortals.* London/Thousand Oaks, CA: Paul Chapman/Corwin.

Fink, D. (in press). *The succession challenge: Building educational leadership capacity through succession management.* Thousand Oaks, California: Corwin.

Fletcher, C., Caron, M., & Williams, W. (1985). *Schools on trial.* Milton Keynes, UK: Open University Press.

Frankl, V. (1997). *Recollections.* New York: Plenum Press.

Frankl, V. (2000). *Man's search for meaning.* Boston: Beacon Press. (Original work published 1959.)

Friedman, T. (2009, June 28). Invent, invent, Invent. *New York Times,* Sunday Opinon Section, p. WK8.

Fullan, M. G. (1991). *The new meaning of educational change.* New York: Teachers College Press.

Fullan, M. G. (1993). *Change forces.* New York: The Falmer Press.

Fullan, M. G. (1996). *What's worth fighting for in your school?* New York: Teachers College Press.

Fullan, M. G. (1997). *What's worth fighting for in the principalship?* New York: Teachers College Press.

Fullan, M. G. (2001a). *Leading in a culture of change.* San Francisco: Jossey-Bass.

Fullan, M. G. (2001b). *The new meaning of educational change* (3rd ed.). New York: Teachers College Press.

Fullan, M. G. (2003a). *Change forces with a vengeance.* New York: Routledge/Falmer.

Fullan, M. G. (2003b). *The moral imperative of school leadership.* Thousand Oaks, CA: Corwin.

Fullan, M. G. (2005). *Leadership & sustainability: System thinkers in action.* Thousand Oaks, CA: Corwin.

Fullan, M. G. (2008). *The six secrets of change: What the best leaders do to help their organizations survive and thrive.* San Francisco: Jossey-Bass.

Fullan, M. G. (2009). *The challenge of change: Start school improvement now* (2nd ed.). Thousand Oaks, CA: Corwin.

Fullan, M., Hill, P., & Crévola, C. (2006). *Breakthrough.* Thousand Oaks, CA: Corwin.

Fullan, M., & Levin, B. (2009, June 17). The fundamentals of whole-system reform: A case study from Canada. *Education Week, 28*(35), 30–31.

Fullan, M., & St. Germain, C. (2006). *Learning places: A field guide for improving the context of schooling.* Thousand Oaks, CA: Corwin.

Galton, M. (2000). "Dumbing down" on classroom standards: The perils of a technician's approach to pedagogy. *Journal of Educational Change, 1*(2), 199–204.

Gardner, J. (1988). *Leadership: An overview.* Washington, DC: Independent Sector.

Gardner, J. (1991). *Building community.* Washington, DC: Independent Sector.

Garmezy, N. (1983). Stressors of childhood. In N. Garmezy & M. Rutter (Eds.), *Stress, coping, and the development in children.* New York: McGraw-Hill.

Garmezy, N. (1994). Reflections and commentary on risk, resilience, and development. In R. J. Haggarty, L. R. Sherrod, N. Garmezy, & M. Rutter (Eds.), *Stress, risk, and resilience in children and adolescents: Processes, mechanisms, and interventions* (pp. 1–18). Cambridge, MA: Cambridge University Press.

Gladwell, M. (2002). *The tipping point: How little things can make a big difference.* Boston: Back Bay Books.

Glasser, W. (1986). *Control theory in the classroom.* New York: HarperCollins.

Glasser, W. (1992). *The quality school: Managing students without coercion.* New York: HarperPerennial.

Glickman, C. (2002). *Leadership for learning: How to help teachers succeed.* Arlington, VA: Association for Supervision and Curriculum Development.

Glickman, C. (2003). *Holding sacred ground: Essays on leadership, courage, and endurance in our schools.* San Francisco: Jossey-Bass.

Goddard, R. D., Hoy, W. K., & Hoy, A. W. (2000). Collective teacher efficacy: Its meaning, measure, and impact on student achievement. *American Educational Research Journal, 37*(2), 479–507.

Goldstein, A. (2001, June 21). How to fix the coming principal shortage. *Time.* Retrieved July 28, 2009, from http://www.time.com/time/nation/article/0,8599,168379,00.html

Goleman, D. (1995). *Emotional intelligence.* New York: Bantam Books.

Goleman, D. Boyatzis, R., & McKee, A. (2002). *Primal leadership: Realizing the power of emotional intelligence.* Boston: Harvard Business School Press.

Goodlad, J. I., McMannon, T. J., & Soder, R. (Eds.). (2001). *Developing democratic character in the young.* San Francisco: Jossey-Bass.

Goodlad, S. J. (Ed.). (2001). *The last best hope.* San Francisco: Jossey-Bass.

Government of Western Australia. (2001). *Managing succession in the Western Australia public sector.* Retrieved June 29, 2003, from www.mpc.wa.gov.au

Gregory, T. (2001). Fear of success? Ten ways alternative schools pull their punches. *Phi Delta Kappan, 82*(8), 577–581.

Guetzloe, E. (1994, Summer). Risk, resilience, and protection. *Journal of Emotional and Behavioral Problems, 3*(2), 2–5.

Hallowell, B. (1997). My nonnegotiables. In G. A. Donaldson (Ed.), *On being a principal: The rewards and challenges of school leadership.* San Francisco: Jossey-Bass.

Hargreaves, A. (2001). Beyond anxiety and nostalgia. *Phi Delta Kappan, 82*(5), 373.

Hargreaves, A. (2003). *Teaching in the knowledge society.* New York: Teachers College Press.

Hargreaves, A. (ed.) (2005). *Extending educational change.* New York: Springer.

Hargreaves, A., Earl, L., Moore, S., & Manning, S. (2001). *Learning to change: Teaching beyond subjects and standards.* San Francisco: Jossey-Bass.

Hargreaves, A., & Fink, D. (2000). The three dimensions of reform. *Educational Leadership, 57*(7), 30–34.

Hargreaves, A., & Fink, D. (2003). Sustaining leadership. *Phi Delta Kappan 84*(9), 693–700.

Hargreaves, A., & Fink, D. (2004). The seven principles of sustainable leadership. *Educational Leadership, 61*(7), 8–13.

Hargreaves, A., & Fink, D. (2005). *Sustainable leadership.* San Francisco: Jossey-Bass.

Hargreaves, A., & Fullan, M. (1998). *What's worth fighting for out there?* New York: Teachers College Press.

Hargreaves, A., Fullan, M., Hopkins, D., & Lieberman, A. (Eds.). (2009, in press). *The second international handbook of educational change.* Dordrecht, The Netherlands: Springer.

Hargreaves, A., & Goodson, I. (2003). *Change over time? A study of culture, structure, time and change in secondary schooling.* Project #199800214. Chicago: Spencer Foundation of the United States.

Hargreaves, A., & Goodson, I. (2006). Educational change over time? The sustainability and non-sustainability of three decades of secondary school change and continuity, *Educational Administration Quarterly, 42*(1).

Hargreaves, A., Halász, G., & Pont, B. (2008). The Finnish approach to system leadership. In B. Pont, D. Nusche, & D. Hopkins (Eds.), *Improving school leadership, Vol. 2: Case studies on system leadership* (pp. 69–109). Paris: OECD.

Hargreaves, A., Shaw, P., Fink, D., Retallick, J., Giles, C., Moore, S., et al. (2000). *Change frames: Supporting secondary teachers in interpreting and integrating secondary school reform.* Toronto: Ontario Institute for Studies in Education/University of Toronto.

Hargreaves, A., & Shirley, D. (2008, October). The fourth way to change. *Educational Leadership, 66*(2), 56–61.

Hargreaves, A., & Shirley, D. (2009). *The fourth way: The inspiring future for educational change.* Thousand Oaks, CA: Corwin.

Harris, A. (2008). *Distributed school leadership: Developing tomorrow's leaders.* London: Routledge.

Harris, A., & Goodall, J. (2008). Do parents know they matter? Engaging all parents in learning. *Educational Research, 50*(3), 277–289.

Haynes, N. M., Emmons, C. L., & Woodruff, D. W. (1998). School development program effects: Linking implementation to outcomes. *Journal of Education for Students Placed at Risk, 3*(1), 71–85.

Heifetz, R. (1999). *Leadership without easy answers.* Cambridge, MA: Belknap Press of Harvard University Press.

Heifetz, R., & Linsky, M. (2002). *Leadership on the line: Staying alive through the dangers of leading.* Boston: Harvard Business School Press.

Henderson, A. (1987). *The evidence continues to grow.* Columbia, MD: National Committee for Citizens in Education.

Henderson, A., & Berla, N. (1995). *A new generation of evidence: The family is critical to student achievement.* Washington, DC: Center for Law and Education.

Higgins, G. (1994). *Resilient adults: Overcoming a cruel past.* San Francisco: Jossey-Bass.

Hill, N. E., & Tyson, D. F. (2009). Parental involvement in middle school: A meta-analytic assessment of the strategies that promote achievement. *Developmental Psychology. 45*(3), 740–763.

Hirsh, S., & Killion, J. (2007). *The learning educator: A new era for professional learning.* Dallas, TX: National Staff Development Council.

Hoffer, E., (1972). *Reflections on the human condition.* New York: HarperCollins.

HOPE Foundation. (2002). *Failure is not an option* [Video series]. Bloomington, IN: HOPE Foundation. Available from www.HopeFoundation.org.

HOPE Foundation. (2009a). *Evaluation of Courageous Leadership Academy I, conducted for Mattoon Community School District #2, Mattoon, IL.* Bloomington, IN: Author.

HOPE Foundation. (2009b). *Failure is not an option 3: Effective assessment for effective learning* [Video series]. Bloomington, IN: HOPE Foundation. Available from www.HopeFoundation.org.

HOPE Foundation (2009c). *Courageous leadership for shaping America's future IV.* Bloomington, IN: Author.

Hopkins, D. (2001). *School improvement for real.* New York: Routledge/Falmer.

Hopkins, D. (2007). *Every school a great school.* Buckingham, UK: Open University Press.

Hopkins, D. (2008, June). Every school a great school: Realizing the potential of system leadership. *Journal of Educational Change, 9*(2).

Hord, S. M. (1997a). *Professional learning communities: Communities of continuous inquiry and improvement.* Austin, TX: Southwest Educational Development Laboratory.

Hord, S. M. (1997b). *Professional learning communities: What are they and why are they important?* Austin, TX: Southwest Educational Development Laboratory.

Hord, S. M., & Hirsh, S. (2008). Making the promise a reality. In A. M. Blankstein, P. D. Houston, & R. W. Cole (Eds.), *Sustaining professional learning communities* (pp. 23–40). Thousand Oaks, CA: Corwin.

Hord, S. M., & Sommers, W. A. (2007). *Leading professional learning communities: Voices from research and practice.* Thousand Oaks, CA: Corwin.

Houston, P. D. (1997). *Articles of faith & hope for public education.* Arlington, VA: American Association of School Administrators.

Houston, P. D., Blankstein, A. M., & Cole, R. W. (Eds.). (2009a). *Leaders as communicators and diplomats.* Thousand Oaks, CA: Corwin.

Houston, P. D., Blankstein, A. M., & Cole, R. W. (Eds.). (2009b). *Out-of-the-box leadership.* Thousand Oaks, CA: Corwin.

Houston, P. D., & Sokolow, S. (2006). *Spirituality in educational leadership.* Thousand Oaks, CA: Corwin.

Huffman, J. B., & Hipp, K. K. (2004). *Reculturing schools as professional learning communities.* Lanham, MD: ScarecrowEducation.

Institute for Educational Leadership. (2000). *Leadership for student learning: Reinventing the principalship.* Washington, DC: Author.

Jackson, K. (2000). *Building new teams: The next generation.* Paper presented at the Future of Work in the Public Sector conference, organized by the School of Public Administration, University of Victoria, British Columbia, Canada. Retrieved June 19, 2003, from www.futurework.telus.com/proceedings.pdf

Johnson, D. (2001, March 29). Maryland's strategy to lure new principals. *Washington Post,* B–2.

Joyce, B., & Showers, B. (1995, May). Learning experiences in staff development. *The Developer,* 3.

Kaiser, B., & Rasminsky, J. S. (2004). *Challenging behavior and social context.* Pearson Allyn Bacon Prentice Hall.

Kegan, R., & Lahey, L. L. (2001). *How the way we talk can change the way we work: Seven languages for transformation.* San Francisco: Jossey-Bass.

Kets de Vries, M. (1993). *Leaders, fools, and imposters: Essays on the psychology of leadership.* San Francisco: Jossey-Bass.

King, M. B., & Newmann, F. (2000). Will teacher learning advance school goals? *Phi Delta Kappan, 81*(8), 576–580.

Korczak, J. (1967). *Selected works of Janusz Korczak.* Warsaw, Poland: Central Institute for Scientific, Technical and Economic Information.

Korczak, J. (1986). *King Matt the first.* New York: Farrar, Straus, and Giroux.

Kotter, J. (1996). *Leading change.* Boston: Harvard Business School Press.

Kouzes, J. M., & Posner, B. Z. (1999). *Encouraging the heart.* San Francisco: Jossey-Bass.

Kozol, J. (2000). *Ordinary resurrection: Children in the years of hope.* New York: Crown.

Kranz, G. (2000). *Failure is not an option: Mission control from Mercury to Apollo 13 and beyond.* New York: Simon & Schuster.

Kruse, S., Louis, K. S., & Bryk, A. S. (1994). *Building professional community in schools.* Madison, WI: Center on Organization and Restructuring of Schools.

Kuhn, T. S. (1996). *The structure of scientific revolutions* (3rd ed.). Chicago: University of Chicago Press.

LaFee, S. (2003). Professional learning communities. *The School Administrator,* 5(60), 6–12.

Lambert, L. (1997). *Who will save our schools? Teachers as constructivist leaders.* Thousand Oaks, CA: Corwin.

Lambert, L. (2002). *The constructivist leader* (2nd ed.). New York: Teachers College Press.

Lambert, L. (2003). *Leadership capacity for lasting school improvement.* Alexandria, VA: Association for Supervision and Curriculum Development.

Land, D., & Stringfield, S. (Eds.). (2002). *Educating at-risk students.* Chicago: National Society for the Study of Education.

Langford, J., Vakii, T., & Lindquist, E. A. (2000). *Tough challenges and practical solutions: A report on conference proceedings.* Victoria, British Columbia, Canada: School of Public Administration, University of Victoria. www.futurework .telus.com/proceedings.pdf

Lawrence, D. (2009, January 28). *Minnesota early childhood summit speech.* Retrieved July 28, 2009, from www.invisiblechildren.org

Leithwood, K., Day, C., Sammons, P., Harris, A., & Hopkins, D. (2006). *Seven strong claims about successful school leadership.* Nottingham, UK: National College of School Leadership.

Lewis, A. C. (2000). Listening to adolescents. *Phi Delta Kappan, 81*(9), 643.

Livsey, R. C., & Palmer, P. J. (1999). *The courage to teach: A guide for reflection and renewal.* San Francisco: Jossey-Bass.

Lortie, D. C. (1975). *School teacher: A sociological study.* Chicago: University of Chicago Press.

Louis, K. S. (2008). Creating and sustaining professional communities. In A. M. Blankstein, P. D. Houston, & R. W. Cole (Eds.), *Sustaining professional learning communities* (pp. 41–58). Thousand Oaks, CA: Corwin.

Louis, K. S., & Kruse, S. D. (1995). *Professionalism and community: Perspectives on reforming urban schools.* Thousand Oaks, CA: Corwin.

Louis, K. S., Kruse, S. D., & Marks, H. M. (1996). Schoolwide professional community. In F. Newmann and Associates (Eds.), *Authentic achievement: Restructuring schools for intellectual quality.* San Francisco: Jossey-Bass.

Louis, K. S., Kruse, S., & Raywid, M. A. (1996). *Putting teachers at the center of reform. NASSP Bulletin, 80*(580), 9–21.

Love, A., & Kruger, A. C. (2005). Teacher beliefs and student achievement in urban schools serving African American students. *Journal of Educational Research, 99*(2), 87–98.

Machiavelli, N. (1999). *The prince* (G. Bull, Trans.). London/New York: Penguin Books. (Original work published 1532.)

MacMillan, R. (1996). *The relationship between school culture and principals' practices during succession.* Unpublished doctoral dissertation, University of Toronto (OISE), Toronto, Ontario, Canada.

MacMillan, R. (2000). Leadership succession, culture of teaching, and educational change. In N. Bascia & A. Hargreaves (Eds.), *The sharp edge of educational change.* London: Falmer Press.

Marx, A. (comp.). (1996). *Annotated bibliography: Research from the Center on Families, Communities, Schools and Learning.* Baltimore, MD: Publications

Department, Center on Families, Communities, Schools and Children's Learning, Johns Hopkins University.

Marzano, R. J. (2003). *What works in schools: Translating research into action.* Alexandria, VA: Association for Supervision and Curriculum Development.

Marzano, R. J. (2007). *The art and science of teaching: A comprehensive framework for effective instruction.* Alexandria, VA: Association for Supervision and Curriculum Development.

Marzano, R. J., Pickering, D. J., & Pollock, J. E. (2001). *Classroom instruction that works: Research-based strategies for increasing student achievement.* Alexandria, VA: Association for Supervision and Curriculum Development.

Marzano, R. J., Waters, T., & McNulty, B. A. (2005). *School leadership that works: From research to results.* Alexandria, VA: Association for Supervision and Curriculum Development.

Maurer, R. (1996). *Beyond the wall of resistance: Unconventional strategies that build support for change.* Austin, TX: Bard Press.

Mason, S. (2002, April). *Turning data into knowledge: Lessons from six Milwaukee public schools.* Paper presented at the annual conference of the American Educational Research Association.

McKenna, J. (2009a, in press). Data without fear. Using relational trust to overcome fear of data. *What's Working in Schools Newsletter, 2*(8).

McKenna, J. (2009b, April 1). From red-flagged to blue ribbon: Using data and collaborative teaming for school success. *What's Working in Schools Newsletter, 2*(4).

McLaughlin, M. (1993). What matters most in teachers' workplace context. In J. W. Lilly & M. McLaughlin (Eds.), *Teachers' work: Individuals, colleagues, and context.* New York: Teachers College Press.

McTighe, J., & O'Connor, K. (2005). Seven practices for effective learning. *Educational Leadership, 63*(3), 10–17.

Meier, D. (1995). *The power of their ideas: Lessons for America from a small school in Harlem.* Boston: Beacon Press.

Mendler, A. N. (1992). *What do I do when . . . ? How to achieve discipline with dignity in the classroom.* Bloomington, IN: Solution Tree.

Merideth, E. M. (2007). *Leadership strategies for teachers, second edition.* Thousand Oaks, CA: Corwin.

Meyer, J. W., & Rowan, B. (1977). Institutional organizations: Formal structures as myth and ceremony. *American Journal of Sociology, 83,* 340–363.

Miles, M. (1998). Finding keys to school change. In A. Hargreaves, A. Lieberman, M. Fullan, & D. Hopkins (Eds.), *International handbook of educational change* (pp. 37–69). Dordrecht, The Netherlands: Kluwer Press.

Montgomery, A. F., & Rossi, R. J. (1994). Becoming at risk of failure in America's schools. In R. J. Rossi (Ed.), *Schools and students at risk: Context and framework for positive change.* New York: Teachers College Press.

Murphy, J., Jost, J., & Shipman, N. (2000). Implementation of the interstate school leaders licensure consortium standards. *International Journal of Leadership in Education, 3*(1), 17–39.

Nanus, B. (1992). *Visionary leadership.* San Francisco: Jossey-Bass.

National Academy of Public Administration. (1997). *Managing succession and developing leadership: Growing the next generation of public service leaders.* Washington, DC: Author.

National Association of Secondary School Principals. (2001). *The principals shortage.* Retrieved June 19, 2003, from www.nassp.org

National Education Goals Panel. (1995). *National education goals report executive summary.* Washington, DC: Author.

National Parent Teacher Association. (1998). *National Standards for Parent/Family Involvement Programs.* Chicago: Author.

National Parent Teacher Association. (n.d.) *National standards for family-school partnerships.* Retrieved August 1, 2009, from http://www.pta.org/documents/National_Standards.pdf

Nespor, J. (1987). The roles of beliefs in the practice of teaching. *Journal of Curriculum Studies, 19,* 317–328.

Newmann, F. M., & Wehlage, G. (1995). *Successful school restructuring.* Madison: Center on Organization and Restructuring of Schools, School of education, University of Wisconsin–Madison.

Nichols, S., & Berliner, D. (2007). *Collateral Damage: How high-stakes testing corrupts American school:* Cambridge, UK: Harvard University Press.

Noer, D. M. (1993). *Healing the wounds.* San Francisco: Jossey-Bass.

Noguera, P. A. (2003). *City schools and the American dream: Reclaiming the promise of public education.* New York: Teachers College Press.

Noguera, P. A. (2009). *The trouble with black boys: And other reflections on race, equity, and the future of public education.* San Francisco: Josey-Bass.

Noguera, P. A., & Wing, J. Y. (Eds.). (2008). *Unfinished business: Closing the racial achievement gap in our schools.* San Francisco: Jossey-Bass.

Novick, B., Kress, J. S., & Elias, M. J. (2002). *Building learning communities with character.* Alexandria, VA: Association for Supervision and Curriculum Development.

O'Connor, K. (2007). *A repair kit for grading: 15 fixes for broken grades.* Portland, OR: Educational Testing Services.

Organization for Economic Cooperation and Development (OECD). (2001). *Schooling for tomorrow: What schools for the future?* Paris: Author.

Ovando, M. N. (1994). *Effects of teachers' leadership on their teaching practices.* Paper presented at the Annual Conference of the University Council of Educational Administration, Philadelphia.

Palmer, P. J. (1998). *The courage to teach: Exploring the inner landscape of a teacher's life.* San Francisco: Jossey-Bass.

Pardini, P. (1999). Making time for adult learning. *Journal of Staff Development, 20*(2).

Pascale, R. (1997–1999). Conversations with change practice consulting teams of Price Waterhouse Coopers and Anderson Consulting, Oxford, England, and Colorado Springs, Colorado.

Pascale, R. (1998, March). Personal communication with David Schneider, partner, North American Change Practice, Price Waterhouse Coopers, Santa Fe, New Mexico.

Pascale, R. T., Millemann, M., & Gioja, L. (2000). *Surfing the edge of chaos.* New York: Three Rivers Press.

Peters, T. (1999). *The circle of innovation: You can't shrink your way to greatness.* New York: Vintage.

Pintrich, P. R. (1990). Implications of psychological research on student learning and college teaching for teacher education. In W. R. Houston (Ed.), *Handbook of research on teacher education* (pp. 826–857). New York: Macmillan.

Pont, B., Nusche, D., & Hopkins, D. (2008). *Improving school leadership: Vol. 2. Case studies on system leadership.* Paris: OECD.

Pont, B., Nusche, D., & Moorman, H. (2008) *Improving school leadership: Vol. 1. Policy and Practice.* Paris: OECD.

Posner, B. Z., & Westwood, R. I. (1995). A cross-cultural investigation of the shared values relationship. *International Journal of Value-Based Management, 11*(4), 1–10.

Purkey, W. W., & Novak, J. M. (1996). *Inviting school success.* Belmont, CA: Wadsworth.

Putnam, R. D. (2000). *Bowling alone: The collapse and revival of American community.* New York: Simon & Schuster.

Putnam, R. D., Leonardi, R., & Nanetti, R. Y. (1993). *Making democracy work: Civic traditions in modern Italy.* Princeton, NJ: Princeton University Press.

Reeves, D. B. (2000). *Accountability in action.* Denver, CO: Advanced Learning Press.

Reeves, D. B. (2002a). *Making standards work* (3rd ed.). Denver, CO: Advanced Learning Press.

Reeves, D. B. (2002b). *The leader's guide to standards: A blueprint for educational equity and excellence.* San Francisco: Jossey-Bass.

Riley, K. (1998). *Whose school is it anyway.* London: Falmer Press.

Riley, K. (2000). Leadership, learning and systemic change. *Journal of Educational Change, 1*(1), 57–75.

Rogers, E. M., & Rogers, E. (2003). *Diffusion of innovations* (5th ed.). New York: Free Press.

Rossi, R. J., & Stringfield, S. C. (1997). *Education reform and students at risk.* Washington, DC: Office of Educational Research and Improvement, U.S. Department of Education.

Sanders, L. (2003, March 16). Medicine's progress, one setback at a time. *New York Times Magazine,* 29.

Sarason, S. (1972). *The creation of settings and the future societies.* San Francisco: Jossey-Bass.

Sarason, S. (1990). *The predictable failure of educational reform.* San Francisco: Jossey-Bass.

Saul, J. R. (1993). *Voltaire's bastards.* Toronto, Canada: Penguin Books.

Schiff, T. (2002, January). Principals' readiness for reform: A comprehensive approach. *Principal Leadership, 2*(5).

Schlechty, P. C. (1992). *Schools for the 21st century: Leadership imperatives for educational reform.* San Francisco: Jossey-Bass.

Schmoker, M. (2004). Tipping point: From feckless reform to substantive instructional improvement. *Phi Delta Kappan, 85*(6), 424–431.

Schorr, L. B. (1988). *Within our reach: Breaking the cycle of disadvantage.* New York: Anchor Press/Doubleday.

Schorr, L. B. (1998, Summer). Searchlights on delinquency. *Journal of Emotional and Behavioral Problems, 7*(2).

Senge, P. M. (1990). *The fifth discipline: The art and practice of the learning organization.* New York: Doubleday/Currency.

Senge, P. M. (in press). Education for an interdependent world: Developing systems citizens. In A. Hargreaves, M. Fullan, D. Hopkins, & A. Lieberman (Eds.), *The second international handbook of educational change.* Dordrecht, The Netherlands: Springer.

Senge, P. M., Ross, R., Smith, B., Roberts, C., & Kleiner, A. (1994). *The fifth discipline fieldbook: Strategies and tools for building a learning organization.* New York: Doubleday.

Sergiovanni, T. J. (1992). *Moral leadership: Getting to the heart of school improvement.* San Francisco: Jossey-Bass.

Sergiovanni, T. J. (1994). *Building community in schools.* San Francisco: Jossey-Bass.

Sergiovanni, T. J. (2000). *The lifeworld of leadership: Creating culture, community, and personal meaning in our schools.* San Francisco: Jossey-Bass.

Shubitz, S. (2008, September 1). 20 Rules for great parent-teacher conferences. *Instructor, 118*(2). Retrieved August 09, 2009, from http://www.thefreeli brary.com/20+Rules+for+great+parent-teacher+conferences.-a0187 672975

Singleton, G. E., & Linton, C. (2006). *Courageous conversations about race: A field guide for achieving equity in schools.* Thousand Oaks, CA: Corwin.

Smith, L. M., Dwyer, D. C., Prunty, J. J., & Kleine, P. F. (1987). *The fate of an innovative school.* London: Falmer Press.

Soder, R. (2001). *The language of leadership.* San Francisco: Jossey-Bass.

Soder, R., Goodlad, J. I., & McMannon, T. J. (2001). *Developing democratic character in the young.* San Francisco: Jossey-Bass.

Solmo, R. (1995, February). Meetings—management; consensus (social sciences). *Social Policy, 44*(2).

Southworth, G. (2009). *Courageous leadership for shaping America's future: A synthesis of best practices guiding school leadership for 21st century education.* Bloomington, IN: HOPE Foundation.

Sparks, D. (2002). *Designing powerful professional development for teachers and principals.* Oxford, OH: National Staff Development Council.

Sparks, D. (2007). *Leading for results.* Thousand Oaks, CA: Corwin.

Spillane, J. P., Halverson, R., & Drummond, J. B. (2001). Investigating school leadership practice: A distributed perspective. *Educational Researcher, 30*(3), 23–28.

Springfield, S. C. (1995). Attempts to enhance students' learning: A search for valid programs and highly reliable implementation techniques. *School Effectiveness and School Improvement, 6,* 67–96.

Standing Bear, L. (1933). *Land of the spotted eagle.* New York: Houghton Mifflin.

Sternberg, R. J. (1996). *Successful intelligence: How practical and creative intelligence determine success in life.* New York: Simon & Schuster.

Stiegelbauer, S. M., & Anderson, S. (1992). *Seven years later: Revisiting a restructured school in northern Ontario.* Paper presented at the American Educational Research Association Meetings, San Francisco.

Stiggins, R. (2004). *Student-involved assessment for learning* (4th ed.). Upper Saddle River, NJ: Prentice Hall.

Stiggins, R., Arter, J. A., Chappuis, J., & Chappuis, S. (2007). *Classroom assessment for student learning: Doing it right—using it well.* Upper Saddle River, NJ: Prentice Hall.

Stoll, L. (1999). Raising our potential: Understanding and developing capacity for lasting improvement. *School Effectiveness and School Improvement, 10*(4), 503–532.

Stoll L., & Fink, D. (1996). *Changing our schools: Linking school effectiveness and school improvement.* Buckingham, UK: Open University Press.

Stoll, L., Fink, D., & Earl, L. (2002). *It's about learning (and it's about time).* London: Routledge/Falmer.

Stoll, L., & Temperley, J. (2009). Creative leadership: A challenge of our times. *School Leadership and Management, 29*(1), 63–76.

Stringfield, S., & Land, D. (Eds.). (2002). *Educating at-risk students.* Chicago: National Society for the Study of Education.

Stringfield, S., Reynolds, D., & Schaffer, E. (2008). Improving secondary students' academic achievement through a focus on reform reliability: 4- and 9-year findings from the High Reliability Schools project. *School Effectiveness and School Improvement, 19*(4), 409–428.

Suzuki, D. (2003). *The David Suzuki reader: A lifetime of ideas from a leading activist and thinker.* Vancouver, Canada: Greystone Press.

Talbert, J., & MacLaughlin, M. (1994). Teacher professionalism in local school contexts. *American Journal of Education, 102,* 123–153.

Teddlie, C., & Stringfield, S. (1993). *Schools make a difference: Lessons learned from a 10-year study of school effects.* New York: Teachers College Press.

Test of wing damage called "smoking gun." (2003, July 8). *redOrbit.* Retrieved July 30, 2009, from http://www.redorbit.com/news/general/16681/test_of_wing_damage_called_smoking_gun/index.html

Tyack, D., & Tobin, W. (1994). The grammar of schooling: Why has it been so hard to change? *American Educational Research Journal, 31*(3), 453–480.

Tyler, R. W. (1949). *Basic principles of curriculum and instruction.* Chicago: University of Chicago Press.

Wallace Foundation. (2003). *Beyond the Pipeline: Getting the principals we need where they are needed most.* Seattle, WA: Center on Reinventing Education.

Walsh, M. (2002, June 27). Supreme court upholds Cleveland voucher program. *Education Week, 21*(42). Retrieved July 28, 2009, from http://www.edweek.org/login.html?source=http://www.edweek.org/ew/articles/2002/06/27/

42voucher_web.h21.html&destination=http://www.edweek.org/ew/articles/2002/06/27/42voucher_web.h21.html&levelId=2100

Weinstein, C. S. (1989). Teacher education students' preconceptions of teaching. *Journal of Teacher Education, 40*(2), 53–60.

Werner, E. E., & Smith, R. S. (1977). Kauai's children come of age. Honolulu: University of Hawaii Press.

Werner, E. E., & Smith, R. S. (1982). *Vulnerable but invincible: A longitudinal study of resilient children and youth.* New York: McGraw-Hill.

Wiggins, G. (1998). *Educative assessment: Designing assessments to inform and improve student performance.* San Francisco: Jossey-Bass.

Wiggins, G., & McTighe, J. (2005). *Understanding by design* (2nd ed.). Alexandria, VA: Association for Supervision and Curriculum Development.

Wiggins, G., & McTighe, J. (2007). *Schooling by design: Mission, action, and achievement.* Alexandria, VA: Association for Supervision and Curriculum Development.

Wilker, K. (1983). *The Lindenhof* (S. Lhotzky, Trans.). Sioux Falls, SD: Augustana College. (Original work published 1920.)

Williams, M. P. (2002, September 25). Reading by the second grade is a strategy to fight crime. *Richmond-Times Dispatch*, p. H4.

Williams, T. (2001). *Unrecognized exodus, unaccepted accountability: The looming shortage of principals and vice-principals in Ontario public school boards.* Toronto, Canada: Ontario Principals' Council.

Wilmore, E. (2007). *Teacher leadership: Improving teaching and learning from inside the classroom.* Thousand Oaks, CA: Corwin.

Woods, E. G. (1995). *School improvement research series, close-up 17: Reducing the drop-out rate.* Portland, OR: Northwest Regional Educational Laboratory.

World Commission on Environment and Development. (1987). *Our common future.* New York: United Nations General Assembly.

Index

CORWIN

A SAGE Company

The Corwin logo—a raven striding across an open book—represents the union of courage and learning. Corwin is committed to improving education for all learners by publishing books and other professional development resources for those serving the field of PreK–12 education. By providing practical, hands-on materials, Corwin continues to carry out the promise of its motto: **"Helping Educators Do Their Work Better."**

The HOPE Foundation logo stands for Harnessing Optimism and Potential Through Education. The HOPE Foundation helps to develop and support educational leaders over time at district- and state-wide levels to create school cultures that sustain all students' achievement, especially low-performing students.

Great Public Schools for Every Student

Our mission is to advocate for education professionals and to unite our members and the nation to fulfill the promise of public education to prepare every student to succeed in a diverse and interdependent world.